The Potential of Generative AI

Transforming technology, business and art through innovative AI applications

Divit Gupta

Anushree Srivastava

www.bpbonline.com

Copyright © 2024 BPB Online

All rights reserved. No part of this book may be reproduced, stored in a retrieval system, or transmitted in any form or by any means, without the prior written permission of the publisher, except in the case of brief quotations embedded in critical articles or reviews.

Every effort has been made in the preparation of this book to ensure the accuracy of the information presented. However, the information contained in this book is sold without warranty, either express or implied. Neither the author, nor BPB Online or its dealers and distributors, will be held liable for any damages caused or alleged to have been caused directly or indirectly by this book.

BPB Online has endeavored to provide trademark information about all of the companies and products mentioned in this book by the appropriate use of capitals. However, BPB Online cannot guarantee the accuracy of this information.

First published: 2024

Published by BPB Online
WeWork
119 Marylebone Road
London NW1 5PU

UK | UAE | INDIA | SINGAPORE

ISBN 978-93-55516-725

www.bpbonline.com

Foreword

It is with great honor and enthusiasm that I contribute a foreword to this extraordinary book on artificial intelligence, authored by my esteemed colleague, Divit. Our collaboration during our tenure at Oracle and my participation in his insightful podcast show have allowed me to witness firsthand the depth of Divit's expertise, the expansiveness of his vision, and the unwavering passion he brings to the field of AI and Gen AI.

Divit possesses a unique ability to seamlessly blend profound knowledge of the AI landscape with a keen understanding of optimizing narratives for search—a clear demonstration of his commitment to delivering excellence in this dynamic field. This book serves as a testament to his insatiable thirst for data, experimentation, and the relentless pursuit of knowledge, all of which contribute to enriching the discourse on artificial intelligence.

Throughout our shared experiences, I have observed Divit's exceptional leadership qualities. Beyond his impressive technical acumen, he embodies the attributes of a visionary leader in the realm of AI and Gen AI. Divit's capacity to absorb diverse ideas, coupled with his decisiveness in making bold and strategic choices, sets him apart. In the complex landscape of AI, he serves as a results-oriented architect, leading by example and demonstrating unparalleled dedication to overcoming challenges.

As you embark on the journey through the pages of this book guided by Divit's expertise, I encourage you to absorb the wealth of knowledge and insights he imparts. It is a journey led by a seasoned professional who not only comprehends the intricate nuances of AI but is also committed to sharing that understanding for the benefit of all. May this book serve as a beacon of enlightenment and inspiration for AI and Gen AI enthusiasts, researchers, and professionals alike.

Warm regards,

– **Dev Patel**
Vice President
Oracle Customer Success Services

Dedicated to

*I would like dedicate this book to my father **Mr. G.K. Srivastava** who has been a lifetime mentor, constant support, my foundation and a guiding star on each and every step of my life. This is for you "Papa," you instilled the belief in my dreams and empowered me to make them a reality.*

-Anushree Srivastava

*To my mother, **Shashi Gupta**, and to the memory of my father, **Pritipal Gupta**, for their sacrifices and for exemplifying the power of determination. To my sons, **Yash** and **Darsh**, who made me understand true love.*

– Divit Gupta

About the Authors

- **Divit Gupta** is a highly accomplished seasoned IT professional with about 20 years of industry experience focusing on strategic architecture-driven initiatives and providing active leadership in multi-pillar sales cycles. He has also led global technical partnerships, set his team's vision & execution model, and nurtured multiple new strategic initiatives.

  Divit is the host of podcast shows Tech Talk with Divit and Live Labs with Divit, Oracle shows that highlight technology initiatives and leadership at Oracle. He was the Oracle TV cloud world correspondent for the year 2022-23.

  At Oracle cloud world 2022-23 Divit interviewed executives/Oracle customers and partners from the C level suite and was streamed live on Oracle TV. This included the executives such as Accenture CTO, Paul Daugherty, Accenture Global CTO Andrea Cesarini, GE CFO, DISH TV VP and more.

  He has a true passion for sharing knowledge which has motivated him to give international conference talks, write technical blogs, and publish books on emerging technologies.

  Divit has presented on Oracle Database technology at the Oracle Cloud world (Official Oracle event attended by 15K professionals) in 2023.

- **Anushree Srivastava** is a seasoned Data and Analytics Architect with over 15 years of experience driving data-driven solutions across diverse industries. She has been leading Generative AI initiatives and enablements at her current role at Google. From the dynamic realm of digital advertising to the intricate infrastructure of finance and healthcare, Anushree has consistently delivered impactful results.

  She has a proven track record in modernizing data platforms, seamlessly integrating disparate data sources, and leveraging cloud analytics to empower informed decision-making.

  Her experience transcends technical expertise. She is a seasoned Data and Analytics Leader, adept at leading and delivering complex projects on time and within budget. Her experience with Agile methodologies allows her to adapt to changing requirements and deliver solutions that meet evolving business needs.

She is passionate about using data to solve real-world problems and improve business outcomes. Her strong interpersonal and communication skills enable her to effectively collaborate with both technical and non-technical stakeholders, bridging the gap between data insights and actionable business strategies.

She is a strong advocate for the transformative power of data. She is committed to building high-performing data teams and fostering a culture of data-driven thinking within organizations. Her passion for using data to unlock new opportunities, enhance decision-making, and drive positive change is a cornerstone of her professional journey.

About the Reviewer

Naresh Kumar Miryala, a distinguished engineering leader at Meta, possesses an extensive background in cloud and platform engineering honed over nearly two decades in the field. His deep understanding of both technical and business intricacies empowers him to provide innovative solutions spanning diverse domains such as database systems, large-scale backend infrastructure, multi-cloud environments (AWS/GCP/OCI/Azure), automation, cloud infrastructure, DevOps, Kubernetes, and Elasticsearch.

Having previously contributed to esteemed organizations like Oracle Corp and Computer Sciences Corporations, Naresh played a pivotal role in migrating or implementing Oracle technologies for over 50 organizations globally, many of which are Fortune 500 entities. His impact spans across various industries, including pharmaceuticals, retail, banking, and gold mining companies worldwide.

Naresh is highly experienced in cloud migrations, particularly involving databases (Oracle/Exadata/MySQL/Postgres) and applications (EBS/Fusion/EPM/GTM). He played a pivotal role in ensuring their seamless execution for large and complex deployments globally.

Naresh's affiliations include membership in IEEE, AIM leadership council, and fellowship at RSA. He holds certifications as a professional in Multi Cloud and Data platforms, and actively engages as a blogger, tech reviewer, and frequent speaker in international conferences.

Acknowledgement

From the depths of my heart, I express profound gratitude to my cherished family and friends. Their unwavering support and encouragement fueled me throughout the long journey of writing this book.

My deepest appreciation goes to BPB Publications for their invaluable guidance and expertise in transforming this manuscript into a tangible reality. This book's journey to fruition would not have been possible without the remarkable contributions of reviewers, technical experts, and editors. Their dedicated efforts and insightful feedback significantly shaped and strengthened this work.

I extend heartfelt thanks to my esteemed colleagues and co-workers in the tech industry. Their invaluable teachings and insightful feedback over the years empowered me to write this book.

Finally, my deepest gratitude goes to all the readers who have taken an interest in this work and supported its realization. Your encouragement has served as a potent fuel, driving me forward at every step.

Preface

Welcome to the fascinating world of Generative AI! This book embarks on a holistic and accessible journey, unveiling the power and potential of this transformative technology. We delve into the intricate workings of generative models, navigating technical complexities with clarity and engaging presentation. By bridging theory and practice, we weave real-world applications into the fabric of complex concepts, rendering them relevant and comprehensible.

This book caters to diverse audiences, extending a welcoming hand to both technical and non-technical readers. Our balanced approach ensures that everyone embarks on a rewarding journey of discovery, regardless of prior expertise. Whether you are a seasoned AI professional or simply curious about this burgeoning field, this book serves as your indispensable guide to unleashing the potential of generative AI.

Through captivating real-world examples and concrete illustrations, we unveil the practical applications of generative AI across a myriad of fields. Case studies delve into the depths of successful projects, offering valuable insights and learning opportunities. This book explores the cutting-edge capabilities and potential of generative AI, illuminating its transformative impact on the technological landscape.

Chapter 1: Introduction to Generative AI - This chapter serves as a foundational exploration of generative AI, introducing its core concepts and tracing its fascinating evolution. We embark on a journey through time, witnessing the groundbreaking advancements that have propelled generative models to their current capabilities. By examining real-world applications, the chapter sheds light on the practical impact of generative AI across diverse domains. Furthermore, it delves into the challenges and ongoing advancements shaping the future of this transformative technology. Finally, the chapter concludes by providing a glimpse into the anticipated future trajectory of generative AI, leaving readers eager to explore the boundless possibilities that lie ahead.

Chapter 2: Generative AI in Industries - This chapter delves into the transformative impact of generative AI across various industries. It unveils the significance of this technology in driving innovation, enhancing efficiency, and unlocking new avenues for growth. We explore a range of industries, including healthcare, finance, entertainment, and manufacturing, highlighting how generative AI is revolutionizing each landscape. Additionally, the chapter addresses the challenges and considerations associated with implementing generative AI in real-world settings, providing valuable insights for businesses and organizations seeking to leverage its potential. Finally, we peer into the future, offering a captivating outlook on the anticipated impact of generative AI on various industries in the years to come.

Chapter 3: Fundamentals of Generative Models - This chapter embarks on a deep dive into the fascinating world of generative models. We begin by providing a comprehensive overview of various generative models, including Generative Adversarial Networks (GANs), Variational Autoencoders (VAEs), and others. By dissecting their architectures and underlying principles, we unravel the complex mechanisms that enable them to generate realistic and diverse data. Furthermore, the chapter delves into the fundamental differences between generative and discriminative models, equipping readers with a clear understanding of their contrasting roles in the machine learning landscape.

Chapter 4: Applications Across Industries - This chapter embarks on a thrilling exploration of the diverse applications of generative AI across countless industries. We delve into the realm of healthcare, where generative models are revolutionizing drug discovery, personalized medicine, and medical imaging. We witness the transformative impact of generative AI in the financial sector, where it is optimizing risk assessment, streamlining fraud detection, and generating personalized financial products. The chapter then ventures into the realm of entertainment, showcasing how generative AI is redefining creative expression through music composition, film production, and game development. Furthermore, we explore its applications in fields ranging from manufacturing and design to education and research, demonstrating its boundless potential to empower innovation and efficiency across the board.

Chapter 5: Creative Expression with Generative AI - This chapter delves into the exciting realm where generative AI meets creative expression. We explore how artists, musicians, and designers are leveraging this powerful technology to push the boundaries of their craft and expand the horizons of artistic creation. We witness the emergence of new artistic movements, where humans and AI collaborate seamlessly, generating unique and captivating works of art that challenge our perceptions and redefine what it means to be creative.

Chapter 6: Generative AI in Business and Innovation - This chapter dives into the transformative power of generative AI in the world of business and innovation. We will explore how companies are leveraging this technology to revolutionize product development and design, optimize manufacturing and supply chain processes, and unlock new avenues for growth and competitive advantage.

Chapter 7: Deep Dive into GANs (Generative Adversarial Networks) - This chapter embarks on a deep dive into the fascinating world of Generative Adversarial Networks (GANs), arguably the most celebrated and impactful class of generative models. We delve into the intricate workings of this architecture, dissecting its core components and the intricate interplay between the generator and discriminator networks that fuel its learning process. Through insightful explanations and illustrative examples, we unravel the complex mechanisms that enable GANs to generate incredibly realistic and diverse data.

Chapter 8: Building and Deploying Generative Models - This chapter transitions from theory to practice, guiding readers through the process of building and deploying generative models. We delve into the practical aspects of model development, providing a step-by-step roadmap for transforming theoretical concepts into real-world applications.

Code Bundle and Coloured Images

Please follow the link to download the
Code Bundle and the *Coloured Images* of the book:

https://rebrand.ly/37cee4

The code bundle for the book is also hosted on GitHub at
https://github.com/bpbpublications/The-Potential-of-Generative-AI
In case there's an update to the code, it will be updated on the existing GitHub repository.

We have code bundles from our rich catalogue of books and videos available at **https://github.com/bpbpublications**. Check them out!

Errata

We take immense pride in our work at BPB Publications and follow best practices to ensure the accuracy of our content to provide with an indulging reading experience to our subscribers. Our readers are our mirrors, and we use their inputs to reflect and improve upon human errors, if any, that may have occurred during the publishing processes involved. To let us maintain the quality and help us reach out to any readers who might be having difficulties due to any unforeseen errors, please write to us at :

errata@bpbonline.com

Your support, suggestions and feedbacks are highly appreciated by the BPB Publications' Family.

Did you know that BPB offers eBook versions of every book published, with PDF and ePub files available? You can upgrade to the eBook version at www.bpbonline.com and as a print book customer, you are entitled to a discount on the eBook copy. Get in touch with us at :

business@bpbonline.com for more details.

At **www.bpbonline.com**, you can also read a collection of free technical articles, sign up for a range of free newsletters, and receive exclusive discounts and offers on BPB books and eBooks.

Piracy

If you come across any illegal copies of our works in any form on the internet, we would be grateful if you would provide us with the location address or website name. Please contact us at **business@bpbonline.com** with a link to the material.

If you are interested in becoming an author

If there is a topic that you have expertise in, and you are interested in either writing or contributing to a book, please visit **www.bpbonline.com**. We have worked with thousands of developers and tech professionals, just like you, to help them share their insights with the global tech community. You can make a general application, apply for a specific hot topic that we are recruiting an author for, or submit your own idea.

Reviews

Please leave a review. Once you have read and used this book, why not leave a review on the site that you purchased it from? Potential readers can then see and use your unbiased opinion to make purchase decisions. We at BPB can understand what you think about our products, and our authors can see your feedback on their book. Thank you!

For more information about BPB, please visit **www.bpbonline.com**.

Join our book's Discord space

Join the book's Discord Workspace for Latest updates, Offers, Tech happenings around the world, New Release and Sessions with the Authors:

https://discord.bpbonline.com

Table of Contents

1. Introduction to Generative AI 1
    Introduction 1
    Structure 2
    Objectives 2
    Defining generative AI and its evolution 2
        Key components and mechanisms 3
        Key components 3
            Generative models 3
            Autoregressive models 4
            Mechanisms 5
            Evaluation 5
    Evolutionary trajectory 5
    Breakthroughs in generative models 7
    Applications in the real world 8
    Challenges and advancements 12
    Anticipated future trajectory 14
    Conclusion 15

2. Generative AI in Industries 17
    Introduction 17
    Structure 17
    Objectives 18
    Significance and impact of generative AI on various industries 18
    Healthcare and drug discovery 19
        Advancing molecular generation 19
        Enhancing biomedical imaging 20
        Targeted drug design and optimization 21
        Personalized medicine and treatment plans 23
        Case studies and success stories 24
        Ethical considerations and future prospects 26

Responsible data use and patient privacy 26
Addressing bias and fairness 27
Informed consent in personalized medicine 29
Transparency in model decision-making 30
Global access to healthcare innovations 32
Ongoing ethical discourse and governance 33

Art and entertainment 35
Generative art 36
Algorithmic composition 36
Evolutionary algorithms in art 36
Interactive generative art 37
Machine learning and style transfer 37
Procedural generation in digital art 37
Collaboration between humans and algorithms 37
Generative art installations 38
Ethical considerations in algorithmic art 38

Creative assistance in content generation 38
Interactive and immersive experiences 39
AI-generated music and composition 39
Visual arts and style transfer 40
AI-enhanced filmmaking and animation 40
Creative chatbots and interactive storytelling 41
Generative AI in virtual fashion design 41
AI-generated literature and poetry 42
Ethical considerations in AI-generated art 42
Marketing and content creation 43
Automated content generation 43
Personalized marketing campaigns 44
Social media management 44
Predictive analytics for customer behaviour 44
Chatbots for customer interaction 44
Visual content generation 44
Sentiment analysis in marketing 45

    Dynamic pricing optimization 45
    Content curation and trend analysis 45
    Email marketing optimization 45

Manufacturing and design 46
    Generative design in product development 46
    Additive manufacturing and 3D printing 46
    Predictive maintenance and quality control 46
    Supply chain optimization 47
    Robotics and automation 47
    Customization and mass personalization 47
    Energy efficiency in manufacturing 47
    Simulations for prototyping and testing 47
    Human-robot collaboration in manufacturing 48

Finance and risk management 48
    Algorithmic trading and quantitative finance 49
    Fraud detection and cybersecurity 49
    Credit scoring and loan approval 49
    Personalized financial advice 49
    Market sentiment analysis 50
    Dynamic risk management 50
    Automated compliance and regulatory reporting 50
    Portfolio optimization and asset allocation 50
    Insurance underwriting and claims processing 51
    Stress testing and scenario analysis 51

Human resources and recruitment 51
    Automated resume screening 52
    Predictive hiring analytics 52
    Candidate matching and recommendations 52
    Diversity and inclusion initiatives 52
    Chatbots for candidate interaction 53
    Employee retention strategies 53
    Skills gap analysis 53
    Automated onboarding processes 53

        Performance management enhancements 53
        Workforce planning and scalability 54
    Robotics and automation 54
        Generative design in robotics 55
        Automated manufacturing processes 55
        Adaptive and learning robotics 55
        Predictive maintenance for robots 55
        Human-robot collaboration 55
        Intelligent vision systems 56
        Autonomous vehicles and drones 56
        AI-enhanced robotic process automation 56
        Warehouse and logistics automation 56
    Urban planning and architecture 57
        Generative design for urban layouts 57
        Smart infrastructure planning 57
        Environmental sustainability in architecture 58
        Traffic flow optimization 58
        Mixed-use development planning 58
        Crisis and disaster response planning 58
        Heritage preservation and adaptive reuse 59
        Public space design and accessibility 59
        Community-driven design through AI feedback 59
    Challenges and considerations 60
    Future outlook 60
    Conclusion 60

3. **Fundamentals of Generative Models** 61
    Introduction 61
    Structure 61
    Objectives 62
    Overview of generative models 62
    Generative adversarial networks 63
        NVIDIA 64
        OpenAI 65

- DALL-E 65
  - Text-to-image synthesis 66
  - Creative AI and beyond 66
  - Continual research contributions 66
  - Ethical considerations 66
  - Collaborative approach 66
  - Education and outreach 66
- Google Brain 67
  - Image-to-image translation 67
  - Style transfer 67
  - Progressive generative adversarial networks 67
  - Conditional generative adversarial networks 67
  - Interactive generative adversarial networks 67
  - Application in TensorFlow 68
  - Collaborations and publications 68
  - AI ethics and fairness 68
- Facebook AI 68
  - Image synthesis and enhancement 68
  - GANs for style transfer 69
  - Deep generative models 69
  - Conditional generative adversarial networks and user interaction 69
  - Generative models for video 69
  - Open-source contributions 69
  - AI research for social good 69
  - Ethical considerations 69
- IBM 70
  - Generative adversarial networks for data augmentation 70
  - Generative models in artificial intelligence research 70
  - Creative applications 70
  - Generative adversarial networks for anomaly detection 70
  - Explainability and interpretability 70
  - Quantum machine learning 71
  - Industry-specific applications 71
  - AI ethics and fairness 71

Using generative adversarial networks 71
Step 1: Defining the problem.. 71
Step 2: Choosing a GAN architecture... 72
Step 3: Data preparation 73
Step 4: Model training 75
Step 5: Optimization and fine-tuning... 76
Step 6: Application deployment 77

Variational autoencoders... 79
Overview of variational autoencoder architecture 79
Training process 80
Example: Image generation with Variational autoencoders......................... 80
Real-world applications of variational autoencoders 80
Challenges and advancements... 81
Examples of variational autoencoders implementations 81
Google's Magenta Studio... 81
OpenAI's DALL-E... 82
DeepChem 82
PyTorch's variational autoencoders implementation.............................. 83
TensorFlow Probability 85
Variational autoencoders implementation framework 86

Autoencoders.. 87
Key concepts 87
Autoencoders implementation framework 90

CycleGAN 91
Key concepts 91
Examples of CycleGAN implementations... 92
ZooGAN.. 92
CycleGAN for art style transfer... 92
CycleGAN for object transfiguration... 93
Pix2PixHD 93
DeepArt.io 93
Using CycleGAN 93

Bidirectional Encoder Representations from Transformers 94
Key concepts 94

Examples of Bidirectional Encoder Representations from Transformers implementations 95
    Hugging Face Transformers library..*95*
    Google's Bidirectional Encoder Representations from Transformers GitHub repository...*96*
    Bidirectional Encoder Representations from Transformers for TensorFlow 2.0........ *96*
    Future directions and ongoing research *96*
DeepDream 96
    Origins and working principle..*96*
    Artistic applications *97*
    Cultural impact *97*
    Challenges and ethical considerations..*98*
Understanding the underlying principles 98
Underlying principles of generative models.. 100
    Mathematical foundations.. *100*
        Probability theory... *100*
        Linear algebra.. *101*
        Generative modelling as mathematical composition............................. *101*
    Generative adversarial networks *101*
    Variational autoencoders *101*
    Training mechanisms *102*
    Loss functions... *102*
        Adversarial loss of generative adversarial networks *102*
        Reconstruction loss of variational autoencoders *102*
        Perceptual loss for Style Transfer and Image Generation *103*
        Cycle consistency loss for CycleGAN *103*
        Balancing act of loss functions... *103*
    Generative model evaluation *103*
    Ethical considerations *103*
    Comparison with discriminative models... *104*
    Transfer learning in generative models *104*
    Case studies and real-world applications *104*
Fundamental differences between generative and discriminative models 105
    Decoding the dichotomy... *105*

| Training methodology 106
| Applications 106
| Uncertainty handling 106
| Trade-offs and synergy 106
| Context in ummary 107
| Conclusion 107

4. Applications Across Industries 109
   Introduction 109
   Structure 109
   Objectives 110
   Exploring generative AI in healthcare, finance, entertainment, and more 110
   Generative AI in healthcare 111
       Medical imaging enhancement 112
           Application in medical imaging 112
           Real-world impact 112
           Example use case 112
           Industry adoption 113
       Drug discovery and molecular design 113
       Application in drug discovery 113
           Real-world impact 113
           Example use case 114
           Industry adoption 114
       Personalized treatment plans 114
           Context and challenges 114
           Generative AI's role 115
           Real-world impact 115
           Example use case 115
           Industry adoption 115
       Medical text generation 116
           Context and challenges 116
           Generative AI's role 116
           Real-world impact 116
           Example use case 117
           Industry adoption 117

Predictive analytics for patient outcomes 117
    Context and challenges 117
    Generative AI's role 118
    Real-world impact 118
    Example use case 118
    Industry adoption 118

Synthetic data generation for research 119
    Context and challenges 119
    Generative AI's role 119
    Real-world impact 119
    Example use case 120
    Industry adoption 120

Generative AI in the financial sector 120

Fraud detection and prevention 121
    Context and importance 121
    Generative AI's role 122
    Real-world impact 122

Algorithmic trading strategies 123
    Context and importance 123
    Generative AI's role 123
    Real-world impact 123

Customer service chatbots 125
    Context and importance 125
    Generative AI's role 125
    Real-world impact 125

Credit scoring and risk assessment 127
    Context and importance 127
    Generative AI's role 127
    Real-world impact 127

Generative AI in the entertainment sector 129

Generative art and design 130

Interactive and immersive experiences 131

AI-generated music and composition 132

Visual arts and style transfer 133

　　　　AI-enhanced filmmaking and animation 135
　　　　Creative chatbots and interactive storytelling 136
　　Ethical considerations in AI-generated art 137
　　Case studies showcasing real-world applications 138
　　　　Healthcare 139
　　　　　　Case study: Medical imaging enhancement in oncology 139
　　　　　　Outcomes 139
　　　　Finance 139
　　　　　　Case study: Fraud detection and prevention in financial transactions 140
　　　　Entertainment 140
　　　　　　Case study: AI-enhanced filmmaking and animation 141
　　　　Manufacturing and design 141
　　　　　　Case study: Generative design in aerospace engineering 141
　　　　Urban planning and architecture 142
　　　　　　Case study: Urban planning with generative AI 142
　　　　Human resources and recruitment 143
　　　　　　Case study: AI-enhanced recruitment in human resources 143
　　　　Robotics and automation 144
　　　　Other sectors 145
　　Future trends and potential disruptions 148
　　　　Gartner 148
　　　　Forrester 150
　　Conclusion 151

5. **Creative Expression with Generative AI** 153
　　Introduction 153
　　Structure 153
　　Objectives 154
　　Generative AI in art, music, and design 154
　　　　Algorithmic artistry 155
　　　　Real-world examples and case studies 155
　　　　Impact and future trends 157
　　Generative adversarial networks in visual arts 158
　　　　Evolution of style transfer 158

- Case study: Google's DeepDream 158
  - Overview of DeepDream 158
  - How DeepDream works 158
  - Visual aesthetics and artistic impact 159
  - Popularization and accessibility 159
  - Impact on the artistic community 159
- Interactive art installations 159
- AI-generated NFT art 160
  - Fusion of technology and creativity 160
  - Unique features of AI-generated NFTs 160
  - Artist collaborations and AI 160
  - Tokenized ownership and digital scarcity 161
  - Impact on the art market: 161

Harmonies of code and melody 161
- Algorithmic musical composition 162
  - Unique melodic patterns 162
  - Collaborative initiatives 162
  - Personalized music experiences 162
  - Real-world examples 162

Aesthetic revolution in design 163
- Algorithmic design creativity 163
- Architectural innovations 163
  - Product and industrial design 163
  - User-centric interfaces 163
- Real-world examples 164
  - Exploration of design options 164
  - Parametric and performance-driven design 164
  - AI-driven decision support 164
  - Real-world applications 165
  - AI-Generated art installations 165

Collaborations between humans and AI 166
- Google's Magenta and music composition 167
  - Examples and use cases 168
  - Value 168

        Human-AI collaboration 169
    NVIDIA's DeepArt and DeepDream in visual arts 169
        Examples and use cases 170
        Value 170
        Human-AI collaboration 170
    Autodesk's generative design in architecture 171
        Examples and use cases 171
        Value 171
        Human-AI collaboration 172
    OpenAI's GPT-3 in creative assistance 172
        Examples and use cases 173
        Value 173
        Human-AI collaboration 173
  Ethical considerations in creative AI 176
    Bias 177
        Bias in creative AI 177
        Types of bias in creative AI 177
        Real-world examples of bias in creative AI 177
        Consequences of bias in creative AI 178
        What can be done to address bias in creative AI 178
    Copyright and ownership 178
    Privacy 180
    Transparency 181
    Examples of ethical concerns in creative AI 182
    How to address ethical concerns in creative AI 184
        Job displacement 184
        Misinformation and disinformation 185
        Weaponization 187
        Autonomy 188
  Conclusion 190

6. Generative AI in Business and Innovation 191
  Introduction 191
  Structure 191

- Enhancing product development and design ... 192
  - Leveraging generative AI in product development ... 193
    - Ford Motor Company ... 194
    - Eli Lilly and Company ... 195
    - Nike ... 196
    - Procter & Gamble ... 197
  - Optimizing existing designs ... 199
  - Personalizing products and services ... 200
    - Retail ... 202
    - Media and entertainment ... 203
    - Financial services ... 204
    - Healthcare ... 206
- Innovations in manufacturing and supply chain ... 207
  - Impact of innovations in manufacturing and supply chain ... 209
- Siemens ... 209
  - Additional benefits of using generative AI to optimize the design of casting molds ... 210
  - Future of generative AI in casting mold design ... 210
- Jet engines ... 211
  - Additional benefits of using generative AI to optimize the production of jet engines ... 212
  - Future of generative AI in jet engine production ... 212
- Walmart ... 212
  - Additional benefits of using generative AI to predict demand and optimize inventory levels ... 213
  - Future of generative AI in demand forecasting and inventory optimization ... 214
- Amazon ... 214
  - Additional benefits of using generative AI to improve route planning ... 215
  - Future of generative AI in route planning ... 215
- Netflix ... 215
  - Additional benefits of using generative AI to recommend movies and TV shows ... 216
  - Future of generative AI in movie and TV show recommendations ... 217
- Spotify ... 217
  - Additional benefits of using generative AI to recommend music ... 218
  - Future of generative AI in music recommendations ... 218
- Strategies for leveraging generative AI in business ... 219

  Implementation roadmaps 219
  Cross-functional collaboration 221
  Data quality and accessibility 222
  Ethical considerations and transparency 223
  Contextual understanding 224
  Intellectual property management 225
  User feedback integration 226
  Regulatory compliance 227
  Strategies for leveraging generative AI in business 228
 Conclusion 229

7. Deep Dive into GANs 231
 Introduction 231
 Structure 231
 Understanding the architecture and training process 232
  Understanding the architecture and training process of generative adversarial networks 232
   Generative adversarial networks applications and success stories 233
   Deep dive into generative adversarial networks 233
   How generative adversarial networks work 234
   Real-world examples 234
   Applications of generative adversarial networks 235
   Examples of generative adversarial networks in use 236
 Challenges and ongoing research in generative adversarial networks 241
  Mode collapse 242
  Training instability 243
  Computational cost 244
  Ethical concerns 246
 Future of generative adversarial networks 247
  New network architectures 247
   Rationale for new network architectures 248
  New training algorithms 249
   Examples of new training algorithms for generative adversarial networks 249
   Rationale for new training algorithms 249

    Examples of how new training algorithms are being used in practice 250
   New objective functions 250
    Examples of new objective functions for generative adversarial networks 251
    Rationale for new objective functions 251
    Examples of how new objective functions are being used in practice 251
  Ethical guidelines 252
  Conclusion 253

8. Building and Deploying Generative Models 255
  Introduction 255
  Structure 255
  Objectives 256
  Practical guide to developing generative models 256
   Generative adversarial networks 259
   Variational autoencoders 259
  Deploying generative models 260
   Examples of generative model deployment 261
   Generative adversarial networks deployment on AWS using CLI 262
   SageMaker Studio 264
   AWS Console 264
   AWS SDKs and APIs 265
  Deploying a variational autoencoder on AWS AI platform 265
   Example of deployment script 266
   Deploying variational autoencoder on AWS SageMaker via console 267
  Deploying a generative adversarial network 268
   Deploying GAN on Google Cloud AI platform 268
   Example of deploying a GAN on Google Cloud using the CLI 268
   Deploying a variational autoencoder on Google Cloud AI Platform using the CLI 270
  Deploying a generative adversarial network on Microsoft Azure 271
   Deploying a variational autoencoder on Microsoft Azure 272
  AI services and tools 273
   AWS: Amazon SageMaker 273
    Value proposition of Amazon SageMaker 273
    Key features 274

Use cases	274
Examples of how Amazon SageMaker is used	275

Google Cloud Platform: AI Platform (Unified) 275

Value proposition of Google AI Platform (Unified)	276
Key features	276
Use cases	277
Examples of how Google AI Platform (Unified) is used	278
Microsoft Azure: Azure Machine Learning	278
Value proposition of Microsoft Azure Machine Learning	278
Key features	279
Use cases	280
Examples of how Microsoft Azure Machine Learning is used	280

Deployment considerations and best practices 283

Considerations	283
Compute resources	283
Training	283
Deployment	284
Model size	285
Model latency	287
Model accuracy	288
Model fairness	289
Best practices	290

Overcoming common challenges in implementation 292

Training data	292
Model architecture	292
Training process	293
Model evaluation	293
Deployment	293

Conclusion 295

Index 297-308

CHAPTER 1
Introduction to Generative AI

Introduction

In this foundational chapter, we embark on a captivating journey into generative AI. We begin by unraveling the essence of generative models, tracing their evolutionary path, and understanding their pivotal role in shaping the landscape of artificial intelligence. Readers will delve into the historical context of generative AI, exploring key milestones that have paved the way for its current prominence.

The chapter serves as a gateway for readers to enter artificial intelligence, specifically focusing on generative models. Here, we navigate through the foundational principles, historical context, and the transformative impact of generative AI across industries.

The readers will gain a clear understanding of the fundamental concepts that underlie generative AI, setting the groundwork for subsequent chapters. This includes an overview of different generative models, the distinctions between generative and discriminative models, and the unique capabilities that make generative AI a powerful force in artificial intelligence. Readers can expect to gain a foundational understanding of generative AI to delve into its intricacies. By the end of the chapter, they will comprehend the historical context, significance, and fundamental principles that drive generative AI. This knowledge will empower them to navigate the intricate landscape of generative models and applications in subsequent chapters.

Structure

The chapter covers the following topics:

- Defining generative AI and its evolution
- Evolutionary trajectory
- Breakthroughs in generative models
- Applications in the real world
- Challenges and advancements
- Anticipated future trajectory

Objectives

By the end of this chapter, readers will have acquired a solid foundation in the basics of generative AI, positioning them to delve deeper into the intricacies of various generative models and their applications across diverse domains. The chapter serves as a gateway to the multifaceted world of generative AI, enticing readers with the promise of unlocking creativity, innovation, and transformative potential. The chapter concludes by inviting readers to embark on a transformative journey through the world of generative AI. It serves as a bridge between theory and application, sparking curiosity about the limitless possibilities that generative models offer. The chapter's narrative paves the way for readers to delve into more specialized topics, ensuring they are well-equipped to explore the multifaceted dimensions of generative AI in the chapters that follow.

Defining generative AI and its evolution

This section offers readers a comprehensive dive into Generative AI, beginning with a clear definition and progressing through its evolutionary journey. It outlines key breakthroughs, such as **general adversarial networks** (**GANs**) and **variational autoencoder** (**VAEs**), and explores their real-world applications, from image synthesis to drug discovery. The section candidly discusses challenges, including ethical considerations and biases. Readers gain insights into the historical context and emerge with a nuanced understanding of the field's evolution, laying a solid foundation for subsequent chapters.

Generative AI represents a paradigm shift in artificial intelligence, distinguished by its ability to create new data instances that resemble, or even innovate beyond, existing datasets. It is a subfield of artificial intelligence. **Artificial intelligence** (**AI**) and generative AI are closely related fields, but they have distinct goals and approaches. While AI encompasses a broad range of techniques that aim to mimic human intelligence, generative AI focuses on creating new content, such as images, music, and text or other forms of data.

It represents a transformative branch of AI focused on creating new, realistic data instances rather than strictly adhering to patterns learned from existing data. At its core, generative AI is about harnessing machines' capacity to imagine, generate, and innovate. The technology primarily relies on sophisticated models designed to understand and replicate patterns present in the training data, enabling the creation of novel content across various domains.

This section serves as a comprehensive exploration of what generative AI entails and how it differs from other branches of AI.

Now let us discuss the key components and mechanisms of generative AI.

Key components and mechanisms

Generative AI models are a powerful tool for creating new data, such as images, music, and text. They are based on a variety of techniques, but they all share some common key components and mechanisms.

Key components

The fundamental key components of generative AI modeling are detailed below:

- **Data:** Generative AI models are trained on large amounts of data. The data can be anything from images and text to audio and video. The quality of the data is critical to the performance of the model.
- **Model architecture:** The model architecture is the design of the neural network. There are many different types of neural networks that can be used for generative AI, but two broad categories are generative adversarial networks and autoregressive models. Let us discuss these two models in detail below:

Generative models

The generative models are defined as follows:

Generative adversarial networks

GANs, a pioneering generative model, consist of a generator and a discriminator engaged in an adversarial training process. The generator's role is to create content, while the discriminator assesses its authenticity. This dynamic interplay refines the generator's ability to produce increasingly realistic outputs. *Figure 1.1* gives an overview of GANs whole system:

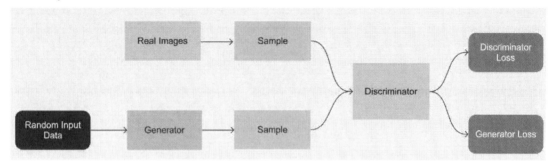

Figure 1.1: *GAN Neural Networks flow diagram*

Variational autoencoders

VAEs adopt a probabilistic approach, focusing on encoding and decoding data distributions. The encoder transforms input data into a probabilistic representation, and the decoder reconstructs this representation into output. VAEs introduce a stochastic element, allowing for the generation of diverse and novel content. *Figure 1.2* illustrates the concept of VAE:

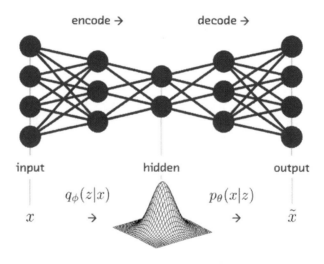

Figure 1.2: *VAE concept diagram*

Autoregressive models

The autoregressive models are defined as follows:

- Autoregressive models, like **Generative Pre-trained Transformer (GPT)**, generate content sequentially, conditioning each step on the preceding ones. These models excel in natural language generation, capturing intricate dependencies and producing coherent and contextually relevant outputs.

- As illustrated in *Figure 1.3*, an autoregressive model's output, h_t, at time **t** depends on not just x_t but also on all the **x's** from previous time steps:

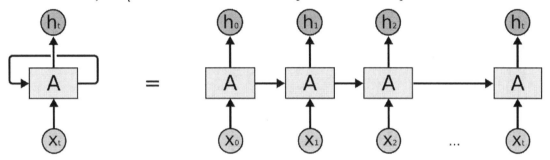

Figure 1.3: Conceptual diagram of autoregressive model, image courtesy Chris Olah

- **Loss function**: The loss function is a measure of how well the model is performing. The loss function is used to train the model by adjusting its weights.
- **Optimizer**: The optimizer is an algorithm that is used to update the weights of the model. The optimizer is responsible for finding the values of the weights that minimize the loss function.

Mechanisms

Enlisted below are some key underlying mechanisms of generative AI models:

- **Learning**: Generative AI models learn from data by adjusting their weights. The weights are adjusted so that the model can generate data that is similar to the data it was trained on.
- **Sampling**: Generative AI models generate new data by sampling from a distribution. The distribution is learned from the data and is used to generate new data that is similar to the data it was trained on.

Evaluation

Generative AI models are evaluated using a variety of metrics. The most common metrics are **Fréchet Inception Distance (FID)** and **Inception Score (IS)**. We will discuss the key components in much more detail in the forthcoming chapters. Let us take a deep dive into how Generative AI has evolved over the years.

Evolutionary trajectory

The evolution of generative AI is a captivating narrative that unfolds across decades of research and innovation. Beginning with foundational work in the mid-20th century, the chapter traverses through landmark moments that have shaped the field. Early concepts, such as Markov models and early attempts at generating text, laid the groundwork. The advent of neural networks, particularly recurrent and convolutional architectures, marked a turning point, enabling more sophisticated generative capabilities. *Figure 1.4* below depicts in summary the evolution of generative AI over years:

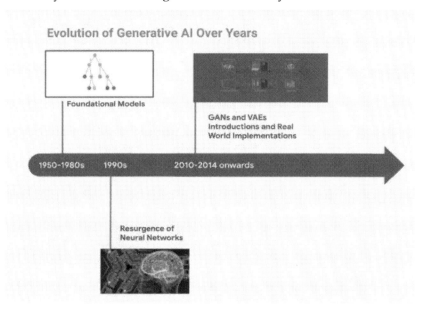

Figure 1.4: *Evolution of Generative AI over years*

- **Early foundations (1950s-1980s)**: The journey of generative AI commences with early foundational work in the mid-20th century. Researchers explored rule-based systems, probabilistic models, and initial attempts at generating text. Early concepts like Markov models laid the groundwork for subsequent advancements.

- **Neural networks resurgence (1990s)**: The 1990s witnessed a resurgence of interest in neural networks, setting the stage for generative AI's evolution. While limited computational power constrained progress, researchers explored **recurrent neural networks (RNNs)** and **convolutional neural networks (CNNs)**, laying the groundwork for future breakthroughs.

- **Introduction of GANs**: A watershed moment in generative AI occurred in 2014 with the introduction of GANs by *Ian Goodfellow* and his collaborators. GANs revolutionized the field with their adversarial training mechanism. This approach pits a generator against a discriminator, leading to the realistic generation of images, videos, and more. GANs quickly became a cornerstone in the generative AI landscape.

- **VAEs and probabilistic approaches**: Parallelly, the introduction of VAEs added a probabilistic dimension to generative modeling. VAEs leveraged probabilistic encodings and decoding, offering a different perspective on generative modeling. This period saw a convergence of deterministic and probabilistic approaches, enriching the field's diversity.

- **Real-world applications (2010s onward)**: Generative AI transcended theoretical frameworks to find practical applications across diverse domains. In image synthesis, GANs produced photorealistic faces through projects like Deepfake. In healthcare, generative models contributed to drug discovery by generating molecular structures. These applications showcased the transformative potential of generative AI beyond academic realms.

- **Ongoing trends and future trajectories**: The evolutionary trajectory of generative AI continues with ongoing trends, including unsupervised learning, federated learning, and ethical considerations. The field is witnessing a convergence with other AI disciplines, promising a future where generative models play a central role in creating, innovating, and solving complex challenges across various domains.

This detailed exploration of the evolutionary trajectory highlights pivotal moments, breakthroughs, and real-world applications that have shaped Generative AI into the dynamic and transformative field it is today.

Breakthroughs in generative models

Key breakthroughs are illuminated, including the introduction of GANs created by *Ian Goodfellow* and his collaborators. GANs, with their adversarial training mechanism, revolutionized the landscape, allowing for the realistic generation of images, videos, and more. VAEs brought another perspective to light, emphasizing probabilistic generative modeling. The following exploration of these models provides readers with a nuanced understanding of the diverse approaches within generative AI.

- **GANs**: A monumental breakthrough, GANs, introduced in 2014, marked a paradigm shift in generative modeling. GANs consist of a generator and a discriminator engaged in an adversarial process. Notable examples include **Deep Convolutional GAN (DCGAN)** for image synthesis and StyleGAN for high-quality, diverse image generation. GANs revolutionized how realistic data, such as images and videos, could be generated.

- **BERT and transformer models for natural language processing**: Generative models extended their influence into **natural language processing (NLP)** with breakthroughs like **Bidirectional Encoder Representations from Transformers (BERT)**. These transformer-based models excel in understanding context and semantics in language. BERT's pre-training on vast corpora followed by fine-tuning for specific tasks led to remarkable advancements in NLP, including question answering and language translation.

- **VAEs**: Another breakthrough came with the introduction of VAEs, emphasizing probabilistic generative modeling. VAEs introduced a different approach, leveraging encodings with probabilistic distributions. Notable applications include image generation and data compression. The probabilistic nature of VAEs added a layer of uncertainty, enabling diverse and creative outputs.

- **Conditional generative models**: Advancements in conditional generative models (cGANs) allowed for the targeted generation of data based on specific conditions. For instance, cGANs demonstrated the ability to generate images conditioned on specific attributes, such as generating images of a particular class. This breakthrough enhanced the practical applicability of generative models in various domains.

- **Style transfer and image-to-image translation:** Generative models showcased breakthroughs in style transfer, where the style of one image could be applied to another. CycleGAN, for instance, demonstrated remarkable capabilities in image-to-image translation without paired training data. These breakthroughs opened avenues for creative applications, such as transforming artistic styles or adapting images across domains.

- **Progressive growing and high-resolution synthesis**: The advent of progressive growing techniques addressed challenges in training GANs for high-resolution image synthesis. StyleGAN, with its progressive growing architecture, demonstrated the synthesis of high-quality images with unprecedented realism and diversity. This breakthrough facilitated the generation of detailed images, impacting fields like digital art and content creation.

- **Cross-modal and multimodal generative models**: Breakthroughs extended to cross-modal and multimodal generative models, enabling the generation of content across different modalities. **Contrastive Language-Image Pretraining (CLIP)** demonstrated the alignment of language and vision, allowing the model to generate images based on textual descriptions. Such models broadened the scope of generative AI to diverse data types and modalities.

These breakthroughs collectively propelled generative models from conceptual frameworks to powerful tools with practical applications. They not only expanded the capabilities of generative AI but also demonstrated its versatility in addressing a wide range of tasks, from creative endeavors to solving real-world challenges.

Applications in the real world

The evolution of generative AI is not merely a theoretical narrative, but one deeply intertwined with its real-world applications. From content creation in the arts to data augmentation in machine learning, generative models have found utility across diverse sectors. This section delves into case studies that highlight the transformative impact of generative AI in areas such as image synthesis, text generation, and even drug discovery.

- **Image synthesis and Deepfake technology**: Generative AI, particularly GANs, has found extensive use in image synthesis. Deepfake technology, powered by GANs, gained notoriety for its ability to create realistic video content by swapping faces. While the ethical implications are profound, the technology showcases the capacity of generative models to alter visual content convincingly. *Figure 1.5* below is a representational picture of image synthesis using Deepfake technology:

Figure 1.5: Representational picture of image synthesis using Deepfake technology

- **Drug discovery and molecular generation**: In the healthcare domain, generative models contribute to drug discovery by generating molecular structures with desired properties. This application streamlines the drug development process by proposing potential compounds for testing. Generative models, including variational autoencoders, have demonstrated their utility in molecular generation, expediting innovation in pharmaceuticals. *Figure 1.6* is a representational image of drug discovery using Gen-AI:

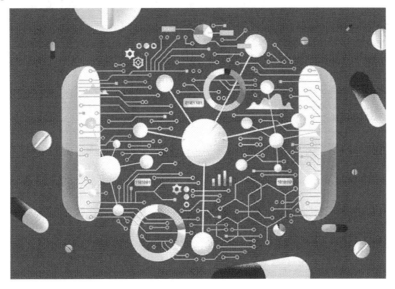

Figure 1.6: Drug discovery using Gen AI, representational image

- **Style transfer in artistic endeavors**: Generative models like neural style transfer enable the transformation of images into artistic styles. Artists and designers leverage this technology to create visually compelling pieces by transferring the stylistic features of famous artworks onto new images. This application demonstrates the intersection of technology and artistic expression. *Figure 1.7* shows a flow diagram of how style transfer works using Gen AI:

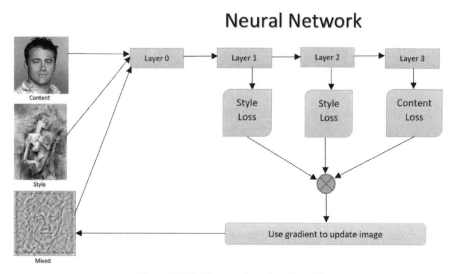

Figure 1.7: *Style transfer using Gen AI*

- **Data augmentation in machine learning**: Generative models play a crucial role in data augmentation for machine learning tasks. By generating diverse instances of existing data, models are trained on more varied inputs, enhancing their robustness and generalization. This application ensures that machine learning models are better equipped to handle real-world scenarios. *Figure 1.8* is an illustration of data augmentation in machine learning:

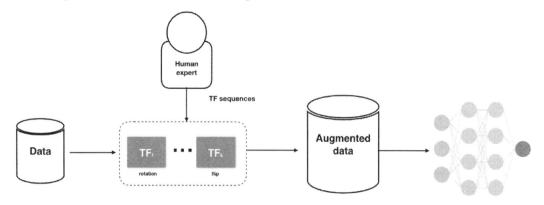

Figure 1.8: *Flow diagram of data augmentation, image courtesy Stanford AI Lab Blog*

- **Text-to-image synthesis**: Generative models have been employed in text-to-image synthesis, enabling the generation of visual content based on textual descriptions. This application has implications in design, advertising, and content creation. For instance, models can generate images based on written prompts, expanding possibilities in creative industries. *Figure 1.9* illustrates the process of Image generation through natural language using Google's Imagen Gen AI model:

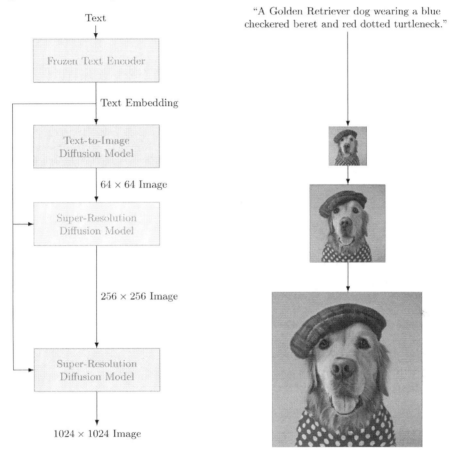

Figure 1.9: *Illustration via Google's Imagen model on how text instructions can be leveraged to create an image*

- **Super-resolution imaging**: Generative models contribute to super-resolution imaging, enhancing the quality and detail of images. Progressive growing techniques, as seen in StyleGAN, enable the synthesis of high-resolution images with unprecedented realism. This application has implications in fields such as satellite imaging, medical imaging, and digital art.
- **Speech synthesis and voice cloning**: Generative models extend their capabilities to speech synthesis and voice cloning. By training on vocal samples, models can generate natural-sounding speech or even clone a person's voice. While this raises

ethical concerns, the technology has applications in voiceovers, virtual assistants, and personalized audio experiences.

- **Cross-modal generation in CLIP**: Cross-modal generative models, like CLIP, align language and vision. CLIP can generate images based on textual descriptions, demonstrating the potential for multimodal applications. This technology opens avenues for content creation based on natural language prompts. *Figure 1.10* illustrates the combination of two different modes, in this case text and image to generate an image:

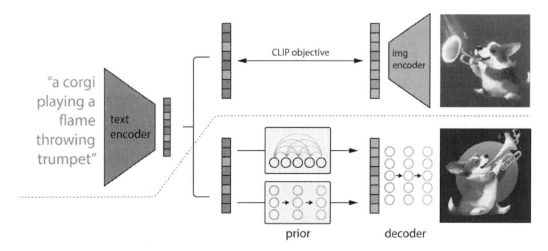

Figure 1.10: Example illustration of multi-modal generative AI model

These real-world applications illustrate the versatility of generative AI across diverse domains, from healthcare and art to machine learning and multimedia content creation. While these applications showcase the transformative potential of generative models, they also prompt discussions around ethical considerations and responsible use in these evolving fields.

Challenges and advancements

The chapter does not shy away from addressing the challenges and limitations faced by generative AI. In this section, we will discuss ethical considerations, biases in generated content, and the interpretability of generative models. Simultaneously, recent advancements, such as the integration of reinforcement learning with generative models, hint at the ongoing evolution of the field.

- **Ethical considerations and biases**: One of the primary challenges in generative AI is the ethical use of technology. Instances of biased content generation, especially in facial recognition applications, have raised concerns. Advancements in research focus on developing algorithms that mitigate biases and ensure fair and ethical outcomes. Ethical AI frameworks and guidelines are emerging to guide practitioners in responsible AI development.

- **Interpretability and explainability**: Generative models, particularly complex ones like GANs, often lack interpretability. Understanding the reasoning behind a model's decision is crucial, especially in critical applications like healthcare. Recent advancements involve developing techniques for explaining the decision-making process of generative models and enhancing transparency and trust in AI systems.

- **Robustness to adversarial attacks**: Generative models are susceptible to adversarial attacks where intentional, small perturbations to input data can lead to incorrect outputs. Research is focused on advancing the robustness of generative models against adversarial attacks, ensuring that models maintain their performance in the presence of deliberately crafted input variations.

- **Data efficiency and training stability**: Training generative models can be resource-intensive and requires large datasets. Advancements are directed at improving data efficiency, enabling models to achieve high-quality outputs with less training data. Additionally, ensuring stability during training, particularly for GANs, is an ongoing challenge. Researchers are exploring techniques to enhance training stability.

- **Long-term dependencies and sequential generation**: Generating coherent and realistic sequences, such as paragraphs of text or video frames, poses challenges due to long-term dependencies. Advancements in recurrent generative models aim to capture and preserve long-term dependencies in sequential data, enhancing the generation of realistic and contextually coherent outputs.

- **Scaling to high-resolution and large models**: Generating high-resolution images or utilizing large models like those in GPT-3 involves significant computational challenges. Advancements focus on scaling generative models efficiently, optimizing training procedures, and exploring novel architectures to handle the computational demands of high-resolution and large-scale generative tasks.

- **Unsupervised and self-supervised learning**: While generative models excel in unsupervised learning scenarios, advancements are being made in self-supervised learning. This involves developing models that can learn from unlabeled data by creating their own supervisory signals. This approach enhances the adaptability of generative models to diverse datasets.

- **Cross-modal and multimodal generative models**: Advancements in generative models extend to cross-modal and multimodal applications, where models can generate content across different modalities (for example, images from textual descriptions). Techniques like CLIP represent progress in aligning language and vision, opening new possibilities for generative AI applications.

These challenges and advancements underscore the dynamic nature of generative AI research. While challenges prompt innovation, advancements drive the field forward, addressing ethical concerns, improving interpretability, enhancing robustness, and expanding the capabilities of generative models across various dimensions. Ongoing research in these areas continues to shape the trajectory of generative AI.

In this section, we covered details on foundational generative AI model. We also talked about the evolution and transformation of generative AI over the years. This section also encompassed various applications of generative AI, its challenges and advancements. In the next section, we will talk about the anticipated future trajectory of generative AI.

Anticipated future trajectory

The chapter concludes by looking forward, offering glimpses into the potential trajectories of generative AI. Trends such as unsupervised learning, federated learning, and ethical AI considerations are discussed, setting the stage for readers to contemplate the future challenges and possibilities that will shape the continual evolution of generative AI.

- **Unsupervised learning and few-shot learning**: The future trajectory of generative AI is anticipated to emphasize unsupervised learning and few-shot learning. Advances in unsupervised learning aim to enable generative models to learn from unannotated data, reducing the reliance on labeled datasets. Few-shot learning, where models generalize from a small number of examples, holds promise for more efficient and adaptable generative AI systems.

- **Federated learning and decentralized generative models**: The shift towards federated learning involves training models across decentralized devices, preserving data privacy. Generative models could benefit from this paradigm, allowing users to contribute to model training without compromising individual data privacy. This approach aligns with the growing emphasis on responsible and privacy-preserving AI.

- **Ethical AI and explainable generative models**: Ethical considerations will play a pivotal role in shaping the future of generative AI. Anticipated advancements involve integrating ethical principles into model design and deployment. The development of explainable generative models is crucial for understanding and justifying model decisions, fostering transparency, and building trust with users and stakeholders.

- **Advancements in reinforcement learning and sequential generation**: Generative models, particularly those handling sequential data, are expected to benefit from advancements in reinforcement learning. Reinforcement learning can guide generative models in creating sequences with improved long-term coherence. This has implications for applications such as natural language generation and video synthesis.

- **Cross-modal integration and multimodal generative models**: The future trajectory involves further integration of cross-modal and multimodal capabilities. Generative models, like CLIP, that understand and generate content across different modalities (text and images) are anticipated to become more sophisticated. This could lead to breakthroughs in tasks requiring multimodal understanding, such as visual storytelling and content creation.

- **AI creativity and co-creation with humans**: Generative AI is poised to become a tool for human-AI co-creation, especially in creative endeavors. Future generative models might collaborate with human users in artistic projects, design tasks, or content creation. This co-creative potential could revolutionize industries where human-AI collaboration is essential.

- **Advancements in transfer learning for generative models**: Transfer learning, where models trained on one task are leveraged for another, is anticipated to play a significant role in generative AI. Pre-trained models could be fine-tuned for specific tasks, enhancing efficiency and adaptability. This approach is particularly relevant for scenarios with limited labeled data.

- **Continued exploration of generative model architectures**: The exploration of novel generative model architectures will persist, with researchers seeking models that balance performance and efficiency. This includes investigating advancements in generative model architectures that can scale to handle high-resolution content and adapt to the complexities of diverse datasets.

These anticipated trajectories in generative AI highlight a future where ethical considerations, privacy preservation, cross-modal capabilities, and co-creation with humans play central roles. As generative AI continues to evolve, these advancements are expected to shape a landscape where AI systems are not only powerful but also aligned with human values and societal needs.

The future of generative AI holds promises of continued innovation. Anticipated developments include advancements in unsupervised learning, ethical considerations, and the integration of generative models with other AI disciplines, paving the way for a future where machines not only learn from the past but actively contribute to creative and innovative endeavors. Generative AI stands as a testament to the evolving landscape of artificial intelligence, pushing the boundaries of what machines can envision and create.

This detailed exploration of defining generative AI and its evolution not only grounds readers in the foundational concepts but also provides a nuanced perspective on the dynamic journey this field has undertaken. It ensures that readers are equipped with the knowledge needed to appreciate the intricacies of subsequent chapters.

Conclusion

The chapter lays the foundation for understanding the transformative force of generative AI. It begins by defining generative AI and tracing its evolutionary trajectory, elucidating how it has evolved from traditional AI models. The readers would have gained a comprehensive understanding of the fundamental concepts surrounding generative AI and its evolution. They would have learned to discern how generative AI differs from traditional AI models, appreciating its creative and innovative capabilities. The chapter equips users with the knowledge to identify scenarios where generative AI can be applied, fostering creative solutions and advancements. Overall, readers would have developed a foundational understanding of the broader implications of generative AI, setting the stage for a deeper dive into its applications across diverse sectors and its potential in shaping the future of technology.

In the next chapter, generative AI in industries, readers can expect a detailed exploration of how generative AI has reshaped industries, revolutionizing the way businesses operate and innovate. The significance of generative AI will be dissected across healthcare, entertainment, marketing, finance, and more. Through real-world examples and case studies, readers will gain insights into the tangible impact of generative AI on diverse sectors. The section will elucidate how generative models contribute to creativity, efficiency, and problem-solving in fields ranging from art and entertainment to finance and urban planning. Additionally, it will address challenges and ethical considerations, providing a comprehensive understanding of the multifaceted role generative AI plays in the contemporary landscape.

Join our book's Discord space

Join the book's Discord Workspace for Latest updates, Offers, Tech happenings around the world, New Release and Sessions with the Authors:

https://discord.bpbonline.com

CHAPTER 2
Generative AI in Industries

Introduction

In this chapter, the readers will learn about the significance of generative AI across various industries, from its roots in research to its real-world applications. We will discuss how generative models contribute to creativity, innovation, and problem-solving, setting the stage for a comprehensive exploration of their principles and functionalities. It delves into the transformative applications of generative models in healthcare, art, entertainment, marketing, finance, manufacturing, human resources, robotics, and urban planning. Through real-world examples and case studies, the section highlights how generative AI contributes to drug discovery, artistic creation, content marketing, financial decision-making, product design, recruitment processes, robotics, and urban design. By the end of this chapter, the readers will gain a good understanding on the multifaceted use cases and implementation of Gen AI across various industries.

Structure

The chapter covers the following topics:

- Significance and impact of Generative AI on various industries
- Healthcare and drug discovery
- Art and entertainment

- Creative assistance in content generation
- Manufacturing and design
- Finance and risk management
- Human resources and recruitment
- Robotics and automation
- Urban planning and architecture
- Challenges and considerations
- Future outlook

Objectives

The objective of this chapter is to explore the profound impact of generative AI across a spectrum of industries. It delves into the transformative applications of generative models in healthcare, art, entertainment, marketing, finance, manufacturing, human resources, robotics, and urban planning. Through real-world examples and case studies, the chapter highlights how generative AI contributes to drug discovery, artistic creation, content marketing, financial decision-making, product design, recruitment processes, robotics, and urban design. It also expands on challenges and considerations whilst using generative AI.

Significance and impact of generative AI on various industries

This part of the chapter extensively explores the profound impact of generative AI across a spectrum of industries. It delves into the transformative applications of generative models in healthcare, art, entertainment, marketing, finance, manufacturing, human resources, robotics, and urban planning. Through real-world examples and case studies, the section highlights how generative AI contributes to drug discovery, artistic creation, content marketing, financial decision-making, product design, recruitment processes, robotics, and urban design. It examines the creative and efficiency-enhancing aspects of generative AI in diverse professional domains. Additionally, the section addresses ethical considerations and challenges associated with the deployment of generative models, providing readers with a comprehensive understanding of the broad and dynamic landscape of generative AI's impact on industries.

Generative AI's significance extends far beyond academic research, impacting a myriad of industries with its transformative capabilities. This section delves into the profound impact of generative AI across diverse sectors, showcasing how this technology has redefined creativity, innovation, and problem-solving. Let us explore Generative AI's impact on various industry sectors.

Healthcare and drug discovery

Generative AI plays a pivotal role in drug discovery by generating molecular structures with desired properties. This accelerates the identification of potential drug candidates, significantly reducing the time and resources required for the discovery process.

Image synthesis techniques are employed to generate realistic biomedical images, aiding in medical imaging research. This has applications in training and validating imaging algorithms, ultimately contributing to improved diagnostics and treatment planning.

Let us discuss some of the aspects of generative AI in healthcare and drug discovery in detail.

Advancing molecular generation

Molecular generation is a machine learning technique used to create new and diverse molecules with desired chemical properties. It involves utilizing algorithms to analyze large datasets of existing molecules, identify key characteristics, and then design new molecules that exhibit specific functionalities or properties.

Generative AI models have revolutionized molecular generation in drug discovery. Traditional methods often rely on trial and error, making the exploration of the vast chemical space for potential drug candidates time-consuming and resource intensive. Generative models, particularly GANs and VAEs, overcome this limitation by learning patterns from existing molecules and proposing novel structures. For instance, GANs trained on molecular datasets can generate diverse compounds with unique structural features, providing researchers with a rich set of potential candidates for further exploration.

Generative AI's impact on drug discovery is particularly pronounced in the domain of molecular generation. Traditional methods for identifying potential drug candidates involve extensive experimentation, limiting the exploration of the vast chemical space. Generative models, such as GANs and VAEs, offer a paradigm shift by harnessing the power of artificial intelligence to propose novel molecular structures.

- **GANs in molecular diversity**: GANs have demonstrated prowess in generating molecular structures with remarkable diversity. Researchers train GANs on large datasets of known molecules, allowing the model to learn the underlying patterns and relationships between different chemical entities. As a result, GANs can generate entirely new molecular structures that may not have been considered through conventional approaches. This capability significantly expands the scope of potential drug candidates.

- **VAEs for latent space exploration**: VAEs contribute by mapping molecules into a latent space where similar structures are clustered together. This enables efficient exploration of molecular diversity. They learn a probabilistic representation of molecules, allowing for the generation of novel structures by sampling from the learned distribution. The inherent probabilistic nature of VAEs aligns with the uncertainty often present in molecular design, providing a more realistic and adaptable approach.

- **Example: GANs in drug design**: Consider the application of GANs in de novo drug design. GANs are trained on a dataset of existing drug molecules, learning the intricate relationships between different chemical groups. When tasked with generating new molecules, GANs produce candidates that adhere to learned patterns of molecular stability and bioactivity. Pharmaceutical researchers can then prioritize synthesized molecules that exhibit promising properties, streamlining the drug discovery process.

- **Application in polypharmacology**: Beyond single-target drug design, generative models excel in addressing the complexity of polypharmacology – the interaction of drugs with multiple targets. GANs, in particular, can propose compounds that modulate multiple targets simultaneously. This polypharmacological approach is crucial for developing drugs that can effectively address diseases with intricate molecular pathways, offering a holistic perspective in drug discovery.

In essence, the advancement in molecular generation powered by generative AI provides researchers with a powerful tool to explore novel chemical spaces efficiently. By leveraging the unique capabilities of GANs and VAEs, drug discovery is propelled into a new era where the potential for identifying innovative therapeutic agents is expanded, offering hope for more rapid and targeted drug development.

Enhancing biomedical imaging

Biomedical imaging plays a crucial role in diagnostics. However, acquiring diverse and extensive datasets for training machine learning algorithms can be challenging. Generative AI addresses this by enabling the creation of synthetic datasets. Models, especially GANs, are trained to generate realistic biomedical images, contributing to algorithm training and validation. This not only addresses data scarcity but also allows for the simulation of various imaging scenarios, enhancing the robustness of algorithms in real-world applications.

The role of generative AI in enhancing biomedical imaging represents a groundbreaking fusion of artificial intelligence and medical diagnostics. Traditional approaches to training machine learning models for medical imaging often encounter challenges related to dataset scarcity and diversity. Generative models, particularly GANs, have emerged as transformative solutions, providing a bridge over these gaps.

- **Synthetic dataset generation with GANs**: GANs are trained on existing medical imaging datasets, learning the intricate patterns and features present in various types of biomedical images. Once trained, GANs can generate synthetic images that closely mimic real-world medical images. This capability addresses the challenge of limited datasets, allowing researchers to create diverse and extensive datasets for training and validating machine learning algorithms.

- **Improving robustness with simulated scenarios**: Biomedical imaging often involves scenarios that are challenging to capture in real-world settings. Generative models enable the simulation of various imaging scenarios, enhancing the robustness of machine learning algorithms. For example, GANs trained on X-ray images can generate synthetic images depicting diverse patient conditions, facilitating the development and validation of algorithms for detecting abnormalities under varying circumstances.

- **Example: GANs in imaging using MRI**: Consider the application of GANs in **Magnetic Resonance Imaging (MRI)**. GANs can generate synthetic MRI images that encompass a wide range of anatomical variations and imaging conditions. These synthetic images serve as valuable additions to training datasets, ensuring that machine learning models are exposed to a comprehensive array of scenarios. This contributes to the development of more robust and versatile MRI interpretation algorithms.

- **Addressing data imbalance**: In biomedical imaging, certain conditions or rare diseases may be underrepresented in datasets. GANs can be employed to generate synthetic images of less common conditions, addressing data imbalance issues. By simulating the imaging characteristics of rare diseases, generative models facilitate more effective training of machine learning models, ensuring that algorithms are proficient in identifying even the less prevalent medical conditions.

- **Simulation of imaging modalities**: Beyond static images, generative models can simulate entire imaging modalities. For instance, GANs can generate synthetic **positron emission tomography (PET)** scans, contributing to the training of machine learning algorithms for image analysis. This extends the applicability of generative AI to a wide range of medical imaging techniques.

The application of generative AI in enhancing biomedical imaging goes beyond addressing data scarcity. It extends to the creation of versatile, diverse, and realistic datasets for training machine learning algorithms. By simulating scenarios and imaging modalities, generative models significantly contribute to the robustness and efficacy of algorithms, ultimately advancing the capabilities of medical diagnostics and imaging interpretation.

Targeted drug design and optimization

Targeted drug design is a strategic approach to developing new medications that specifically target a particular disease-causing molecule or pathway. This differs from traditional drug discovery, which often involves screening large libraries of compounds for potential activity against a disease with less focus on the specific molecular mechanism.

Generative models are applied to design drugs with a targeted approach. By learning from datasets containing information on molecular interactions, these models can propose compounds optimized for specific biological targets. This targeted design accelerates the drug discovery process by focusing on molecules with higher binding affinity and efficacy. The efficiency of generative models in proposing optimized compounds brings a precision medicine approach to drug design, aligning with the growing emphasis on personalized and effective therapeutics.

Generative AI's impact on drug design transcends traditional methodologies by offering a targeted and efficient approach. Focusing on specific biological targets, these models, especially GANs, have revolutionized the optimization of drug candidates for enhanced binding affinity and efficacy.

- **Learning from molecular interactions**: Generative models are trained on vast datasets containing information about molecular interactions. GANs, in particular, learn the complex relationships between molecular structures and their interactions with specific biological targets. This knowledge forms the foundation for generating novel compounds optimized for binding to these targets.

- **Optimizing binding affinity**: The primary objective in drug design is often to enhance the binding affinity of a compound to a specific target. Generative models excel in proposing molecular structures that exhibit high affinity, guided by learned patterns from training data. For instance, if a GAN is trained on datasets of known ligands and their binding affinities, it can generate new ligands with predicted high affinities for the target.

- **Example: GANs in protein-ligand binding**: Consider the application of GANs in protein-ligand binding. GANs trained on a diverse set of known protein-ligand interactions can generate novel ligands with characteristics that align with successful binding profiles. This accelerates the drug discovery process by suggesting potential candidates that are more likely to exhibit the desired therapeutic effects.

- **Polypharmacology and multi-target optimization**: Generative AI extends its capabilities to polypharmacology, where a drug may interact with multiple targets. GANs can propose compounds that are optimized for interacting with multiple targets simultaneously. This polypharmacological approach is crucial for diseases with complex molecular pathways, allowing for the design of drugs that can address multiple facets of a condition.

- **In silico lead optimization**: In drug discovery, the lead optimization phase involves refining initial drug candidates to enhance their properties. Generative models aid in this process by suggesting modifications to existing compounds that may improve their bioactivity, pharmacokinetics, or safety profiles. This in silico optimization accelerates the iterative nature of drug development.

- **Rational drug design**: The rationale behind targeted drug design with generative models is rooted in rational drug design principles. By leveraging learned insights from molecular interactions, these models contribute to a rational and systematic approach to designing drugs. This stands in contrast to traditional methods that often rely on serendipity in discovering effective compounds.

Generative AI in targeted drug design and optimization embodies a paradigm shift in the precision and efficiency of pharmaceutical innovation. By harnessing the power of deep learning, these models contribute to the creation of novel compounds with enhanced binding affinity and efficacy, offering a transformative approach to drug discovery that is guided by learned molecular insights.

Personalized medicine and treatment plans

Generative AI is instrumental in ushering in the era of personalized medicine. By analyzing patient data, including genetic information, these models contribute to the formulation of personalized treatment plans. For example, a generative model can analyze a patient's genetic makeup to recommend personalized drug regimens, accounting for factors such as drug metabolism and potential side effects. This personalized approach not only enhances treatment efficacy but also minimizes adverse reactions, marking a significant shift from generic treatment strategies.

Generative AI has ushered in a new era of healthcare by facilitating the advent of personalized medicine. The ability to analyze patient-specific data, including genetic information, empowers generative models to contribute significantly to the formulation of personalized treatment plans. This approach goes beyond the conventional one-size-fits-all paradigm, considering individual variations to optimize treatment efficacy. Some of the practical use cases of personalized medicine are enlisted below:

- **Genetic analysis for precision**: Generative models, when fed with genetic data, can discern patterns and relationships that influence drug metabolism, response, and potential side effects. For instance, if a patient has a genetic predisposition to metabolize a drug slowly, a generative model can propose alternative medications or dosage adjustments tailored to the individual's unique genetic makeup.

- **Tailoring drug selection**: In personalized medicine, the selection of drugs is customized based on a patient's genetic, molecular, and clinical profile. Generative models can analyze diverse datasets to propose optimal drug combinations that align with the specific biological characteristics of an individual. This tailoring ensures that prescribed medications are more likely to be effective with fewer adverse effects.

- **Example: Individualized cancer treatment**: Consider a scenario where a patient is diagnosed with cancer. Generative models, trained on vast datasets of cancer genomics and treatment outcomes, can assist oncologists in devising a personalized treatment plan. By analyzing the genetic mutations specific to the patient's cancer cells, the model may recommend a combination of targeted therapies tailored to inhibit the unique pathways driving the malignancy.

- **Dose optimization for patient variability**: Patient responses to medications can vary significantly. Generative models can account for this variability by proposing dose optimizations based on individual patient characteristics. For instance, if a patient has a higher tolerance for a particular drug, the model may suggest an increased dosage to ensure therapeutic efficacy.

- **Integration of multi-omics data**: Personalized medicine often involves the integration of multi-omics data, encompassing genomics, transcriptomics, proteomics, and more. Generative models are adept at comprehensively analyzing these multi-dimensional datasets to extract meaningful insights. This holistic approach enables healthcare providers to formulate treatment plans that consider the intricate interplay of various biological factors.

- **Real-time adjustments**: Generative models can contribute to the dynamism of personalized treatment plans by facilitating real-time adjustments. As a patient's health status evolves or new data becomes available, the model can continuously analyze and recommend modifications to the treatment plan. This adaptability enhances the responsiveness of healthcare strategies.

In essence, personalized medicine and treatment plans powered by generative AI represent a transformative shift toward patient-centric healthcare. By leveraging the wealth of information encoded in individual genomes and health data, generative models contribute to the realization of tailored treatment strategies that optimize therapeutic outcomes while minimizing the risk of adverse effects. This patient-specific approach marks a paradigm shift in healthcare, aligning interventions with the unique characteristics of each individual.

Case studies and success stories

Real-world case studies and success stories illustrate the tangible impact of generative AI in healthcare and drug discovery. Pharmaceutical companies and research institutions leveraging generative models report notable reductions in the time and resources required for drug discovery. These success stories highlight the practical implications of generative AI in addressing longstanding challenges in the healthcare industry, providing concrete evidence of its transformative power.

The application of generative AI in healthcare and drug discovery is substantiated by a plethora of compelling case studies and success stories. These real-world examples underscore the transformative potential of generative models in addressing challenges and accelerating breakthroughs in the medical and pharmaceutical domains:

- **Accelerating drug discovery at Insilico Medicine**: *Insilico Medicine*, a biotechnology company, utilized GANs to expedite drug discovery processes.

By training GANs on vast datasets of molecular structures and their associated bioactivities, the company generated novel compounds with desired properties. This approach significantly reduced the time and resources traditionally required for identifying potential drug candidates, demonstrating the efficiency gains afforded by generative AI in the pharmaceutical industry.

- **Synthetic data for medical imaging at PathAI**: *PathAI*, a company specializing in pathology solutions, leveraged generative models to address data scarcity in medical imaging datasets. GANs were employed to generate synthetic pathology images, augmenting limited datasets for training machine learning algorithms. This synthetic data approach enhanced the robustness of the algorithms, leading to more accurate and reliable diagnoses in pathology, particularly in scenarios with a shortage of diverse real-world images.

- **Polypharmacology in drug design at Atomwise**: *Atomwise*, a company utilizing AI for drug discovery, implemented generative models to explore polypharmacology. By considering multiple targets simultaneously, generative models proposed compounds with broader therapeutic effects. This polypharmacological approach proved invaluable in developing drugs that could address complex diseases with intricate molecular pathways. *Atomwise*'s success demonstrates the potential of generative AI in designing multi-target drugs for enhanced therapeutic outcomes.

- **Personalized treatment plans at Tempus**: *Tempus*, a technology company focused on precision medicine, utilized generative models to analyze patient data for personalized treatment plans. By incorporating genetic information, clinical data, and outcomes, generative AI facilitated the identification of optimal treatment strategies tailored to individual patients. This approach showcased the potential of generative models in reshaping the landscape of healthcare toward personalized and more effective interventions.

- **In silico lead optimization at Numerate**: *Numerate*, a drug design company, applied generative AI for in silico lead optimization. Generative models suggested modifications to existing drug candidates to improve their properties, such as bioactivity and pharmacokinetics. This approach streamlined the lead optimization phase, enabling the rapid iteration and improvement of drug candidates. *Numerate*'s success exemplifies how generative AI can enhance the efficiency of the drug development pipeline.

These case studies exemplify the tangible impact of generative AI in diverse aspects of healthcare and drug discovery. From accelerating drug discovery to addressing data scarcity in medical imaging and optimizing treatment plans, these success stories underscore the versatility and efficacy of generative models in pushing the boundaries of what is achievable in the realms of medicine and pharmaceutical innovation.

Ethical considerations and future prospects

As generative AI becomes increasingly integrated into healthcare, ethical considerations become paramount. Ensuring responsible use, addressing biases in models, and safeguarding patient privacy are critical aspects of ethical deployment. Looking to the future, ongoing ethical discourse is essential to navigate the challenges and potentials of generative AI in advancing personalized medicine, drug discovery, and overall healthcare delivery.

As generative AI continues to redefine possibilities in healthcare and drug discovery, a critical lens on ethical considerations becomes imperative. Anticipating future prospects involves not only technological advancements but also responsible deployment of these innovations to ensure equitable, transparent, and ethical practices.

Responsible data use and patient privacy

One of the foremost ethical considerations revolves around data privacy. Generative models often require access to vast and diverse datasets, including patient records and genomic information. Ethical practices necessitate robust measures to safeguard patient privacy, ensuring that sensitive information is anonymized and protected against unauthorized access. Striking a balance between data utility and privacy is crucial to maintain public trust in the use of generative AI.

Responsible data use and patient privacy stand as pillars of ethical considerations in generative AI for healthcare and drug discovery. The transformative potential of artificial intelligence in these fields comes with a responsibility to handle sensitive patient data with the utmost care, ensuring privacy, confidentiality, and ethical use. The following highlight the ways in which data privacy and confidentiality is taken care of when being used by generative AI models:

- **Data anonymization and de-identification**: Generative AI often relies on large datasets that may include identifiable patient information. To navigate the ethical landscape, responsible data use begins with the anonymization and de-identification of sensitive data. This involves removing or encrypting personally identifiable information to prevent the identification of individuals. Striking a balance between data utility and privacy protection is a delicate yet crucial task.

- **Secure data transmission and storage**: The entire data lifecycle, from transmission to storage, requires robust security measures. Generative AI models may be trained on distributed datasets from various healthcare institutions. Ensuring secure data transmission prevents unauthorized access during data sharing. Additionally, secure storage practices, including encryption and access controls, are essential to protect patient data from breaches and unauthorized use.

- **Informed consent and patient empowerment**: Responsible data use emphasizes the importance of informed consent from patients whose data contributes to generative AI models. Informed consent ensures that individuals understand how their data will be used, for what purposes, and with whom it may be shared. Transparent communication fosters trust and empowers patients to actively participate in the decision-making process regarding the use of their health data for AI-driven healthcare solutions.

- **Ethical data governance and oversight**: Establishing ethical data governance frameworks and oversight mechanisms is critical. This involves defining clear policies and procedures for data collection, storage, and sharing. Ethical review boards or committees can provide oversight to ensure that generative AI projects align with ethical standards and regulatory requirements. Such governance structures promote accountability and ethical conduct throughout the data lifecycle.

- **Mitigating risks of re-identification**: Even with anonymization efforts, there is always a risk of re-identification, especially as datasets grow in size and diversity. Generative AI developers must implement techniques to mitigate these risks, such as differential privacy, which adds noise to the data to prevent the identification of individual records. By understanding and addressing re-identification risks, developers can uphold patient privacy even in the face of evolving technologies.

- **Education and awareness**: Ensuring responsible data use requires a concerted effort to educate all stakeholders involved, including healthcare professionals, data scientists, and patients. Raising awareness about the ethical considerations of data use in generative AI fosters a culture of responsible and ethical practices. Healthcare institutions and organizations should invest in training programs to equip their personnel with the knowledge and skills necessary to navigate the complexities of data privacy in AI applications.

Addressing bias and fairness

Generative models can inadvertently perpetuate biases present in training data, impacting the fairness of healthcare interventions. For instance, if a model is trained predominantly on data from certain demographics, it may not generalize well to underrepresented groups. Ethical considerations involve continuous efforts to identify and mitigate biases, employing techniques such as fairness-aware training and auditing to ensure that generative AI contributes to equitable healthcare outcomes.

Addressing bias and ensuring fairness in generative AI applications is paramount to building ethical and equitable healthcare systems. The potential biases present in training data and the outputs of AI models demand careful consideration and proactive measures to avoid perpetuating or exacerbating existing disparities in healthcare.

- **Diverse and representative training data**: The first step in mitigating bias is to ensure that the training data used for generative AI models is diverse and representative of the entire population. If the training data predominantly represents certain demographics, the model may inadvertently learn and replicate biases present in that data. For example, in medical imaging, ensuring diverse representation across age, gender, ethnicity, and other demographic factors is crucial to building fair models.

- **Fairness-aware training techniques**: Researchers are developing fairness-aware training techniques to mitigate bias during the model training process. These techniques involve adjusting the learning process to explicitly account for fairness considerations. For instance, in drug discovery, the training process might be adjusted to ensure that the generative model does not favor certain types of drugs or therapeutic approaches over others based on demographic or socioeconomic factors.

- **Algorithmic audits and bias assessments**: Conducting algorithmic audits and bias assessments is essential to identify and rectify biases in generative AI models. This involves systematically evaluating the model's outputs for potential biases and assessing their impact on different demographic groups. For instance, in personalized medicine, biases in treatment recommendations based on demographic factors need to be systematically identified and addressed to ensure fair and equitable healthcare.

- **Explainability and interpretability**: Building transparency into generative AI models enhances their explainability and interpretability. Understanding how a model arrives at specific decisions allows healthcare practitioners to identify and address potential biases. For instance, if a generative model recommends certain treatments over others, healthcare professionals should have insights into the features or factors influencing these recommendations to ensure they align with ethical and unbiased healthcare practices.

- **Ongoing monitoring and adaptation**: Addressing bias is an iterative process that requires ongoing monitoring and adaptation. Generative AI models should be continuously evaluated for biases, especially as they are deployed in real-world healthcare settings. Regular assessments ensure that any emerging biases are promptly identified and mitigated. This is particularly crucial in applications like clinical decision support systems, where biases can have direct implications for patient care.

- **Community engagement and stakeholder involvement**: Community engagement and involving stakeholders in the development and evaluation of generative AI models contribute to a more inclusive and fair process. Collaborating with diverse communities and involving patients, clinicians, and ethicists in decision-making processes helps identify potential biases that may not be apparent to the model developers alone. This participatory approach is essential for building generative AI systems that serve the needs of diverse populations fairly.

Informed consent in personalized medicine

The personalized nature of treatment plans generated by AI raises questions about informed consent. Patients should have a clear understanding of how their data is being used, the role of generative AI in formulating treatment plans, and the potential implications of personalized interventions. Transparent communication and consent mechanisms are paramount to uphold ethical standards in the era of personalized medicine.

In personalized medicine, where generative AI plays a pivotal role in tailoring treatment plans based on individual characteristics, obtaining informed consent becomes a critical ethical consideration. Informed consent ensures that patients are actively engaged in decisions about the use of their health data and have a comprehensive understanding of how generative AI will influence their personalized treatment.

- **Transparent communication about AI's role**: Obtaining informed consent begins with transparent communication regarding the role of generative AI in personalized medicine. Patients should be informed about how AI algorithms analyze their genetic, clinical, and other health data to derive personalized treatment recommendations. Providing clear explanations, potentially through patient-friendly material and educational resources, is essential to ensure that individuals can make informed decisions about participating in AI-driven healthcare interventions.

- **Clarifying data usage and storage**: Patients must be made aware of how their health data will be used and stored. This includes details about whether their data will be anonymized, aggregated for research purposes, or retained in identifiable forms. Explicitly stating the purposes for which AI algorithms will leverage their data ensures that patients understand the scope of their participation and can make informed decisions about the privacy implications of sharing their health information.

- **Potential benefits and risks**: Informed consent should outline the potential benefits and risks associated with the use of generative AI in personalized medicine. Patients should be informed about the potential advantages, such as more tailored and effective treatment plans, and the inherent uncertainties and risks, including the possibility of algorithmic biases or errors. This comprehensive understanding allows patients to weigh the potential benefits against the risks and make informed decisions aligned with their preferences and values.

- **Voluntary participation and withdrawal rights**: Patients should have the autonomy to decide whether to participate in AI-driven personalized medicine. Moreover, they should be assured that their participation is entirely voluntary. Furthermore, patients should be informed about their right to withdraw consent at any time without facing negative consequences. This empowers individuals to actively engage in their healthcare decisions and aligns with principles of respect for autonomy.

- **Long-term implications and follow-up**: Given the dynamic nature of personalized medicine, patients need to understand the potential long-term implications of participating in AI-driven healthcare. This includes considerations such as how their data may contribute to ongoing research, updates to treatment recommendations, and the evolving nature of AI algorithms. Providing information about the long-term implications ensures that patients can make informed choices in light of potential future developments.

- **Interactive consent processes**: In the context of generative AI, where complexity may be involved in explaining technical aspects, interactive consent processes can be beneficial. This might involve multimedia presentations, interactive platforms, or even consultations with healthcare professionals who can answer questions and address concerns. This interactive approach ensures that patients have ample opportunities to seek clarifications and actively engage in the consent process.

- **Ethical considerations in pediatric and vulnerable populations**: Special attention must be given to ethical considerations in populations such as pediatrics and vulnerable individuals. Informed consent processes in personalized medicine involving generative AI should be adapted to the developmental and decision-making capacities of pediatric patients and should involve additional safeguards for vulnerable populations, such as those with cognitive impairments.

Transparency in model decision-making

Generative AI models, particularly deep neural networks, are often considered *black-box* systems, making it challenging to interpret their decision-making processes. Ethical AI demands increased transparency to understand how generative models arrive at specific recommendations. Research into explainability techniques and the development of interpretable AI models are essential to provide healthcare practitioners and patients with insights into the rationale behind AI-generated treatment plans.

Transparency in the decision-making processes of generative AI models is imperative to build trust among healthcare practitioners and patients. As these models often operate as complex, *black-box* systems, understanding how they arrive at specific recommendations is crucial for ethical deployment in healthcare. Here are key considerations and examples that illuminate the concept of transparency in model decision-making:

- **Explainability techniques**: To enhance transparency, researchers are actively developing explainability techniques for generative AI models. These techniques aim to make the decision-making process more interpretable and understandable. For example, methods like **Local Interpretable Model-agnostic Explanations (LIME)** provide insights into specific model predictions by approximating the decision boundaries around a particular instance. By visualizing how changes in input data affect the output, these techniques contribute to the interpretability of generative AI models.

- **Feature importance and contributions**: Transparency involves elucidating the importance of different features in influencing model predictions. Generative AI models, especially those used in personalized medicine, can highlight the contribution of various patient-specific factors, such as genetic markers or clinical parameters, in shaping treatment recommendations. By providing insights into feature importance, healthcare practitioners gain a clearer understanding of the factors driving the model's decisions.

- **Clinical guidelines alignment**: Transparent models should align with established clinical guidelines and medical knowledge. For instance, a generative AI model recommending personalized treatment plans should be able to justify its suggestions in the context of evidence-based medicine. If a model recommends a certain course of action, it should be able to reference relevant medical literature or guidelines that support its decision, providing a bridge between AI-derived insights and existing medical knowledge.

- **Interactive decision support**: Transparency can be enhanced through interactive decision support interfaces. Interfaces that allow healthcare practitioners to interact with the model's decision-making process foster a deeper understanding rather than presenting static outputs. This can involve exploring different scenarios, adjusting input parameters, and observing how these changes impact the model's recommendations. Such interactivity promotes a more nuanced comprehension of the model's functioning.

- **Education and training**: Ensuring transparency also involves educating healthcare professionals about the underlying principles of generative AI. Training programs that familiarize practitioners with the basics of AI, its limitations, and interpretation of model outputs contribute to a more informed and discerning user base. This education empowers healthcare professionals to critically evaluate AI-driven recommendations and integrate them judiciously into their clinical decision-making processes.

- **Use of intelligible model architectures**: The choice of model architecture itself contributes to transparency. Intelligible model architectures, such as decision trees or rule-based models, can be preferred in certain contexts where interpretability is crucial. While more complex models like deep neural networks might offer superior performance, the trade-off between complexity and interpretability must be carefully considered based on the application and its implications.

- **Real-time explanation and feedback**: In dynamic healthcare settings, real-time explanation and feedback mechanisms are essential. Generative AI models should be designed to provide explanations for their recommendations in real time, allowing healthcare practitioners to grasp the rationale behind decisions promptly. This real-time feedback loop enables practitioners to intervene if the model's suggestions deviate from established clinical norms or if unexpected scenarios arise.

By incorporating these strategies, the transparency of generative AI models can be significantly enhanced, contributing to responsible and ethical deployment in healthcare. Transparency not only addresses concerns related to the *black-box* nature of AI but also empowers healthcare professionals to make informed decisions collaboratively with AI-driven insights.

Global access to healthcare innovations

Anticipating the future prospects of generative AI involves considerations of global accessibility. The benefits of AI-driven healthcare innovations should not be confined to affluent regions or high-income countries. Ensuring equitable access to AI-powered diagnostics, treatment plans, and drug discoveries is an ethical imperative. Collaborative efforts are needed to bridge the digital divide and address healthcare disparities on a global scale.

Ensuring global access to healthcare innovations driven by generative AI is a complex and crucial ethical consideration. The goal is not only to harness the benefits of AI advancements but also to address healthcare disparities globally. Here are key considerations and examples that underscore the importance of global access:

- **Equitable distribution of technological infrastructure**: Access to generative AI innovations begins with addressing the disparities in technological infrastructure. High-income countries often have more robust digital infrastructures, including high-speed internet and advanced computing resources. Efforts should be directed toward ensuring that low and middle-income countries have equitable access to the technological foundations required for deploying and benefiting from generative AI applications.

- **Affordability of healthcare technologies**: Generative AI applications, especially those in healthcare, should be designed with affordability in mind. High costs associated with AI-driven diagnostics, treatment planning, or drug discovery can exacerbate healthcare inequalities. Striking a balance between technological sophistication and cost-effectiveness ensures that the benefits of AI are accessible to healthcare systems with varying financial capacities.

- **Open data sharing for global collaboration**: Encouraging open data sharing facilitates global collaboration and democratizes access to diverse datasets. Initiatives that promote the sharing of anonymized health data for research purposes can foster a more inclusive AI landscape. For example, collaborative platforms that bring together researchers, healthcare institutions, and data contributors globally enable the development of more robust and generalizable AI models.

- **Tailoring solutions to resource-limited settings**: Generative AI solutions need to be adaptable to resource-limited settings. This involves developing models that can function efficiently with smaller datasets, accommodating variations in data quality, and considering the constraints of healthcare infrastructures in regions with limited resources. Tailoring solutions to these settings ensures that the benefits of generative AI are not confined to technologically advanced environments.

- **Capacity building and training programs**: Investing in capacity building and training programs is essential for enabling healthcare professionals in diverse settings to leverage generative AI technologies effectively. This includes providing education on the use and interpretation of AI-driven insights, as well as training in the ethical considerations associated with these technologies. Empowering local healthcare practitioners enhances their ability to integrate AI into patient care in a culturally sensitive and contextually relevant manner.

- **Adapting to cultural and ethical contexts**: Generative AI applications should be designed with sensitivity to cultural and ethical contexts. Healthcare practices, norms, and patient expectations vary across regions. Adapting AI solutions to these variations ensures that recommendations align with local values and preferences. This adaptability is particularly crucial in the context of personalized medicine, where cultural factors may influence individual healthcare decisions.

- **Public-private partnerships for global health**: Collaboration between public and private entities is instrumental in promoting global access. Public-private partnerships can support initiatives to make AI technologies available and affordable in underserved regions. Such collaborations can include technology transfer, joint research efforts, and the development of scalable solutions that cater to the unique challenges faced by diverse healthcare systems.

- **Telehealth and remote healthcare delivery**: Leveraging generative AI in telehealth initiatives can extend healthcare services to remote or underserved areas. For example, AI-driven diagnostic tools can be integrated into telehealth platforms to provide remote consultations and diagnostic support. This approach enhances access to healthcare expertise beyond geographical constraints.

By addressing these considerations, the global impact of generative AI in healthcare can be maximized, contributing to more inclusive, equitable, and ethically responsible healthcare systems worldwide. The ethical deployment of generative AI involves not only technological advancements but also a commitment to reducing healthcare disparities and ensuring that the benefits of innovation are accessible to all.

Ongoing ethical discourse and governance

Ethical considerations in generative AI are dynamic and should be subject to ongoing discourse and governance. The establishment of ethical frameworks, standards, and regulatory oversight is crucial to guide the responsible development and deployment of AI technologies in healthcare. Engaging stakeholders, including healthcare professionals, researchers, ethicists, and the general public, in ethical discussions ensures a collective and inclusive approach to shaping the future of AI in medicine.

Ensuring ethical governance and ongoing discourse around generative AI is imperative to respond to evolving challenges and opportunities. The dynamic nature of AI technologies requires adaptive frameworks that uphold ethical standards. Here are key considerations and examples that underscore the importance of ongoing ethical discourse and governance:

- **Establishment of ethical review boards**: In the context of generative AI applications, especially in healthcare, the establishment of ethical review boards becomes crucial. These boards, comprising multidisciplinary experts, can provide ongoing ethical oversight and review of AI projects. Their role involves evaluating the ethical implications, potential biases, and adherence to privacy standards, ensuring that projects align with evolving ethical norms.

- **Regular ethical audits and impact assessments**: Conducting regular ethical audits and impact assessments helps organizations proactively identify and address ethical considerations in generative AI deployments. These assessments should not be static but evolve with the technology and its applications. For instance, an impact assessment might focus on the ethical implications of deploying a new generative AI model for personalized medicine, considering factors such as equity, fairness, and privacy.

- **Adaptation to regulatory changes**: The ethical landscape surrounding AI is subject to regulatory changes and advancements. Organizations involved in generative AI should proactively adapt to these changes, aligning their practices with emerging ethical standards and legal requirements. For example, changes in data protection regulations may necessitate adjustments in how healthcare data is handled and used by AI models.

- **International collaboration on ethical standards**: Given the global nature of AI development and deployment, international collaboration on ethical standards is essential. Organizations, governments, and research institutions should engage in dialogue to establish common ethical frameworks that transcend geographical boundaries. Forums for international collaboration can facilitate the exchange of best practices and contribute to the development of globally accepted ethical norms for generative AI.

- **Inclusion of diverse stakeholders in ethical deliberations**: Ethical discourse should involve diverse stakeholders, including not only AI researchers and developers but also healthcare practitioners, patients, ethicists, and representatives from marginalized or vulnerable communities. Including a broad spectrum of perspectives ensures that ethical considerations are comprehensive and account for the varied interests and values of different stakeholders.

- **Ethics training for AI practitioners**: Training programs that incorporate ethics into the education of AI practitioners are essential. AI developers, data scientists, and engineers should receive training on the ethical implications of their work, emphasizing the responsible use of AI technologies. Integrating ethics education into academic and professional training programs fosters a culture of ethical awareness within the AI community.

- **Public awareness and engagement**: Ethical discourse should extend beyond academic and industry circles to include the general public. Raising awareness about the ethical dimensions of generative AI, especially in healthcare, enables informed public discourse. Engaging the public in discussions about the ethical use of AI in areas like disease diagnosis, treatment planning, and drug discovery helps build trust and ensures that AI technologies align with societal values.

- **Continuous ethical guidelines for AI in healthcare**: Establishing and updating continuous ethical guidelines specific to AI in healthcare is essential. These guidelines should address issues such as consent, privacy, fairness, transparency, and the responsible handling of sensitive health data. Regular reviews and updates ensure that the guidelines remain relevant and effective in guiding ethical practices in the rapidly evolving field of generative AI.

- **Whistleblower protection and reporting mechanisms**: Encouraging a culture of ethical reporting and whistleblower protection mechanisms within organizations is crucial. Individuals within AI development teams should feel empowered to raise ethical concerns without fear of reprisal. Establishing clear reporting mechanisms and protections for whistleblowers contributes to a culture of accountability and ethical responsibility.

By actively engaging in ongoing ethical discourse and governance, generative AI can navigate the complexities of technological advancements while upholding ethical principles. This iterative and adaptive approach ensures that ethical considerations remain at the forefront of AI development and deployment, contributing to the responsible evolution of generative AI technologies.

Ethical considerations and future prospects in generative AI for healthcare and drug discovery underscore the need for a conscientious and inclusive approach. Balancing technological advancements with ethical principles is not only foundational to the responsible use of AI but also pivotal in fostering trust, ensuring equity, and maximizing the positive impact of generative AI in transforming the landscape of healthcare and pharmaceutical innovation.

Art and entertainment

Generative models contribute to creating novel and visually striking content in art and entertainment. Artists leverage these models for style transfer, creating unique pieces by merging different artistic styles. This technology fosters a new era of collaboration between human creativity and AI. Generative AI is employed in game development for the generation of landscapes, characters, and other visual elements. This not only expedites the game design process but also introduces dynamic and adaptive content, enhancing the gaming experience.

The intersection of generative AI and art and entertainment has ushered in a new era of creativity, enabling artists and creators to explore novel expressions and push the boundaries of traditional artistic practices. This section delves into the diverse ways in which generative AI is shaping the landscape of art and entertainment, offering innovative tools, generating unique content, and challenging preconceived notions of creativity.

Generative art

Generative art refers to artworks created with the assistance of autonomous systems, such as generative algorithms or machine learning models. Artists input parameters and rules into these systems, autonomously producing visual or auditory compositions. Following is an example use case and implementation of generative AI in generative art.

Example: **Artificial Intelligence Virtual Artist (AIVA)** is an AI system that composes classical music. It analyzes patterns in existing compositions and generates entirely new pieces, demonstrating the contribution of generative AI to music compositions that evoke emotions and resonate with listeners.

Generative art represents a paradigm shift in artistic creation, where algorithms and computational processes take center stage in the generation of visual or auditory expressions. The fusion of art and generative algorithms results in artworks that are not predefined but emerge from the interaction between human artists and computational systems. Here, we delve deeper into the nuances of generative art:

Algorithmic composition

Generative art often involves using algorithms to dictate the composition of visual or auditory elements. Artists program algorithms that generate patterns, colors, shapes, or sounds, allowing for the creation of dynamic and evolving artworks. Following is an example of algorithmic composition.

Example: The algorithmic art of *Casey Reas*, co-creator of the programming language *Processing*, exemplifies this approach. His works, such as *Software Structures*, are created through the execution of algorithms that define the visual elements, resulting in intricate and evolving visual compositions.

Evolutionary algorithms in art

Evolutionary algorithms, inspired by biological evolution, are employed to iteratively generate and refine artistic elements. This process involves selecting and mutating elements based on predefined criteria to simulate a form of creative evolution. The following example illustrates.

Example: *Karl Sims'* interactive installation *Galápagos* uses evolutionary algorithms to generate virtual creatures. Viewers can influence the evolution of these creatures by selecting those they find visually appealing, illustrating how generative algorithms can mimic natural selection in the creation of virtual entities.

Interactive generative art

Generative art can be interactive, responding to user input or environmental stimuli. This engagement introduces an element of unpredictability as the artwork evolves in real time based on the interaction with its audience.

Example: The *Rain Room* installation by *Random International* is an interactive generative artwork that responds to the presence of visitors. As individuals move through the space, sensors detect their presence and temporarily *pause* the rain falling in a specific area, creating an immersive and participatory experience.

Machine learning and style transfer

Machine learning techniques, particularly style transfer algorithms, are employed to imbue artworks with the characteristics of renowned artists or visual styles. This enables the creation of pieces that blend traditional artistic influences with modern computational methods. Following is an example of using generative AI for style transfer.

Example: *Starry Night AI*, an artwork by *Leon Gatys*, employs neural style transfer to reinterpret *Vincent van Gogh*'s *Starry Night* in the style of various artists. This demonstrates how generative algorithms can be used to remix and reinterpret classic artworks in novel ways.

Procedural generation in digital art

Procedural generation involves using algorithms to create visual elements in a systematic manner. This approach is often employed in digital art, where complex and intricate visuals can be generated through mathematical procedures. Following is an example of implementing generative AI in digital art.

Example: The video game *Minecraft* utilizes procedural generation to create vast and diverse landscapes. The terrain, structures, and even the placement of vegetation are generated algorithmically, contributing to the uniqueness of each player's gaming experience.

Collaboration between humans and algorithms

Generative art blurs the boundaries between human creativity and algorithmic processes, often involving collaborative efforts where artists guide and influence the output of generative algorithms. The following is an example of using generative AI for collaboration between humans and algorithms.

Example: The collaboration between artist *Mario Klingemann* and the AI system *Memories of Passersby I* exemplifies this synergy. *Klingemann* provided artistic direction, and the AI-generated continuously evolving portraits based on a dataset of faces it had been trained on, resulting in a dynamic and collaborative artistic creation.

Generative art installations

Generative art extends beyond traditional canvases into immersive installations. These installations leverage algorithms to create dynamic, transformative, and multisensory experiences for viewers. The following is an example of using generative AI in art installations.

Example: *Unnumbered Sparks* by *Janet Echelman* and *Aaron Koblin* is a generative art installation where a net of interactive lights responds to the audience's movements. This large-scale piece transforms urban spaces into dynamic canvases, showcasing the potential of generative art in shaping public environments.

Ethical considerations in algorithmic art

The rise of generative art raises ethical questions concerning authorship, attribution, and the role of algorithms in the creative process. These considerations challenge traditional notions of the artist as the sole creator. The following example illustrates how a Gen AI-enabled artwork took care of ethical considerations.

Example: The sale of an AI-generated artwork by *Beeple* for millions of dollars prompted discussions about the valuation and ownership of algorithmically generated art. This highlights the need for ethical frameworks that navigate the complexities of attribution and ownership in the context of generative art.

Generative art not only expands the possibilities of creative expression but also challenges our perceptions of authorship and creativity in the digital age. It exemplifies a symbiotic relationship between human imagination and computational algorithms, where the canvas becomes a playground for the fusion of art and code.

Creative assistance in content generation

Generative AI assists content creators by automating or suggesting elements of the creative process. This can include generating plot ideas, character designs or even assisting in screenplay writing. The following example illustrates implementation of Gen AI in creative assistance.

Example: OpenAI's GPT-3 has been utilized to generate creative content. For instance, it can help generate dialogue for characters in a screenplay or assist in brainstorming ideas for a creative project. This showcases how AI can act as a collaborative tool for human creators, enhancing the efficiency of content generation.

Generative AI plays a pivotal role in providing creative assistance to content creators across various domains. By leveraging machine learning models and algorithms, content generation becomes a collaborative process where AI acts as a catalyst for human creativity. For instance, in literature, AI models like OpenAI's GPT-3 can assist authors by suggesting plot ideas, generating character dialogues, or even in development of complete narratives. This creative collaboration extends to fields like design, where AI tools can propose visual elements based on input or streamline the creative workflow. The rationale behind this approach is to enhance efficiency, inspire new ideas, and break creative blocks by leveraging the vast knowledge and patterns learned by the AI models. This synergy between human intuition and AI capabilities showcases the potential for generative AI to act as a supportive partner in the creative process, enriching the final output with a fusion of human ingenuity and computational insights.

Interactive and immersive experiences

Generative AI contributes to interactive and immersive experiences in entertainment, such as video games or **virtual reality (VR)** environments. These environments adapt to user interactions, providing dynamic and personalized experiences. The following is an example of implementation of using Gen AI in interactive and immersive experiences.

Example: The game *No Man's Sky* uses procedural generation to create an entire universe of planets, each with unique ecosystems. The procedural generation ensures that players encounter diverse and unexpected environments, showcasing how generative AI can enhance the richness and variability of interactive experiences.

Generative AI transforms the landscape of interactive and immersive experiences, particularly in domains like gaming and virtual reality. The incorporation of generative algorithms allows for dynamic and personalized interactions, making each user experience unique. In video games, procedural generation techniques create ever-evolving environments, ensuring that no two gameplay sessions are identical. This not only enhances the replay ability of games but also introduces an element of unpredictability. In virtual reality, generative AI adapts experiences based on user actions, creating immersive worlds that respond in real time. The rationale behind leveraging generative AI in interactive experiences is to break away from static content and provide users with engaging, adaptive, and personalized encounters. By infusing a sense of dynamism and responsiveness, generative AI elevates interactive and immersive experiences to new heights, captivating users in digital realms that evolve in harmony with their actions and preferences.

AI-generated music and composition

Generative AI is employed in the creation of music, ranging from composition to performance. AI models can generate melodies, harmonies, and even entire pieces, collaborating with human musicians or acting autonomously. The following is an example of implementation of using Gen AI in music and composition.

Example: Google's *Magenta* project explores the intersection of AI and music. *Magenta*'s AI models can generate melodies, suggest chord progressions, and even improvise in response to human input. This illustrates the potential for AI to contribute to the music composition process and inspire new creative directions.

Generative AI has found a melodious niche in music composition, acting as a collaborator in the creative process. Machine learning models, such as those employed by Google's *Magenta* project, can analyze vast musical datasets to learn intricate patterns and styles. This enables the AI to generate unique melodies, suggest harmonious progressions, and even improvise in response to human input. The transformative potential of AI-generated music lies not just in its ability to mimic existing styles but in exploring novel compositions that evoke emotional responses. This symbiotic relationship between human musicians and AI algorithms showcases how technology can augment and inspire the creative journey, leading to harmonious blends of human intuition and artificial ingenuity.

Visual arts and style transfer

Generative AI is used in visual arts for style transfer, where the style of one image is applied to another. This allows artists to experiment with different visual aesthetics and create novel artworks. The following is an example of implementation of using Gen AI for visual arts.

Example: *DeepArt*, a platform that uses neural networks, enables users to apply the style of famous artworks to their images. This democratizes the exploration of artistic styles, allowing individuals to create personalized artworks inspired by renowned masterpieces.

Generative AI, particularly through style transfer algorithms, is making a significant impact in the realm of visual arts. Style transfer allows artists and creators to reimagine their works by applying the distinctive visual characteristics of renowned artists or styles to their creations. For instance, platforms like *DeepArt* leverage neural networks to facilitate this process, enabling users to experiment with different artistic aesthetics. The rationale behind incorporating style transfer in visual arts is to democratize artistic exploration, allowing individuals to blend their unique perspectives with the influences of established artistic styles. This innovative fusion of human creativity and AI algorithms not only expands the horizons of visual expression but also challenges traditional notions of artistic influence and inspiration.

AI-enhanced filmmaking and animation

Generative AI contributes to filmmaking and animation by automating certain aspects of the production process, enhancing visual effects, and even assisting in scriptwriting the following is an example implementation of using Gen AI in filmmaking and animation.

Example: AI-based tools like Runway ML have been used in filmmaking to automate tasks such as rotoscoping, a process that involves tracing over live-action footage to create animated effects. This showcases how AI can streamline complex tasks in the filmmaking pipeline.

Generative AI is scripting a new chapter in filmmaking and animation, ushering in innovations that streamline production processes and enhance visual effects. Tools like Runway ML are being utilized to automate intricate tasks in filmmaking, such as rotoscoping. This application of AI contributes to the efficiency of the filmmaking pipeline, allowing creators to focus more on storytelling and creative direction. The rationale behind incorporating AI in filmmaking is to leverage its capabilities in visual processing, facilitating the creation of captivating scenes, and augmenting the overall cinematic experience. As AI continues to evolve, it stands poised to become an indispensable collaborator in the visual storytelling industry, opening doors to new possibilities in narrative exploration and visual expression.

Creative chatbots and interactive storytelling

Generative AI is employed in the development of chatbots that engage users in creative conversations and interactive storytelling. These chatbots often leverage natural language processing and understanding to respond dynamically to user input. The following is an example of leveraging Gen AI in creative chatbots and interactive storytelling.

Example: *Replika* is a conversational AI chatbot designed to engage users in meaningful and creative conversations. It adapts the responses based on user input, providing a unique and personalized conversational experience.

Generative AI finds a compelling application in creative chatbots and interactive storytelling, transforming conventional narratives into dynamic and personalized experiences. Platforms like *Replika* showcase the potential of AI in engaging users in meaningful and creative conversations. These chatbots, fueled by natural language processing, adapt their responses based on user input, blurring the lines between scripted storytelling and spontaneous dialogue. The rationale behind incorporating generative AI in this context is to provide users with interactive narratives that respond dynamically to their choices and preferences. By enabling a collaborative storytelling experience, AI-driven chatbots contribute to the evolution of interactive fiction, offering users a glimpse into the future of immersive and personalized storytelling interactions.

Generative AI in virtual fashion design

Generative AI is revolutionizing the fashion industry by assisting in the design process. AI models can generate unique fashion designs, predict trends, and even assist in virtual fitting experiences. The following is an example of implementing Gen AI in virtual fashion designs.

Example: IBM's AI-powered fashion advisor uses machine learning to analyze fashion trends and generate design recommendations. This showcases how AI can be a valuable tool in the creative process of fashion design.

Generative AI is reshaping the landscape of fashion design by offering innovative solutions in a virtual fashion. AI-powered tools, like IBM's fashion advisor, utilize machine learning to analyze trends and generate design recommendations. This marks a departure from traditional design processes, allowing for the creation of unique and trend-responsive fashion pieces. The rationale behind integrating generative AI in virtual fashion design is to streamline the creative process, predict emerging styles, and enhance the overall design workflow. By leveraging AI, fashion designers can explore novel design avenues, ensuring that their creations are not only aesthetically appealing but also aligned with the ever-evolving trends in the fashion industry. The synergy between human creativity and algorithmic insights is redefining the runway, offering a glimpse into the future of fashion where virtual design meets real-world style.

AI-generated literature and poetry

Generative AI is employed in the generation of literature and poetry, showcasing its ability to mimic and extend human creative expression in written language. The following is an example of implementing Gen AI in literature and poetry.

Example: OpenAI's GPT-3 has been utilized to generate poetry and prose that mimic the styles of different authors. This demonstrates the potential of generative AI to contribute to literary exploration and experimentation.

Generative AI steps in literary expression, contributing to the creation of literature and poetry that mirrors human creativity. Open AI's GPT-3 has shown its ability to create text that resembles the writing of various authors.

This transformative capability extends beyond imitation, allowing for the exploration of new literary landscapes. The rationale behind incorporating AI in literature and poetry is to expand the possibilities of language and narrative, pushing the boundaries of what can be expressed and imagined. As AI models continue to evolve, they stand as literary companions, sparking innovative ideas, challenging traditional writing norms, and serving as tools for authors to explore uncharted realms of literary expression. This collaborative dance between artificial intelligence and human ingenuity redefines the art of storytelling and poetic composition.

Ethical considerations in AI-generated art

As generative AI becomes increasingly involved in artistic creation, ethical considerations regarding issues such as authorship, ownership, and the potential for bias in training data arise. The following is an example of using Gen AI to incorporate ethical considerations in AI-generated art.

Example: The sale of an AI-generated artwork by the artist *Beeple* for a significant sum raised questions about the ownership and value of AI-generated creations. This exemplifies the need for ethical frameworks that consider the unique challenges posed by AI in the art world.

The rise of AI-generated art prompts profound ethical considerations that extend beyond aesthetics. Questions of authorship, attribution, and the commercial value of AI-created pieces challenge traditional art paradigms. The ethical discourse delves into issues of transparency, ensuring that viewers are aware of the involvement of algorithms in the creative process. Moreover, concerns about bias, especially in AI models trained on biased datasets, underscore the need for responsible and inclusive AI practices in the art world. Striking a balance between pushing the boundaries of creativity and upholding ethical standards becomes paramount as AI continues to shape the artistic landscape. The ongoing discourse seeks to establish governance frameworks that embrace the transformative potential of AI-generated art while safeguarding the principles of fairness, transparency, and cultural sensitivity.

Marketing and content creation

Generative models aid in the creation of personalized and engaging ad content. By understanding user preferences and trends, these models can generate advertisements that resonate with specific audiences, improving marketing effectiveness.

Content creation for blogs, websites, and social media can be automated using generative AI. This streamlines the content generation process, ensuring a consistent flow of relevant and engaging material.

In marketing and content creation, generative AI has emerged as a transformative force, revolutionizing how brands engage with their audiences and produce compelling content. This chapter explores various facets of how AI is reshaping marketing strategies, content creation processes, and audience interactions.

Automated content generation

AI-driven tools are automating the creation of diverse content types, from articles and blog posts to social media updates. For instance, tools like OpenAI's GPT-3 can generate coherent and contextually relevant content, reducing the time and effort traditionally required for content creation. The following example illustrates usage of Gen AI in content generation.

Example: ChatGPT-based chatbots are employed by businesses to interact with customers on websites, providing instant responses and personalized information.

Personalized marketing campaigns

Generative AI analyzes user data to create highly personalized marketing campaigns. This involves tailoring content, offers, and messaging to individual preferences, increasing engagement and conversion rates. The following example illustrates usage of Gen AI in personalized marketing campaigns.

Example: E-commerce platforms use recommendation engines powered by AI to suggest products based on a user's browsing and purchase history.

Social media management

AI tools assist in managing social media accounts by scheduling posts, analyzing engagement metrics, and even generating captions and hashtags. This streamlines the social media workflow for businesses. The following example illustrates usage of Gen AI in social media management.

Example: *Buffer*, a social media management platform, employs AI to suggest optimal posting times and analyze post-performance.

Predictive analytics for customer behaviour

AI algorithms analyze historical data to predict customer behavior, helping marketers anticipate trends, identify potential leads, and optimize marketing strategies. The following example illustrates usage of Gen AI in predictive analytics for customer behavior.

Example: Salesforce's *Einstein Analytics* utilizes machine learning to provide insights into customer behaviors, enabling businesses to make data-driven marketing decisions.

Chatbots for customer interaction

Chatbots powered by generative AI enhance customer interactions by providing instant responses to queries, handling routine tasks, and offering personalized recommendations. The following example illustrates usage of Gen AI in creating chatbots for customer interaction.

Example: Many companies implement AI-driven chatbots on their websites to engage with visitors, answer FAQs, and guide users through the sales funnel.

Visual content generation

AI is employed to generate visual content, including images, graphics, and videos. This not only speeds up the content creation process but also ensures a consistent visual identity.

Example: *Canva* uses AI to suggest design elements, layouts, and color schemes, assisting users in creating visually appealing graphics.

Sentiment analysis in marketing

AI-driven sentiment analysis tools assess public sentiment towards a brand or product by analyzing social media mentions, reviews, and comments. This helps marketers understand and respond to consumer perceptions.

Example: Brands use tools like *Brandwatch* to monitor social media sentiment and adjust marketing strategies based on public opinion.

Dynamic pricing optimization

AI algorithms analyze market conditions, competitor pricing, and customer behavior to dynamically adjust pricing strategies. This ensures competitiveness and maximizes revenue.

Example: Airlines use AI-powered pricing systems to dynamically adjust ticket prices based on factors like demand, time until departure, and competitor pricing.

Content curation and trend analysis

AI tools curate content by analyzing trends, user preferences, and industry developments. This ensures that marketers stay relevant and capitalize on emerging trends.

Example: News aggregators use AI algorithms to curate and personalize news feeds for users based on their interests and reading habits.

Email marketing optimization

AI is employed to optimize email marketing campaigns by analyzing user behavior, segmenting audiences, and delivering personalized content. This increases email engagement and conversion rates.

Example: AI-powered email marketing platforms like Mailchimp use predictive analytics to suggest optimal sending times and content for different audience segments.

Rationale: Generative AI transforms marketing and content creation by automating routine tasks, personalizing interactions, and providing data-driven insights. The rationale behind these applications is to enhance efficiency, improve targeting, and deliver more engaging and relevant content to audiences. The ability of AI to process vast amounts of data quickly and make predictions based on patterns empowers marketers to make informed decisions and adapt strategies in real time. As businesses increasingly embrace digital channels and data-driven approaches, the integration of generative AI in marketing becomes not just a trend but a fundamental aspect of staying competitive in the dynamic landscape of the digital age.

Manufacturing and design

Generative design techniques are applied in manufacturing to optimize product designs based on specific criteria such as material efficiency and structural integrity. This results in innovative and efficient designs that may not have been intuitive to human designers.

In prototyping, generative AI assists in creating and iterating through various design possibilities. This accelerates the prototyping phase, enabling faster product development cycles.

Generative design in product development

Generative design leverages AI algorithms to explore countless design possibilities based on defined parameters such as materials, manufacturing constraints, and performance requirements. This process enables the creation of complex, optimized structures that might not be immediately apparent to human designers. The following is an example of implementing Gen AI in product development.

Example: Autodesk's generative design tool helps engineers and designers create innovative designs for components like brackets or supports by iteratively exploring and testing numerous design variations.

Additive manufacturing and 3D printing

AI enhances the capabilities of additive manufacturing by optimizing designs for 3D printing, reducing material waste, and improving structural integrity. Generative algorithms can create intricate geometries that are challenging for traditional manufacturing methods. The following is an example of leveraging Gen AI in 3D printing.

Example: Airbus utilizes generative design and 3D printing to produce lightweight and complex components for aircraft, leading to improved fuel efficiency.

Predictive maintenance and quality control

AI-driven predictive maintenance models analyze sensor data from machinery to predict when equipment will likely fail. This proactive approach minimizes downtime and extends the lifespan of manufacturing equipment. AI also aids in quality control by detecting defects in real time. The following is an example of leveraging Gen AI in predictive maintenance and quality control.

Example: General Electric uses AI for predictive maintenance in its aircraft engines, predicting potential issues and scheduling maintenance before critical failures occur.

Supply chain optimization

AI algorithms optimize supply chain operations by predicting demand, identifying potential disruptions, and recommending efficient logistics strategies. This results in reduced costs, improved inventory management, and enhanced overall efficiency. The following is an example of leveraging Gen AI in supply chain optimization.

Example: Companies like Amazon employ AI for demand forecasting, ensuring that products are strategically distributed to warehouses based on anticipated demand.

Robotics and automation

Generative AI plays a crucial role in optimizing the programming of robots for manufacturing tasks. AI-driven robotics enable flexible automation, allowing robots to adapt to different tasks and work collaboratively with human workers. The following is an example of using Gen AI in robotics and automation.

Example: BMW uses AI-powered robotic systems in its manufacturing plants for tasks such as painting, welding, and assembly, improving precision and efficiency.

Customization and mass personalization

AI facilitates mass customization by enabling the efficient production of customized products at scale. This is achieved through generative design, which tailors' products to individual preferences while maintaining cost-effectiveness. The following example is an implementation of Gen AI in customization and personalization.

Example: Adidas utilizes generative design to create personalized midsoles for its running shoes, considering factors like an individual's running style and foot shape.

Energy efficiency in manufacturing

AI-driven algorithms optimize energy consumption in manufacturing processes by analyzing patterns and adjusting operations for maximum efficiency. This not only reduces environmental impact but also lowers operational costs. The following example shows how Gen AI was leveraged in driving energy efficiency in manufacturing.

Example: Siemens employs AI for energy optimization in industrial processes, ensuring that machinery operates at peak efficiency while minimizing energy consumption.

Simulations for prototyping and testing

AI-powered simulations enhance the prototyping and testing phases of product development. These simulations provide insights into how designs will perform under various conditions, reducing the need for physical prototypes and speeding up the development cycle. The following example illustrated how Gen AI was leveraged in simulations for prototyping and testing.

Example: SpaceX utilizes AI-driven simulations to test and refine designs for its rocket components, enabling rapid iteration and reducing development time.

Human-robot collaboration in manufacturing

AI enables safe and efficient collaboration between humans and robots on the factory floor. Collaborative robots, or cobots, are equipped with AI algorithms that allow them to work alongside human workers, performing tasks that require precision and strength. The following example illustrates usage of Gen AI in human robot collaboration in manufacturing.

Example: Nissan employs collaborative robots in its manufacturing plants, where AI algorithms enable robots to work in close proximity to human workers, enhancing overall efficiency.

Rationale: Generative AI is transforming manufacturing and design by revolutionizing the product development lifecycle, optimizing operational processes, and enabling new levels of customization. The rationale behind these applications lies in the pursuit of efficiency, cost-effectiveness, and innovation. AI-driven design processes not only accelerate the creation of optimized products but also contribute to sustainability efforts by reducing material waste. The integration of AI in manufacturing operations enhances the overall agility and responsiveness of industries, allowing them to adapt to changing market demands and stay at the forefront of technological advancement. As manufacturing becomes increasingly connected and data-driven, the role of generative AI in shaping the future of industry innovation becomes indispensable.

Finance and risk management

Generative models are utilized for scenario generation in finance. By simulating various economic and market scenarios, these models aid in risk assessment and strategic decision-making for investment portfolios.

In finance, generative AI contributes to fraud detection by generating anomaly detection models. These models can learn patterns of normal behavior and identify anomalies that may indicate fraudulent activities.

Finance and risk management in the era of generative AI represents a paradigm shift, ushering in unprecedented advancements across various facets of the financial landscape. This chapter navigates through the transformative impact of AI on traditional financial practices, exploring key areas such as algorithmic trading, fraud detection, credit scoring, and dynamic risk management. From reshaping investment strategies to fortifying cybersecurity measures, generative AI is at the forefront of revolutionizing decision-making processes in finance. As we delve into the intricacies of portfolio optimization, personalized financial advice, and regulatory compliance automation, it becomes evident that AI is not merely a technological enhancement but a strategic enabler for institutions seeking agility, precision, and adaptability in an ever-evolving financial environment.

The subsequent sections explore some of the aspects of the field.

Algorithmic trading and quantitative finance

Generative AI is employed in algorithmic trading to analyze vast datasets, identify patterns, and execute trades at speeds impossible for human traders. Quantitative finance models utilize AI algorithms to predict market trends and optimize investment strategies. The following example illustrates usage of Gen AI in algorithmic trading and quantitative finance.

Example: Hedge funds like Renaissance Technologies leverage generative AI algorithms to inform their trading decisions, achieving significant returns through data-driven strategies.

Fraud detection and cybersecurity

AI-driven models analyze transactions, user behavior, and network activity to detect anomalies and potential fraudulent activities. Machine learning algorithms continuously adapt to evolving fraud patterns, enhancing the security of financial transactions. The following example illustrates usage of Gen AI in fraud detection and cybersecurity.

Example: Banks utilize AI-powered fraud detection systems to identify unusual spending patterns, irregular transactions, and potential identity theft, preventing financial losses for both institutions and customers.

Credit scoring and loan approval

Generative AI models assess creditworthiness by analyzing diverse data points, including credit history, transaction patterns, and alternative data sources. This facilitates more accurate and fair credit scoring, improving loan approval processes. The following example illustrates usage of Gen AI in credit scoring and loan approval.

Example: Fintech companies like *ZestFinance* use AI algorithms to assess credit risk for individuals with limited credit history, enabling more inclusive lending practices.

Personalized financial advice

AI-driven financial advisory platforms analyze individual financial profiles, goals, and market conditions to provide personalized investment advice. This enhances the quality of financial guidance for investors. The following example illustrates the usage of Gen AI in personalized financial advice.

Example: Robo-advisors such as *Wealthfront* use generative algorithms to create customized investment portfolios based on an individual's risk tolerance, financial goals, and market conditions.

Market sentiment analysis

AI algorithms analyze social media, news articles, and other textual data to gauge market sentiment. This information is valuable for predicting short-term market movements and making informed trading decisions. The following example illustrates usage of Gen AI in market sentiment analysis.

Example: Traders and investment firms use tools like *RavenPack* to perform sentiment analysis on news articles and social media feeds, gaining insights into market sentiment.

Dynamic risk management

AI enables dynamic risk management by continuously assessing market conditions, economic indicators, and geopolitical events. This allows financial institutions to adapt risk strategies in real time. The following example illustrates usage of Gen AI dynamic risk management.

Example: Insurance companies use AI-driven risk models to assess changing factors, such as climate patterns or economic trends, to dynamically adjust their risk exposure and pricing.

Automated compliance and regulatory reporting

AI automates compliance checks by analyzing transactions against regulatory requirements. It also streamlines the process of generating accurate and timely reports for regulatory bodies, reducing the risk of non-compliance. The following example illustrates usage of Gen AI in automated compliance and regulatory reporting.

Example: Banks deploy AI systems to ensure adherence to **anti-money laundering (AML)** regulations by automating the detection of suspicious transactions and generating required reports.

Portfolio optimization and asset allocation

AI-driven portfolio optimization models analyze historical data, market trends, and risk factors to create diversified and optimized investment portfolios. This enhances returns while managing risk. The following example illustrates the usage of Gen AI in portfolio optimization and asset allocation.

Example: Institutional investors use AI algorithms to dynamically adjust asset allocations based on changing market conditions, optimizing the risk-return profile of their portfolios.

Insurance underwriting and claims processing

AI assesses risk factors for insurance underwriting, ensuring more accurate premium calculations. Claims processing is expedited through AI, which analyzes documentation and assesses the validity of claims. The following example illustrates usage of Gen AI in insurance underwriting and claims processing.

Example: Insurtech companies use AI to analyze diverse data sources, including IoT devices and social media, to assess risk and offer personalized insurance policies.

Stress testing and scenario analysis

AI facilitates stress testing by simulating various economic scenarios and assessing the resilience of financial institutions and portfolios. This aids in identifying potential vulnerabilities. The following example illustrates the usage of Gen AI in stress testing and scenario analysis.

Example: Central banks and financial institutions use AI models to simulate economic scenarios, such as recessions or market crashes, to assess the resilience of the financial system.

Rationale: Generative AI in finance and risk management serves as a catalyst for data-driven decision-making, risk mitigation, and improved customer experiences. The rationale behind these applications is rooted in the need for precision, efficiency, and adaptability in the financial landscape. AI models can analyze vast datasets at speeds beyond human capacity, providing insights that inform trading strategies, enhance fraud detection, and optimize investment portfolios. In the context of risk management, AI offers dynamic and real-time assessments, ensuring that financial institutions can respond effectively to changing conditions. The integration of generative AI in finance aligns with the industry's shift toward more proactive, data-centric, and personalized approaches to decision-making and risk mitigation.

Human resources and recruitment

Generative models assist in the automated generation of job descriptions based on industry standards and specific organizational requirements. This enhances the efficiency of the recruitment process. By analyzing candidate profiles and job requirements, generative models contribute to the automated matching of candidates with suitable job opportunities, streamlining the hiring process.

The integration of generative AI with human resources and recruitment emerges as a transformative force, reshaping traditional practices and elevating talent management strategies. This section explores the multifaceted impact of AI, from automating resume screening to predicting candidate success, fostering diversity and inclusion, and optimizing workforce planning. Delve into the future of HR, where AI-driven innovations enhance efficiency, objectivity, and strategic decision-making, ensuring organizations thrive in the ever-evolving landscape of talent acquisition and management.

Automated resume screening

Generative AI automates the initial screening of resumes by analyzing key criteria and matching them against job requirements. This expedites the recruitment process and ensures a more objective initial assessment. The following example illustrates the usage of Gen AI in automated resume screening.

Example: Companies like Unilever use AI-powered tools to screen resumes, enabling recruiters to focus on evaluating candidates with the best fit for the organization.

Predictive hiring analytics

AI-driven predictive analytics assess historical hiring data to identify patterns and trends. This helps in predicting the success of candidates and making informed decisions during the recruitment process. The following example illustrates usage of Gen AI in predictive hiring analytics.

Example: IBM's Watson Recruitment uses AI to analyze data from past hires, enabling organizations to predict candidate success and make data-driven hiring decisions.

Candidate matching and recommendations

Generative AI analyzes candidate profiles and job requirements to provide personalized matching recommendations. This ensures that recruiters focus on candidates whose skills align closely with the job specifications. The following example illustrates usage of Gen AI in candidate matching and recommendations.

Example: *LinkedIn*'s AI-based matching algorithm suggests potential candidates to recruiters based on skills, experience, and industry relevance.

Diversity and inclusion initiatives

AI assists in promoting diversity and inclusion by minimizing biases in the recruitment process. Algorithms can focus on skills and qualifications rather than demographic information. The following example illustrates the usage of Gen AI in diversity and inclusion initiatives.

Example: Textio uses AI to analyze job descriptions, providing feedback to ensure language is inclusive and appealing to a diverse pool of candidates.

Chatbots for candidate interaction

AI-powered chatbots engage with candidates during the application process, providing information, answering queries, and even conducting initial assessments. This enhances the candidate experience and improves efficiency. The following example illustrates usage of Gen AI in chatbots and candidate interaction.

Example: *Olivia* by *Paradox* is an AI chatbot that interacts with candidates, schedules interviews, and provides information about the company, streamlining the initial stages of recruitment.

Employee retention strategies

Generative AI analyzes employee data to identify factors contributing to employee turnover. This insight enables organizations to implement targeted retention strategies and improve overall employee satisfaction. The following example illustrates usage of Gen AI in employee retention strategies.

Example: IBM's AI-driven *Employee Attrition Prediction* model helps companies predict which employees are at risk of leaving, allowing proactive measures to retain valuable talent.

Skills gap analysis

AI conducts skills gap analyses within the organization, identifying areas where employees may need additional training. This ensures that the workforce remains adaptable and aligned with evolving job requirements. The following example illustrates usage of Gen AI in skill gap analysis.

Example: Skillsoft's Percipio uses AI to assess the skills of employees and provides personalized learning paths to bridge any identified gaps.

Automated onboarding processes

AI streamlines the onboarding process by automating paperwork, providing new employees with relevant information, and facilitating a smoother transition into the organization. The following example illustrates the usage of Gen AI automated onboarding processes.

Example: BambooHR's AI-driven onboarding tools automate administrative tasks, allowing HR professionals to focus on creating a positive onboarding experience.

Performance management enhancements

Generative AI contributes to performance management by analyzing employee performance data and providing insights for more objective evaluations and targeted development plans. The following example illustrates usage of Gen AI performance management enhancements.

Example: *Lattice*'s AI-driven performance management tools help organizations provide timely feedback, set goals, and create development plans for employees.

Workforce planning and scalability

AI aids in workforce planning by analyzing data on current workforce capabilities and predicting future needs. This ensures that organizations can scale effectively in response to changing business requirements. The following example illustrates usage of Gen AI in workforce planning and scalability.

Example: Workday's AI-driven workforce planning tools help organizations anticipate talent needs, enabling proactive hiring and skill development initiatives.

Rationale: Generative AI in human resources and recruitment aligns with the need for efficiency, objectivity, and strategic talent management. By automating repetitive tasks such as resume screening and onboarding processes, AI allows HR professionals to focus on strategic initiatives that enhance the overall employee experience. Predictive hiring analytics and skills gap analysis ensure that organizations are not only recruiting the right talent but also nurturing the skills needed for future success. Additionally, AI contributes to diversity and inclusion efforts by minimizing biases in candidate selection, fostering a more equitable and inclusive workplace. Overall, this chapter explores how generative AI is reshaping the HR landscape, optimizing processes, and contributing to strategic workforce planning.

Robotics and automation

Generative AI is applied in robotics for motion planning and control. This includes generating optimal trajectories for robotic arms, facilitating precise and efficient movements in manufacturing and automation settings. In autonomous systems, generative models contribute to behavior synthesis. This involves generating adaptive behaviors based on environmental stimuli, enabling robots to navigate complex and dynamic environments. Robotics and automation, fueled by the capabilities of generative AI, stands at the forefront of industrial evolution. This transformative synergy not only streamlines manufacturing processes through intelligent design and predictive maintenance but also ushers in a new era of adaptive and learning robotics. From enhancing human-robot collaboration in shared workspaces to revolutionizing logistics through autonomous vehicles and drones, this section delves into how generative AI is reshaping industries, optimizing efficiency, and propelling the paradigm of intelligent automation into the future.

Generative design in robotics

AI-driven generative design enables the creation of innovative robotic structures and components by exploring numerous design possibilities. This accelerates the development of highly efficient and specialized robots for diverse applications. The following example illustrates usage of Gen AI in robotics.

Example: Autodesk's generative design tools facilitate the creation of lightweight and structurally optimized robotic components, enhancing overall performance and energy efficiency.

Automated manufacturing processes

Generative AI optimizes manufacturing processes by analyzing data to identify inefficiencies and suggesting improvements. This leads to the automation of complex tasks, streamlining production lines and reducing operational costs. The following example illustrates usage of Gen AI in automated manufacturing processes.

Example: Siemens' AI-powered manufacturing solutions enhance efficiency by automating production planning, quality control, and maintenance processes.

Adaptive and learning robotics

AI enables robots to adapt to dynamic environments and learn from experience. This fosters the development of robots that can optimize their actions based on real-time data, enhancing flexibility in various applications. The following example illustrates usage of Gen AI in adaptive and learning robotics.

Example: Boston Dynamics' robots, equipped with AI, demonstrate adaptive behaviors, learning to navigate and perform tasks in changing environments.

Predictive maintenance for robots

Generative AI analyzes data from robotic sensors to predict maintenance needs, preventing unexpected breakdowns and optimizing the lifespan of robotic systems. The following example illustrates usage of Gen AI in predictive maintenance for robots.

Example: IBM's Watson IoT platform utilizes AI for predictive maintenance, ensuring that robotic systems operate at peak efficiency with minimal downtime.

Human-robot collaboration

AI facilitates seamless collaboration between humans and robots in shared workspaces. This enhances efficiency and safety by enabling robots to understand human intent and adapt their actions accordingly. The following example illustrates usage of Gen AI in human robot collaboration.

Example: Universal Robots' collaborative robots use AI to safely work alongside humans, with sensors and machine learning enabling them to respond to human movements.

Intelligent vision systems

Generative AI enhances robotic vision systems, enabling robots to perceive and interpret visual data more intelligently. This is crucial for tasks such as object recognition, navigation, and quality control. The following example illustrates usage of Gen AI in intelligent vision systems.

Example: NVIDIA's Jetson platform provides AI capabilities to robotic vision systems, enabling real-time object detection and analysis.

Autonomous vehicles and drones

AI plays a pivotal role in the autonomy of vehicles and drones, enabling them to navigate and make decisions based on real-time data. This has implications for industries such as logistics, transportation, and agriculture. The following example illustrates usage of Gen AI in autonomous vehicles and drones.

Example: *Waymo*, an autonomous vehicle company, employs AI algorithms for real-time decision-making, ensuring safe navigation in diverse environments.

AI-enhanced robotic process automation

Generative AI enhances **robotic process automation (RPA)** by enabling robots to perform more complex tasks that involve decision-making and learning from data. This expands the scope of automation in various business processes.

Example: UiPath's AI-driven RPA capabilities enable robots to handle tasks that require cognitive skills, such as understanding natural language and making informed decisions.

Warehouse and logistics automation

AI-powered robots streamline warehouse and logistics operations by automating tasks such as sorting, picking, and packing. This improves efficiency, reduces errors, and accelerates order fulfillment.

Example: Amazon's use of Kiva robots in its warehouses showcases how AI-driven automation enhances the speed and accuracy of order processing.

Generative AI's integration into robotics and automation signifies a paradigm shift in industrial operations, ushering in an era of intelligent and adaptive systems. By leveraging generative design, robots can be customized for specific tasks, optimizing performance and resource utilization. The automation of manufacturing processes ensures precision and efficiency, reducing operational costs. Adaptive and learning robotics enhance flexibility in applications where dynamic responses are essential. Predictive maintenance prolongs the lifespan of robotic systems, minimizing downtime. Human-robot collaboration promotes safer and more efficient shared workspaces. Intelligent vision systems empower robots with enhanced perception, crucial for tasks requiring visual interpretation. The application of AI in autonomous vehicles and drones transforms transportation and logistics. AI-enhanced RPA expands the capabilities of robotic automation to include cognitive tasks. Warehouse and logistics automation exemplify how AI-driven robots revolutionize order fulfillment processes. This chapter unravels the transformative potential of generative AI in reshaping the landscape of robotics and automation, propelling industries toward unprecedented levels of efficiency and innovation.

Urban planning and architecture

Urban planners and architects leverage generative AI for designing and optimizing urban spaces. This includes generating layouts, architectural designs, and landscape plans that balance functionality and aesthetics. Generative models contribute to optimizing building designs for energy efficiency. By exploring various design configurations, these models help identify solutions that minimize energy consumption and environmental impact.

In urban planning and architecture, the infusion of generative AI marks a revolutionary juncture, fundamentally transforming how cities are envisioned and constructed. This chapter unveils the pivotal role of AI in optimizing urban layouts, streamlining infrastructure planning, fostering environmental sustainability in architecture, and revolutionizing traffic management. From crisis preparedness to adaptive heritage preservation, AI-driven solutions redefine the very fabric of urban living. Explore how generative AI becomes the visionary architect, contributing to smarter, more resilient, and community-centric urban landscapes.

Generative design for urban layouts

AI-driven generative design assists in creating optimal urban layouts by considering factors such as traffic flow, green spaces, and accessibility. This accelerates the planning phase and ensures efficient land use. The following example illustrates usage of Gen AI in creating designs for urban layouts.

Example: Autodesk's generative design tools have been used to create urban layouts that prioritize sustainability, transportation efficiency, and aesthetic appeal.

Smart infrastructure planning

Generative AI analyzes data to optimize the planning and placement of infrastructure elements, such as roads, utilities, and public amenities. This results in the creation of smart and efficient urban environments. The following example illustrates usage of Gen AI in smart infrastructure planning.

Example: Singapore's use of generative AI for infrastructure planning ensures optimal utilization of space and resources, contributing to the city-state's reputation as a smart city.

Environmental sustainability in architecture

AI-driven simulations and analyses aid architects in designing environmentally sustainable structures. This includes considerations for energy efficiency, natural light utilization, and materials with low environmental impact. The following example illustrates the usage of Gen AI in environmental sustainability in architecture.

Example: The Edge, a building in Amsterdam, employs generative AI for sustainable design, incorporating features like energy-efficient systems and solar panels.

Traffic flow optimization

Generative AI models analyze traffic patterns to optimize road networks and transportation systems. This contributes to reduced congestion, improved commuting experiences, and enhanced overall urban mobility. The following example illustrates usage of Gen AI in traffic flow optimization.

Example: Los Angeles utilizes AI-powered traffic management systems to dynamically adjust traffic signal timings based on real-time conditions, optimizing traffic flow.

Mixed-use development planning

AI assists in planning mixed-use developments that combine residential, commercial, and recreational spaces. This ensures vibrant and balanced urban environments that cater to diverse community needs. The following example illustrates usage of Gen AI in mixed use development planning.

Example: Toronto's Quayside project incorporates generative AI in planning a mixed-use neighborhood that prioritizes sustainability, innovation, and inclusivity.

Crisis and disaster response planning

Generative AI models aid in predicting and planning for crisis scenarios, such as natural disasters or pandemics. This ensures that urban environments are resilient and equipped to handle emergencies. The following example illustrates usage of Gen AI in crisis and disaster response planning.

Example: Tokyo's earthquake-resistant urban planning incorporates AI-based simulations to anticipate and mitigate the impact of seismic events.

Heritage preservation and adaptive reuse

AI contributes to preserving cultural heritage by assisting in the adaptive reuse of historical structures. This involves repurposing old buildings for contemporary needs while respecting their architectural and historical significance. The following example illustrates usage of Gen AI in heritage preservation and adaptive reuse.

Example: London's King's Cross redevelopment project employs AI to adaptively reuse historic buildings, blending modern functionality with heritage preservation.

Public space design and accessibility

Generative AI considers accessibility parameters in designing public spaces, ensuring inclusivity for individuals with diverse mobility needs. This results in urban environments that are welcoming and accessible to all. The following example illustrates usage of Gen AI in public space design and accessibility.

Example: Barcelona's urban planning initiatives leverage AI to design public spaces that prioritize accessibility, making the city more inclusive for residents and visitors.

Community-driven design through AI feedback

AI tools gather and analyze feedback from communities to inform urban planning and architectural decisions. This ensures that the design process is inclusive and aligned with the needs and preferences of residents. The following example illustrates usage of Gen AI in creating community driven designs.

Example: Helsinki's use of AI-powered citizen feedback platforms enables residents to participate in the city planning process, contributing to the creation of more livable urban spaces.

Generative AI's integration into urban planning and architecture epitomizes a shift toward smarter, more sustainable, and inclusive cities. By leveraging generative design, urban layouts are optimized for efficiency and aesthetics. Smart infrastructure planning ensures that cities are equipped with advanced technologies for enhanced living. Environmental sustainability becomes a focal point in architectural design, contributing to a greener urban landscape. Traffic flow optimization addresses one of the major challenges in urban areas, improving mobility and reducing congestion. Mixed-use development planning fosters vibrant communities that cater to diverse needs. Crisis and disaster response planning ensure cities are resilient and well-prepared. Heritage preservation and adaptive reuse honor the past while embracing the future. Public space design prioritizes accessibility, creating inclusive environments. Lastly, community-driven design through AI feedback ensures that urban planning decisions are reflective of the diverse needs and preferences of the residents, fostering a sense of ownership and belonging. This chapter delves into the innovative ways in which generative AI is reshaping urban environments, emphasizing sustainability, resilience, and community-centric design.

In this section we learnt about various Gen AI use cases and their implementations spanning different industries. We talked about how Gen AI has enhances user experience and minimized human efforts by making the systems and processes more efficient.

Challenges and considerations

While the impact of generative AI is profound, it comes with its set of challenges and considerations. Ethical concerns regarding the potential misuse of generated content, the need for interpretability in critical applications, and ongoing efforts to address biases in generative models are paramount. Responsible development and deployment practices are essential to ensure that the benefits of generative AI are realized without compromising ethical standards. We will cover the challenges and considerations in detail in the forthcoming chapters.

Future outlook

The section concludes by highlighting the ongoing trends and future trajectories of generative AI in various industries. These include advancements in unsupervised learning, the integration of generative models with other AI disciplines, and the continued focus on ethical and responsible AI practices. Generative AI stands at the forefront of technological innovation, reshaping industries and fostering a future where human-AI collaboration drives progress and creativity.

Conclusion

The chapter delves into the significance and profound impact of generative AI across various industries. Highlighting its role as a catalyst for innovation, the discussion spans healthcare, art and entertainment, marketing, manufacturing, finance, and beyond. As a driving force behind creative advancements and problem-solving, generative AI emerges as a cornerstone technology reshaping the landscape of diverse sectors. The chapter sets the stage for an exploration of generative AI's role in revolutionizing industries and its potential to shape the future of technology and human experiences.

The upcoming chapter, *Fundamentals of Generative Models,* is a comprehensive exploration of the essential concepts underpinning generative AI. Readers can anticipate an insightful overview of prominent generative models, including GANs, VAEs, and more. The chapter unravels the underlying principles that govern these models, offering a clear understanding of their functioning and the distinctive features that set them apart. Emphasis is placed on elucidating how generative models differ fundamentally from discriminative models. Readers can expect to gain a solid grasp of the theoretical foundations of generative models, paving the way for a nuanced comprehension of their applications and the intricacies of their design and training.

CHAPTER 3
Fundamentals of Generative Models

Introduction

In this chapter, the readers will embark on a journey into the core principles that underpin the world of generative AI. The chapter provides a comprehensive guide to essential concepts, providing readers with a robust foundation to navigate the intricate landscape of generative models. By the end of this chapter, readers can expect to gain a deep understanding of key models such as **generative adversarial networks (GANs)** and **variational autoencoders (VAEs)**, appreciating their applications and nuances. The exploration of underlying principles will empower readers to comprehend the mechanics of these models and distinguish them from discriminative models. Topics covered include an overview of generative models, an exploration of model principles, and a nuanced understanding of the distinctions that make generative models unique. As readers delve into the fundamentals, they will be equipped with the knowledge needed to unravel the potential and intricacies of generative AI applications across various domains.

Structure

The chapter will cover the following topics:

- Overview of generative models
- Generative adversarial networks

- Variational autoencoders
- Autoencoders
- CycleGAN
- Bidirectional Encoder Representations from Transformers implementations
- DeepDream
- Understanding the underlying principles
- Underlying principles of generative models
- Fundamental differences between generative and discriminative models

Objectives

The objective of this chapter is to introduce readers to the world of generative AI and its fundamental principles. It will provide a comprehensive overview of essential concepts in generative AI, including generative adversarial networks and variational autoencoders. The details in this chapter will help the readers gain a deep understanding of the applications, nuances, and underlying mechanics of generative models. Additionally, it will help them distinguish generative models from discriminative models and appreciate their unique capabilities.

It will equip readers with the knowledge and skills necessary to unravel the potential and intricacies of generative AI applications across various domains.

These objectives align with the overall purpose of the chapter, which is to provide readers with a strong foundation in generative AI and prepare them to explore its advanced applications.

Overview of generative models

This section serves as a gateway into the diverse landscape of generative models, with a spotlight on prominent models such as GANs, VAEs, and more. Readers will embark on a journey of exploration, gaining a comprehensive overview of these models, their architectural structures, and the principles that drive their generative capabilities. By delving into the intricacies of each model, users will acquire a nuanced understanding of their strengths, limitations, and real-world applications. This knowledge is pivotal for readers seeking to navigate the expanding field of generative AI, enabling them to make informed decisions about model selection based on the specific requirements of their projects. As users progress through this section, they will lay the groundwork for a deeper dive into the practical implementation and creative potential of generative models across diverse domains.

This section provides a detailed exploration of key generative models, illuminating their architecture, functioning, and real-world applications. It equips readers with a profound understanding of these generative models, elucidating their mechanisms and showcasing diverse applications. By grasping the intricacies of GANs, VAEs, and other models, readers will be empowered to navigate the rich landscape of generative AI and make informed decisions in their own creative and problem-solving endeavors.

Let us discuss some of the key models in detail.

Generative adversarial networks

GANs introduce a unique adversarial training framework where a generator creates data, and a discriminator evaluates its authenticity. The interplay between these components leads to the generation of remarkably realistic outputs.

StyleGAN, an extension of GANs, has been influential in creating highly realistic and diverse synthetic images, demonstrating the potential for creative applications in art and design.

GANs represent a paradigm shift in artificial intelligence, introducing a captivating framework for generating realistic and novel data. Conceived by *Ian Goodfellow* and his colleagues in 2014, GANs have since become a driving force behind a myriad of creative applications, from realistic image synthesis to innovative artwork generation.

At the heart of GANs lies a compelling duality – a generator and a discriminator engaged in an adversarial dance. The generator's mission is to craft data indistinguishable from authentic samples, while the discriminator endeavors to differentiate between genuine and synthetic data. This adversarial interplay leads to continual refinement of the generator's skills, resulting in the creation of increasingly realistic outputs.

One notable example of GANs' prowess is exemplified by StyleGAN, an extension that excels in creating highly detailed and diverse synthetic images. StyleGAN has demonstrated an unparalleled ability to generate lifelike faces, landscapes, and even fictional characters. This technology has found applications not only in creative domains but also in scenarios where realistic data augmentation is crucial, such as training machine learning models for facial recognition.

GANs have also been instrumental in image-to-image translation, enabling the transformation of one type of image into another without the need for paired training data. **Cycle generative adversarial network** (**CycleGAN**), for instance, has been employed in artistic endeavors, allowing photographs to be transformed into the stylistic nuances of famous paintings. This not only showcases the technical prowess of GANs but also underscores their potential as tools for artistic expression.

The impact of GANs extends beyond the visual domain. In natural language processing, GANs have been adapted to generate coherent and contextually relevant text. This has implications for applications like chatbots and conversational AI, where generating human-like responses is paramount. The bidirectional capabilities of GANs, allowing both data generation and discrimination, make them a versatile choice for various text-related tasks.

Despite their groundbreaking capabilities, GANs pose challenges, notably in terms of training stability and the potential for mode collapse, where the generator produces limited diversity in its outputs. Researchers continue to refine GAN architectures and training methodologies to address these issues, highlighting the evolving nature of this transformative technology.

GANs have been implemented by various tech companies and researchers across different domains. Here are some notable examples and use cases:

NVIDIA

NVIDIA has been at the forefront of GAN research, particularly in generating high-quality images. They introduced StyleGAN and StyleGAN2, which have been influential in generating realistic faces and diverse synthetic images. NVIDIA has been a pioneering force in the advancement of GANs, contributing significantly to the development and understanding of these generative models. We will discuss these innovations and applications of GANs by NVIDIA in this section:

StyleGAN and StyleGAN2: NVIDIA introduced StyleGAN and later enhanced it with StyleGAN2, focusing on the generation of high-resolution and highly realistic images.

Key contributions: The two major key contributions of these models are enlisted below:
- These models have set benchmarks in the field of image synthesis. StyleGAN, in particular, demonstrated the ability to generate diverse and highly detailed faces of non-existent individuals.
- StyleGAN2 further refined this capability, addressing issues related to image quality and training stability.

Data-driven image synthesis: NVIDIA's research in GANs emphasizes a data-driven approach to image synthesis.

Key features: The key features of this research and innovation are enlisted below:
- The models are trained on large datasets to capture diverse features and characteristics, enabling the generation of images that exhibit impressive realism.
- The research also explores techniques for transfer learning, where pre-trained models can be fine-tuned for specific tasks or domains. This approach enhances the adaptability of GANs to different creative applications.

Interactive GANs: NVIDIA's work has extended beyond static image generation to interactive and controllable GANs. These innovations allow users to manipulate specific features of generated images, offering a level of control and customization that goes beyond conventional generative models.

Collaborations and open-source contributions: NVIDIA actively engages with the research community, contributing to open-source projects related to GANs. This collaborative approach fosters knowledge sharing and accelerates advancements in the broader field of generative AI.

AI art and creativity: NVIDIA's GANs, particularly those focused on artistic applications, have opened new avenues for creative expression. Artists and researchers alike have leveraged these models to create visually stunning and imaginative artworks that blur the lines between human and machine creativity.

Educational initiatives: NVIDIA has played a crucial role in disseminating knowledge about GANs through educational initiatives, tutorials, and workshops. This commitment to education has contributed to a broader understanding of GANs and their potential applications.

NVIDIA's contributions to the GAN landscape extend beyond technological innovations; they represent a commitment to pushing the boundaries of the possibilities in generative AI. As GAN research evolves, NVIDIA continues to be a key player, driving progress in both the theoretical and practical aspects of these transformative models.

OpenAI

OpenAI stands at the forefront of artificial intelligence research, dedicated to developing and deploying AI in a way that benefits all of humanity. Founded in 2015 with a bold mission, OpenAI is a non-profit research company composed of leading researchers, engineers, and entrepreneurs. Unlike traditional tech giants, their focus is not on profit but on ensuring that powerful AI technology is developed responsibly and safely.

OpenAI, a research lab focused on artificial intelligence, has explored GANs for various applications. Notably, they developed DALL-E, a GAN-based model capable of generating creative and coherent images from textual descriptions. OpenAI, a forefront research lab in artificial intelligence, has been instrumental in advancing the field of GANs, introducing novel models, and pushing the boundaries of what is achievable in creative AI applications. Some of the major innovations and applications of OpenAI have been discussed below in this section.

DALL-E

OpenAI gained widespread attention with the introduction of DALL-E, a GAN-based model capable of generating diverse and coherent images from textual descriptions.

Key innovative output: The key innovative outputs of DALL-E are highlighted below:

- DALL-E demonstrated the capacity to create imaginative visuals, generating images of objects and scenes that do not exist in the real world based on textual prompts.
- This extends the capabilities of GANs beyond traditional image synthesis.

Text-to-image synthesis

OpenAI has been focused on research in the GenAI domain. OpenAI's work in GANs extends to text-to-image synthesis, where the model translates textual input into visually plausible images. This aligns with their broader mission to develop AI systems that can understand and generate content across different modalities.

Creative AI and beyond

OpenAI's exploration of GANs goes beyond practical applications, delving into artistic expression. The models they develop showcase the potential of AI not only as a tool for problem-solving but also as a medium for creativity and imagination.

Continual research contributions

OpenAI maintains an active role in research and development, continually exploring ways to enhance the capabilities of GANs. Their commitment to advancing the field is evident in their regular contributions to conferences, publications, and open-source projects.

Ethical considerations

OpenAI places a strong emphasis on ethical considerations in AI development. They actively engage in discussions around transparency, safety, and responsible AI use, addressing concerns related to potential misuse of generative models.

Collaborative approach

OpenAI adopts a collaborative approach, often collaborating with other research institutions and organizations. This approach fosters a collective effort to tackle challenges and push the boundaries of AI research.

Education and outreach

OpenAI is dedicated to knowledge sharing and education. They provide resources, research papers, and insights to the broader AI community, contributing to the democratization of AI knowledge.

OpenAI's work in GANs not only showcases technical prowess but also reflects a commitment to leveraging AI for creative endeavors. Their innovative models inspire new possibilities in AI-generated content, emphasizing the potential for technology to amplify human creativity.

Google Brain

Researchers at Google Brain have applied GANs to tasks such as image-to-image translation and style transfer. They have explored the potential of GANs in enhancing image quality and generating visually appealing outputs. Google Brain, Google's AI research division, has been at the forefront of exploring and advancing the capabilities of GANs, contributing to various applications that span image synthesis, style transfer, and more.

Image-to-image translation

Google Brain researchers have extensively explored GANs for image-to-image translation tasks. This includes transforming images from one domain to another without paired training data, showcasing the versatility of GANs in visual content manipulation.

Style transfer

GANs have been applied to the domain of style transfer, allowing users to apply artistic styles to their images. Google Brain's contributions in this area have led to advancements that enable the transfer of artistic characteristics from famous paintings to photographs, enhancing the aesthetic appeal of images.

Progressive generative adversarial networks

Google Brain has been making major contributions in research. It has made notable contributions to developing progressive GANs. This architecture facilitates the generation of high-resolution images in a progressive manner, addressing challenges associated with training stability and quality in GANs.

Conditional generative adversarial networks

Google Brain's research is versatile in a way where it includes the exploration of conditional GANs, which can generate images based on specific conditions. This capability is particularly useful in tasks where users want to control certain attributes or features of the generated content.

Interactive generative adversarial networks

Google Brain's research has been focused on user driven outputs. Google Brain's research in GANs extends to interactive models, allowing users to have more control over the generated outputs. This interactive aspect is crucial for applications where user customization is desired, such as creative design projects.

Application in TensorFlow

Google Brain's TensorFlow, an open-source machine learning library, provides tools and frameworks for implementing GANs. TensorFlow's support for GANs has empowered researchers and developers to leverage GANs in their projects. This has been its contribution towards open-source frameworks.

Collaborations and publications

Researchers at Google Brain actively collaborate with the broader AI research community. Their publications, shared insights, and collaborations contribute to the collective understanding of GANs and their applications.

AI ethics and fairness

Google Brain, as part of Google's broader commitment, is actively engaged in discussions surrounding AI ethics and fairness. This includes addressing biases and ensuring responsible use of AI technologies, including those based on GANs.

Google Brain's involvement in GAN research showcases a commitment to advancing the state-of-the-art in generative models. Their contributions not only drive technical innovation but also emphasize the importance of ethical considerations in the development and deployment of AI technologies.

Facebook AI

Facebook AI has utilized GANs for tasks such as image synthesis and enhancement. GANs generate high-resolution and realistic images, contributing to improved user experiences on the platform.

Facebook AI, the artificial intelligence research division of Facebook, has made significant contributions to the field of GANs, leveraging these models for tasks related to image synthesis, enhancement, and creative applications.

Image synthesis and enhancement

Facebook AI has employed GANs for image synthesis, creating realistic and high-quality images. The focus extends to image enhancement, where GANs are used to improve the visual quality of images, making them more appealing and engaging.

GANs for style transfer

Researchers at Facebook AI have explored the application of GANs in style transfer, allowing users to apply artistic styles to their images. This capability enhances creative expression by transforming photos into visually distinct and stylized artworks.

Deep generative models

Facebook AI has been involved in the development and exploration of deep generative models, including GANs. Their research contributions help advance the capabilities of generative models, making them more effective in capturing and generating complex patterns.

Conditional generative adversarial networks and user interaction

Facebook AI's research extends to conditional GANs, enabling the generation of images based on specific conditions. This versatility is valuable in applications where user interaction and customization play a crucial role, such as interactive creative projects.

Generative models for video

Facebook AI has ventured into applying generative models, including GANs, to videos. This involves generating realistic and coherent video sequences, opening up possibilities for content creation and video editing.

Open-source contributions

Facebook AI actively contributes to the open-source community, sharing insights, models, and tools related to GANs. This collaborative approach fosters knowledge exchange and accelerates advancements in the broader AI research community.

AI research for social good

Facebook AI's mission includes leveraging AI for social good. While GANs are powerful tools for creative applications, there is also a commitment to exploring how AI technologies, including generative models, can contribute positively to societal challenges.

Ethical considerations

Responsible AI: Facebook AI is involved in addressing ethical considerations in AI development. This includes ensuring responsible and fair use of AI technologies, addressing potential biases, and considering the broader societal impacts of generative models.

Facebook AI's contributions to GAN research align with the broader mission of Facebook to connect people and foster creativity. Their research not only advances the technical capabilities of generative models but also emphasizes responsible and ethical AI practices.

IBM

IBM has explored the use of GANs in various applications, including data augmentation, for improved model training. GANs can generate diverse synthetic data, enhancing the robustness of machine learning models. IBM, a global leader in technology and innovation, has made notable contributions to the field of GANs, exploring applications that span creative domains, data generation, and AI research.

Generative adversarial networks for data augmentation

IBM has explored the use of GANs for data augmentation, enhancing the diversity and size of datasets. This application is particularly valuable in machine learning tasks where having a diverse dataset is crucial for model performance.

Generative models in artificial intelligence research

IBM has a dedicated focus on leveraging generative models, including GANs, in various AI research initiatives. This includes exploring new architectures, training techniques, and applications that contribute to the advancement of generative AI.

Creative applications

IBM's research extends to creative applications of GANs, showcasing their potential in generating artistic content. This includes applications in generating artwork, music, and other forms of creative expression.

Generative adversarial networks for anomaly detection

IBM has investigated the use of GANs for anomaly detection in data. By training GANs on normal patterns, deviations from these patterns can be identified, making GANs a valuable tool in cybersecurity and fraud detection.

Explainability and interpretability

IBM's research considers challenges related to the interpretability of generative models. Understanding and explaining the decisions made by GANs are crucial for their broader adoption in various industries, and IBM contributes to addressing these challenges.

Quantum machine learning

IBM is at the forefront of exploring the intersection of quantum computing and machine learning. While not exclusive to GANs, this exploration could influence the development of more powerful models, including generative models.

Industry-specific applications

IBM's approach involves tailoring generative models to address industry-specific challenges. Whether in healthcare, finance, or other sectors, IBM explores how GANs can be customized to provide solutions that meet specific industry needs.

AI ethics and fairness

IBM is actively involved in discussions around AI ethics and fairness. As part of their commitment to responsible AI, they contribute to frameworks and practices that ensure the ethical use of generative models.

IBM's engagement with GANs reflects a multifaceted approach, encompassing not only creative applications but also practical solutions in data science, anomaly detection, and industry-specific challenges. Their commitment to addressing ethical considerations aligns with the responsible deployment of generative models in various domains.

Using generative adversarial networks

Implementing GANs typically involves the following steps.

Step 1: Defining the problem

Identify the specific task or problem you want GANs to address, for example, image generation, style transfer, or data augmentation.

Defining the problem is a critical first step when leveraging GANs for a specific task. This involves precisely outlining the objectives and constraints of the problem you aim to solve using GANs. Here are key considerations in this initial phase:

- **Problem formulation**: Clearly articulate the problem you intend to address. Whether it is image synthesis, data augmentation, style transfer, or another application, defining the problem sets the foundation for the GAN's purpose.

- **Scope and constraints**: Identify the scope of the problem and any constraints that need to be considered. This includes factors such as data availability, computational resources, and specific requirements of the application.

- **Desired output characteristics**: Define the characteristics of the desired outputs that the GAN should generate. This could involve specifying the visual style, level of realism, or other features relevant to the task.

- **Data requirements**: Assess the data required to train the GAN. Determine the nature of the input data and any labeled or unlabeled data that might be needed. Understanding the data landscape is crucial for successful GAN implementation.

- **Evaluation metrics**: Establish metrics for evaluating the performance of the GAN. Employing well-defined evaluation criteria, including quantitative measures like **Fréchet inception distance (FID)** for image generation and domain-specific metrics, is crucial for gauging the effectiveness of GAN models.

- **Stakeholder input**: Engage with stakeholders or end-users to gather their insights and expectations. Understanding the perspectives of those who will interact with the GAN-generated outputs ensures that the model aligns with real-world needs.

- **Ethical considerations**: Consider ethical implications associated with the problem. This includes addressing issues such as bias in data, potential misuse of generated content, and ensuring that the GAN aligns with ethical guidelines and regulations.

- **Project timeline**: Establish a realistic timeline for the project. GAN training can be computationally intensive, and defining a timeline helps manage expectations and allocate resources effectively.

By rigorously defining the problem, practitioners lay the groundwork for a successful GAN implementation. This clarity not only guides the subsequent steps in the process but also ensures that the GAN solution aligns with the specific needs and objectives of the problem at hand.

Step 2: Choosing a GAN architecture

Select a GAN architecture suitable for your task. Common architectures include vanilla GANs, **Deep Convolutional GAN (DCGAN)**, and more specialized variants like StyleGAN for image generation.

Selecting the appropriate GAN architecture is a crucial decision in the implementation process. Different GAN architectures are designed for specific tasks and data types. Here are key considerations when choosing a GAN architecture:

- **Task compatibility**: Understand the nature of the task you are addressing. Different GAN architectures excel in specific applications, such as image synthesis (for example, DCGAN), style transfer (for example, CycleGAN), or conditional generation (for example, cGAN). Choose an architecture aligned with your task.

- **Data characteristics**: Analyze the characteristics of your dataset. If you are working with high-resolution images, architectures like BigGAN might be suitable. For smaller datasets, architectures with techniques for improved training stability, such as **Wasserstein GAN (WGAN)**, could be beneficial.

- **Generator and discriminator complexity**: Consider the complexity of the generator and discriminator networks. More intricate architectures may capture finer details but could be computationally expensive. Balance the complexity based on the available computational resources and the level of detail required in generated outputs.

- **Conditional or unconditional GAN**: Decide if your task requires a conditional or unconditional GAN. **Conditional GANs (cGANs)** allow you to generate outputs based on specific conditions, adding a level of control to the generation process. Unconditional GANs are simpler but may be suitable for certain tasks.

- **Architecture variants**: Explore variations of popular architectures. For example, StyleGAN introduces style-based generator architecture for more control over image styles. Such variants might offer improved performance or features relevant to your task.

- **Training techniques**: Assess the training techniques incorporated into the architecture. Techniques like spectral normalization (used in SN-GAN) or progressive growing (used in Progressive GAN) can enhance training stability and scalability.

- **Open-source implementations**: Leverage open-source implementations and pre-trained models. Popular deep learning frameworks like TensorFlow and PyTorch have a variety of GAN implementations available. Pre-trained models can save training time and resources.

- **Community and research impact**: Consider the impact and community support for a specific GAN architecture. Architectures with widespread use in research and practical applications often benefit from a larger community, which can be advantageous for problem-solving and updates.

- **Resource requirements**: Evaluate the computational resources required for training and inference. Some GAN architectures demand significant GPU power and memory. Ensure that your infrastructure can support the selected architecture.

Choosing the right GAN architecture involves a careful assessment of the task, data characteristics, and available resources. It is a crucial step that significantly influences the performance and applicability of the GAN for your specific use case.

Step 3: Data preparation

Prepare a dataset relevant to your task. High-quality and diverse training data are essential for GANs to learn meaningful patterns.

Effective data preparation is a fundamental step in leveraging GANs for various applications. Well-prepared data contributes to the successful training and generation of realistic outputs. Here are key considerations for data preparation:

- **Data cleaning and preprocessing**: Cleanse the dataset of any anomalies, outliers, or irrelevant information. Preprocess the data to ensure uniformity in features, scales, and formats. Standardize or normalize numerical values and handle missing data appropriately.

- **Dataset size and diversity**: Assess the size and diversity of the dataset. GANs often benefit from large and diverse datasets to capture a wide range of features. Augment the dataset if needed to increase its size and variety, enhancing the model's ability to generate diverse outputs.

- **Labeling for conditional GANs**: If working with a **conditional GAN (cGAN)** where outputs are conditioned on specific labels, ensure the dataset is properly labeled. This includes assigning accurate labels to data points based on the desired conditions for generation.

- **Data augmentation**: Apply data augmentation techniques to increase the variability of the dataset. Techniques such as rotation, flipping, or cropping can introduce diversity, especially when working with limited data.

- **Image quality and resolution**: Consider the quality and resolution of images in the dataset. GANs designed for high-resolution image synthesis, like BigGAN, may require datasets with images of sufficient quality to generate realistic outputs.

- **Noise addition**: Introduce controlled noise to the dataset. GANs learn to generate realistic outputs by discerning patterns in data, and adding noise can enhance the model's ability to generalize and produce more diverse outputs.

- **Handling imbalanced datasets**: Address class imbalances if present in the dataset. Imbalanced datasets can lead to biased generation. Techniques such as oversampling minority classes or using class weights during training can help mitigate this issue.

- **Data splitting**: Split the dataset into training, validation, and testing sets. The training set is used for model training, the validation set helps tune hyperparameters, and the testing set evaluates the model's generalization performance.

- **Consideration of domain-specific features**: If the dataset contains domain-specific features or characteristics, ensure that the GAN architecture is designed to capture and reproduce these features. Understanding the domain-specific nuances is crucial for generating meaningful outputs.

- **Data privacy and ethical considerations**: Adhere to data privacy regulations and ethical considerations. Ensure that the use of the dataset complies with privacy standards, especially when working with sensitive or personally identifiable information.

Properly prepared data forms the foundation for successful GAN implementation. Rigorous data cleaning, augmentation, and consideration of domain-specific features contribute to the model's ability to generate realistic and diverse outputs.

Step 4: Model training

Train the GAN on the prepared dataset. This involves training the generator to create realistic data and the discriminator to differentiate between real and synthetic samples.

Training a GAN is a complex process that involves optimizing both the generator and discriminator networks through adversarial training. Here are key considerations for successful GAN model training:

- **Loss function selection**: Choose an appropriate loss function for both - generator and discriminator. Common choices include binary cross-entropy or Wasserstein loss. The selection depends on the specific GAN architecture and task requirements.

- **Adversarial training dynamics**: Understand the dynamics of adversarial training. The generator and discriminator are trained iteratively, each attempting to outperform the other. Achieving a balance in training dynamics is crucial for the GAN to converge to a stable solution.

- **Hyperparameter tuning**: Tune hyperparameters such as learning rates, batch sizes, and momentum terms. These parameters significantly impact training stability and convergence. Experiment with different values to find the optimal configuration for your specific task.

- **Regularization techniques**: Apply regularization techniques to prevent overfitting. Techniques like dropout or weight regularization can be beneficial, especially when dealing with limited datasets or complex architectures.

- **Gradient clipping**: Implement gradient clipping, particularly in architectures like Wasserstein GANs, to stabilize training. This prevents exploding gradients and contributes to smoother convergence.

- **Monitoring and visualization**: Monitor the training process and visualize key metrics. Plotting the generator and discriminator losses over time helps identify convergence patterns and potential issues. Visualization aids in understanding the learning dynamics.

- **Early stopping**: Implement early stopping, if necessary. If the model performance on a validation set plateaus or starts degrading, early stopping prevents unnecessary overfitting and allows you to save the model at an optimal point.

- **Checkpointing**: Implement model checkpointing to save intermediate models during training. This ensures that, in case of unexpected interruptions, you can resume training from the last checkpoint rather than starting from scratch.

- **Data augmentation during training**: Continue data augmentation during training to introduce diversity. This is especially relevant when working with GANs for image generation or data synthesis. Augmenting the dataset dynamically during training enhances the model's ability to generalize.

- **Training on appropriate hardware**: Utilize appropriate hardware for training. GANs, especially large architectures, may require substantial computational resources. Training on GPUs or TPUs accelerates the process and allows for experimentation with different configurations.

- **Monitoring mode collapse**: Watch for mode collapse, a common challenge in GAN training where the generator produces limited diversity. Techniques like mini-batch discrimination or architectural modifications can mitigate mode collapse.

- **Understanding convergence**: Understand what convergence means in the context of your task. For some applications, achieving a perfect match to the training data may not be desirable, and a balance between diversity and fidelity is crucial.

Model training in GANs is an intricate process that demands careful consideration of hyperparameters, regularization, and dynamic adjustments during training. Continuous monitoring and experimentation contribute to the successful convergence and generation of high-quality outputs.

Step 5: Optimization and fine-tuning

Optimize the GAN parameters, and fine-tune the model based on feedback from the discriminator. This iterative process aims to improve the quality of generated outputs.

Optimization and fine-tuning are crucial steps in harnessing the full potential of GANs. These steps involve refining the model's performance, addressing issues that may arise during training, and preparing the deployment model. Here are key considerations for optimization and fine-tuning:

- **Learning rate scheduling**: Implement learning rate scheduling to dynamically adjust the learning rate during training. This technique can help achieve faster convergence in the early stages of training and finer adjustments as the model approaches convergence.

- **Batch normalization**: Consider the use of batch normalization, especially in deeper architectures. Batch normalization helps stabilize training by normalizing input activations, leading to improved convergence and preventing issues such as vanishing or exploding gradients.

- **Transfer learning**: Explore transfer learning, if pre-trained models are available. Transfer learning involves leveraging knowledge gained from a model trained on a related task. Fine-tuning a pre-trained GAN can significantly reduce training time and resource requirements.

- **Architecture modifications**: Experiment with architecture modifications. Adjusting the architecture, such as adding or removing layers, may be necessary to address specific challenges encountered during training, like mode collapse or instability.

- **Regularization techniques**: Continue or refine regularization techniques during fine-tuning. Regularization methods such as dropout or L2 regularization can prevent overfitting, especially when working with limited datasets.

- **Evaluation metrics**: Reevaluate and fine-tune based on evaluation metrics. Metrics such as FID or Inception Score can provide insights into the quality and diversity of generated outputs. Optimize the model to achieve desirable metrics.

- **Hyperparameter grid search**: Conduct a hyperparameter grid search. Fine-tune hyperparameters systematically to identify the combination that yields the best performance. This may involve adjusting learning rates, regularization strengths, and other hyperparameters.

- **Addressing mode collapse**: Implement strategies to address mode collapse. Techniques like feature matching, minibatch discrimination, or adjusting the architecture can mitigate mode collapse, ensuring the model generates diverse outputs.

- **Data augmentation refinement**: Refine data augmentation techniques. Depending on the outputs generated by the model, adjusting data augmentation strategies during fine-tuning can enhance the diversity and realism of generated samples.

- **Ensemble techniques**: Explore ensemble techniques. Combining multiple GAN models can lead to improved performance and more robust generation. Ensemble methods can mitigate individual model weaknesses.

- **Understanding failure modes**: Analyze failure modes. Understand the specific scenarios where the model struggles and iteratively refine the model to address these challenges. This may involve adjusting loss functions or introducing new architectural elements.

- **Cross-validation**: If applicable, perform cross-validation. Evaluate the model's generalization performance on different subsets of the dataset to ensure robustness across various scenarios.

Optimization and fine-tuning in GANs are iterative processes that involve continuous evaluation, adjustment, and experimentation. Fine-tuning addresses specific challenges encountered during training, refines model behavior, and ensures that the GAN is well-suited for its intended application

Step 6: Application deployment

Once the GAN is trained and optimized, deploy it for the specific application. This could involve integrating the model into a larger system, using it for creative projects, or incorporating it into a machine learning pipeline.

Deploying a GAN for real-world applications involves considerations beyond training and optimization. Application deployment ensures that the generated outputs are integrated into practical scenarios. Here are key considerations for deploying GANs in applications:

- **Model serialization**: Serialize and save the trained GAN model. Convert the trained model into a serialized format, such as TensorFlow's SavedModel or PyTorch's TorchScript. Serialization enables easy storage, sharing, and deployment of the model.

- **Scalability**: Design the deployment architecture for scalability. Consider the scalability requirements of the application. GAN deployment may involve serving requests from multiple users or handling large-scale data, requiring scalable and efficient deployment solutions.

- **Hardware considerations**: Choose appropriate hardware for deployment. The hardware used during training may differ from what is suitable for deployment. Ensure that the selected hardware can efficiently handle the computational requirements of real-time inference.

- **Inference speed optimization**: Optimize the model for fast inference. Techniques such as model quantization, that reduce the precision of model weights, can significantly speed up inference without sacrificing too much performance.

- **API integration**: Integrate the GAN model into existing systems through APIs. Develop an API that allows other applications or services to interact with the GAN for generating outputs. RESTful APIs or GraphQL interfaces are common choices for seamless integration.

- **User interface design**: Design a user interface for interaction. If the GAN-generated outputs are intended for human consumption, develop a user interface that allows users to interact with and customize the generated content. Consider **user experience (UX)** principles in interface design.

- **Real-time versus batch processing**: Decide between real-time and batch processing. Depending on the application requirements, determine whether real-time generation or batch processing is more suitable. Real-time applications may require low-latency inference, while batch processing can be efficient for offline tasks.

- **Security measures**: Implement security measures. Ensure that the deployed GAN model is secured against potential attacks, such as adversarial attacks or unauthorized access. Employ encryption, authentication, and authorization mechanisms as needed.

- **Monitoring and logging**: Set up monitoring and logging. Implement monitoring tools to track the performance of the deployed GAN model. Logging critical events and metrics helps in diagnosing issues and ensuring the reliability of the deployed system.

- **Continuous Integration and Deployment (CI/CD)**: Establish CI/CD pipelines. Implement CI/CD practices to automate the deployment process. This ensures that updates to the GAN model can be seamlessly deployed, reducing downtime and streamlining the development lifecycle.

- **Compliance with regulations**: Ensure compliance with regulations. If the generated outputs contain sensitive or regulated information, adhere to data privacy and compliance standards. This is particularly crucial in healthcare, finance, or other industries with strict regulatory requirements.

- **Feedback mechanism**: Incorporate a feedback mechanism. Design a mechanism for collecting feedback on the generated outputs. User feedback can be valuable for continuous improvement and refinement of the GAN model.

Application deployment is the final step in bringing GAN-generated outputs into practical use. By addressing considerations related to scalability, hardware, security, and user interaction, the deployed GAN can seamlessly integrate into diverse applications, providing value in various domains.

> Note: GANs can be resource-intensive and require careful tuning. Additionally, ethical considerations, such as preventing bias in generated outputs, should be considered when deploying GANs in real-world applications.

Variational autoencoders

VAEs leverage probabilistic techniques to generate new data by encoding input into a latent space. This model enables the generation of diverse outputs by sampling from the learned distribution. In healthcare, VAEs have been used to generate synthetic medical images for training machine learning models without compromising patient privacy.

VAEs represent a powerful class of generative models that extend the capabilities of traditional autoencoders. Introduced by *Kingma* and *Welling* in 2013, VAEs have found widespread applications in diverse fields, from image generation to drug discovery. This section delves into the intricacies of VAEs, exploring their architecture, training process, and real-world applications.

Overview of variational autoencoder architecture

VAEs have two main components - a probabilistic encoder and a generative decoder. The encoder maps input data to a probability distribution in a latent space, and the decoder reconstructs the input data from samples drawn from this distribution. The latent space introduces a continuous and probabilistic element, enabling VAEs to generate diverse and realistic outputs.

Training process

The training of VAEs involves two primary objectives - reconstruction loss and the **Kullback-Leibler (KL)** divergence. The reconstruction loss ensures that the generated outputs closely resemble the input data, while the KL divergence regularizes the latent space, promoting smoother transitions between data points. This dual-objective training allows VAEs to learn meaningful and continuous latent representations.

Example: Image generation with Variational autoencoders

Consider the task of generating realistic images using VAEs. The encoder maps images to a distribution in the latent space, and the decoder generates new images by sampling from this distribution. The continuous nature of the latent space allows for the interpolation between different images. For instance, moving along a trajectory in the latent space can smoothly transition an image of a cat into an image of a dog, demonstrating the model's ability to generate diverse outputs.

Real-world applications of variational autoencoders

In this section we will be discussing some of the real-world applications of VAE. We will discuss how VAEs have been contributing in innovation and day to day application.

- **Drug discovery**: VAEs play a crucial role in molecular generation for drug discovery. By encoding molecular structures into a latent space, VAEs can generate novel molecular structures with desired properties. This application accelerates the process of identifying potential drug candidates.

- **Anomaly detection**: VAEs excel in anomaly detection tasks. By learning the distribution of normal data, VAEs can effectively identify deviations from the norm. This is valuable in various domains, including cybersecurity, where anomalies in network traffic can signify potential security threats.

- **Natural language processing (NLP)**: In NLP, VAEs are employed for tasks such as text generation and semantic representation learning. The continuous latent space enables the generation of diverse and coherent textual outputs, making VAEs a valuable tool in creative text generation.

- **Medical imaging**: VAEs contribute to medical image analysis by providing a means to generate synthetic images for data augmentation. Additionally, VAEs aid in encoding and decoding medical images, facilitating tasks such as image reconstruction and segmentation.

Challenges and advancements

While VAEs offer remarkable capabilities, they are not without challenges. One common issue is the tendency of VAEs to produce blurry outputs. Researchers are actively exploring architectural modifications and training strategies to address this limitation. Advances in disentangled representation learning aim to enhance the interpretability of the learned latent space, allowing for more explicit control over the generated outputs.

Examples of variational autoencoders implementations

Enlisted below are some implementations of VAEs.

Google's Magenta Studio

Magenta Studio, developed by Google's Magenta team, leverages VAEs for creative applications in music. It allows musicians and artists to generate new musical compositions by exploring the latent space of musical features.

Google's Magenta Studio stands as a remarkable testament to the creative potential of VAEs. Developed by Google's Magenta team, Magenta Studio is an open-source project that fuses machine learning with artistic expression, specifically focusing on the domain of music generation.

Key insights: Let us investigate key insights and applications of Google's Magenta Studio.

- **Music generation with VAEs**: Magenta Studio employs VAEs to unlock the latent space of musical features. This enables musicians and artists to explore and navigate a continuous and probabilistic representation of musical elements. By doing so, Magenta Studio provides a unique platform for generating novel musical compositions.

- **Latent space exploration**: VAEs in Magenta Studio allow users to traverse the latent space of musical attributes. Musicians can manipulate and interact with various dimensions of this space, influencing aspects such as melody, harmony, and rhythm. This interactive exploration enables the creation of diverse and personalized musical pieces.

- **User-friendly interface**: Magenta Studio is designed with a user-friendly interface, making it accessible to both experienced musicians and those with limited technical background. The interface provides intuitive controls for navigating the latent space, adjusting parameters, and influencing the generated musical output.

- **Collaboration and inspiration**: The collaborative nature of Magenta Studio fosters inspiration and exploration. Musicians can use the platform individually or collaborate with others, creating a dynamic space for musical discovery. This collaborative aspect aligns with the broader vision of Magenta, which aims to explore the possibilities at the intersection of machine learning and the arts.

- **Integration with music creation tools**: Magenta Studio seamlessly integrates with existing music creation tools. This integration allows artists to incorporate the AI-generated musical elements into their larger compositions. The synergy between human creativity and AI-generated content opens up new avenues for musical innovation.

- **Educational potential**: Magenta Studio serves as an educational resource, demonstrating the capabilities of VAEs in a creative context. It provides insights into how machine learning models can be harnessed not only for automation but also as tools for artistic inspiration and experimentation.

- **Open-source community**: Being an open-source project, Magenta Studio encourages contributions from the broader community. This collaborative approach enables the continuous refinement of the platform, with artists, developers, and researchers contributing to its evolution.

Google's Magenta Studio, driven by the power of VAEs, represents a harmonious blend of technology and artistry. By providing a canvas for musicians to explore the latent space of music, it exemplifies how generative models can transcend traditional boundaries, inspiring new forms of creative expression in the digital age.

OpenAI's DALL-E

DALL-E is a project by OpenAI that uses a VAE-based generative model for creating diverse and imaginative images based on textual descriptions. It demonstrates the potential of VAEs in generating novel visual content.

DeepChem

DeepChem, an open-source library for drug discovery, incorporates VAEs to generate molecular structures. The VAE-based molecular generation is employed for exploring chemical space and identifying potential drug candidates.

It is a groundbreaking open-source library that harnesses the capabilities of VAEs to revolutionize the field of drug discovery. Developed to address the complex challenges of molecular design, DeepChem showcases the transformative potential of VAEs in computational chemistry.

Let us look into some key insights of DeepChem in this section:

- **Molecular generation for drug discovery**: At the core of DeepChem's functionality is the application of VAEs for molecular generation. By encoding molecular structures into a latent space, VAEs within DeepChem enable the generation of novel molecular structures with desired properties. This capability accelerates the process of identifying potential drug candidates.

- **Encoding and decoding molecular structures**: DeepChem's VAEs facilitate the encoding and decoding of molecular structures. The encoding process involves transforming complex molecular representations into a latent space, while decoding reconstructs these representations from the latent space. This bidirectional capability enhances the understanding of molecular properties and relationships.

- **Chemical space exploration**: VAEs in DeepChem contribute to the exploration of chemical space. The continuous and probabilistic nature of the latent space allows for the generation of diverse molecular structures. This exploration is instrumental in discovering novel compounds and optimizing chemical structures for specific therapeutic purposes.

- **Data augmentation for model training**: DeepChem utilizes VAEs for data augmentation in the context of model training. By generating synthetic molecular structures, the dataset's diversity is enhanced, leading to more robust models. This approach mitigates challenges associated with limited and biased training data.

- **Generative models for molecular design**: The generative capabilities of VAEs in DeepChem empower researchers to iteratively design molecules with desired properties. This iterative design process aligns with the principles of rational drug design, allowing for the creation of compounds tailored to specific biological targets.

- **Integration with cheminformatics tools**: DeepChem seamlessly integrates with existing cheminformatics tools and workflows. This integration ensures that the insights gained from VAE-generated molecular structures can be readily incorporated into the broader drug discovery pipeline. The compatibility with industry-standard tools enhances the practicality and adoption of DeepChem.

- **Community collaboration**: As an open-source project, DeepChem encourages collaboration and contributions from the scientific community. The collaborative nature of the platform fosters the sharing of knowledge, methodologies, and advancements in the domain of computational chemistry and drug discovery.

DeepChem's utilization of VAEs exemplifies the synergy between machine learning and life sciences. By transforming molecular design into a generative and exploratory process, DeepChem contributes to the acceleration of drug discovery, offering new possibilities for the development of innovative therapeutic interventions.

PyTorch's variational autoencoders implementation

PyTorch, a popular deep learning framework, provides tools and libraries for implementing VAEs. The PyTorch implementation includes modules for building the encoder, decoder, and defining the loss functions necessary for training VAEs.

PyTorch, a widely adopted deep learning framework, has played a pivotal role in democratizing the implementation of VAEs. PyTorch's VAE implementation empowers researchers and practitioners by providing a flexible and intuitive platform for developing generative models and exploring latent spaces.

Here are some key insights into PyTorch's VAE framework and its capabilities:

- **Dynamic computational graphs**: PyTorch's dynamic computational graph nature facilitates the construction of VAEs with dynamic structures. Unlike static graph frameworks, PyTorch allows for dynamic adjustments during runtime, offering flexibility in model architecture and adaptation to diverse data types.

- **Autograd for automatic differentiation**: The Autograd functionality in PyTorch automates the process of computing gradients. This is crucial for VAEs, where gradient-based optimization algorithms, such as stochastic gradient descent, are employed for model training. Autograd simplifies the implementation of backpropagation in the VAE architecture.

- **Torch distribution for probabilistic modeling**: PyTorch's torch distributions module provides a rich set of tools for probabilistic modeling, aligning with the probabilistic nature of VAEs. Researchers can easily define and manipulate probability distributions, facilitating the modeling of latent variables and the generative process.

- **Flexible model definition**: PyTorch's modular design allows for a clear and concise definition of VAE architectures. Researchers can easily define the encoder and decoder components, specify the structure of the latent space, and experiment with various architectural choices. This flexibility encourages innovation in model design.

- **Ease of debugging and visualization**: The dynamic nature of PyTorch simplifies debugging during model development. Researchers can inspect and visualize intermediate results within the computation graph, aiding in the identification and resolution of issues. This transparency is crucial for understanding the intricate workings of VAEs.

- **Integration with TorchVision**: PyTorch seamlessly integrates with TorchVision, a computer vision library, making it convenient for researchers working on image-related VAE applications. This integration streamlines tasks such as data preprocessing, augmentations, and visualization, enhancing the overall efficiency of VAE-based image generation.

- **Growing ecosystem and community support**: PyTorch's vibrant ecosystem and strong community support contribute to the widespread adoption of its VAE implementation. Researchers benefit from a wealth of tutorials, documentation, and community-contributed models, accelerating the learning curve and enabling collaborative exploration.

- **Transfer learning and pre-trained models**: PyTorch's ecosystem facilitates transfer learning with pre-trained models. Researchers can leverage pre-trained VAEs on large datasets, allowing for faster convergence and adaptation to specific tasks with limited data availability.

PyTorch's VAE implementation serves as a catalyst for advancements in generative modeling. By providing a user-friendly yet powerful platform, PyTorch empowers researchers to unlock the potential of VAEs, fostering innovation in diverse domains such as image generation, molecular design, and natural language processing.

TensorFlow Probability

TensorFlow Probability (TFP), an extension of TensorFlow for probabilistic modeling, includes components for implementing VAEs. TFP provides a high-level interface for building probabilistic models, making it accessible for researchers and practitioners.

TFP stands at the forefront of probabilistic programming and generative modeling, offering a comprehensive suite of tools for researchers and practitioners. TFP, built on the TensorFlow framework, facilitates the seamless integration of probabilistic models like VAEs into deep learning workflows.

Let us look into some key insights of TFP and its capabilities:

- **Probabilistic layers for uncertainty modeling**: TFP introduces probabilistic layers, a fundamental concept for uncertainty modeling in deep generative models like VAEs. With these layers, researchers can explicitly model uncertainty in both the encoder and decoder components, enabling a more nuanced representation of uncertainty in the latent space.

- **Rich probabilistic distributions**: TFP provides an extensive collection of probability distributions, allowing for flexible and expressive modeling of probabilistic relationships. Researchers working with VAEs in TFP can leverage distributions beyond the standard Gaussian, tailoring the model to the specific characteristics of the data being modeled.

- **Joint distribution for complete model specification**: TFP's emphasis on probabilistic programming is manifested in its `JointDistribution` class, enabling the concise specification of complex generative models. Researchers can express the joint distribution of latent variables and observed data, simplifying the process of defining and training VAEs.

- **Bayesian neural networks integration**: TFP seamlessly integrates with **Bayesian neural networks (BNNs)**, allowing researchers to extend VAEs with Bayesian principles. By incorporating uncertainty in the neural network weights, TFP supports the exploration of model uncertainty and robustness, particularly in scenarios with limited data.

- **Distribution-aware optimization**: TFP offers distribution-aware optimization techniques that align with the probabilistic nature of generative models. This includes methods for variational inference and stochastic optimization tailored to the challenges posed by probabilistic models, ensuring more effective and stable training of VAEs.

- **Hierarchical modeling capabilities**: TFP enables hierarchical modeling, facilitating the incorporation of structured dependencies within generative models. This capability is particularly beneficial for applications where the data exhibits hierarchical structures, such as in healthcare or social sciences.

- **Integration with TensorFlow ecosystem**: TFP seamlessly integrates with the broader TensorFlow ecosystem. This integration enables researchers to leverage TensorFlow's high-performance computation graph and benefit from features such as distributed training, hardware acceleration, and compatibility with TensorFlow Serving for deployment.

- **Community-driven development**: TFP benefits from an active and growing community of researchers and developers contributing to its development. This collaborative environment ensures ongoing advancements, a rich set of tutorials, and a repository of models and tools that empower researchers working on VAEs and probabilistic generative models.

TensorFlow Probability, with its focus on probabilistic programming, extends the capabilities of TensorFlow into the realm of uncertainty-aware generative modeling. Through its rich set of probabilistic tools and seamless integration with TensorFlow, TFP remains a pivotal framework for researchers exploring the frontiers of generative models like VAEs.

Variational autoencoders implementation framework

In this section, we will discuss in detail VAEs implementation framework. This framework will give step-by-step guidance on how to use a VAE for various use cases:

1. **Defining the problem**: The first step is to clearly define the problem you want to solve using VAEs. Whether it is image generation, molecular design, or anomaly detection, understanding the problem is the first step.

2. **Choosing a VAE architecture**: Second step is to select an appropriate VAE architecture based on the nature of your data and the complexity of the task. Common architectures include convolutional VAEs for images and variational recurrent neural networks for sequential data.

3. **Data preparation**: Once you have chosen a VAE architecture that should be used, prepare your dataset for training. Ensure that the data is preprocessed

and normalized appropriately. Data preparation is crucial for the model to learn meaningful representations.

4. **Model training**: In the next step, train the VAE using the dual objective of reconstruction loss and KL divergence. Experiment with hyperparameters such as learning rates and regularization strengths to achieve optimal performance.

5. **Evaluation metrics**: Evaluate the trained model using appropriate metrics for your task. For image generation, metrics like Inception Score or FID may be used. For other tasks, task-specific metrics can be defined.

6. **Application deployment**: If the goal is real-world application, deploy the trained VAE model in a production environment. This involves serialization of the model, designing an API for integration, and considering factors like scalability and security.

7. **Continuous improvement**: Iterate on your model based on feedback and performance evaluation. Continuous improvement may involve adjusting hyperparameters, exploring different architectures, or incorporating advancements from the research community.

8. **Community resources**: Leverage community resources and pre-existing implementations. Frameworks like TensorFlow and PyTorch have a wealth of documentation, tutorials, and open-source projects that can accelerate the implementation and understanding of VAEs.

By following the given steps and adapting them to the specifics of your problem, you can effectively use VAEs for a wide range of applications, contributing to advancements in generative modeling and data representation.

Autoencoders

Autoencoders consist of an encoder and decoder, working together to reconstruct input data. In generative tasks, they can produce novel outputs by manipulating the encoded representation. Autoencoders find applications in image denoising, where they learn to reconstruct clean images from noisy inputs.

Autoencoders, a class of neural networks, have emerged as powerful tools for unsupervised learning, dimensionality reduction, and generative modeling. The fundamental principle behind autoencoders involves learning compact and informative representations of input data by encoding and subsequently decoding it. This process enables the network to capture essential features, making autoencoders versatile across various domains.

Key concepts

In this section we will be discussing key concepts of Autoencoders:

- **Encoder-decoder architecture**: At the core of autoencoders lies an encoder-decoder architecture. The encoder compresses input data into a lower-dimensional latent space, and the decoder reconstructs the original input from this representation. The synergy between encoding and decoding fosters the extraction of meaningful features.

- **Varieties of autoencoders**: Autoencoders come in various forms, each tailored for specific tasks. Variants include vanilla autoencoders, convolutional autoencoders (for image data), denoising autoencoders (trained to reconstruct from noisy inputs), and variational autoencoders (incorporating probabilistic modeling for generative tasks).

- **Applications in image compression**: Autoencoders find extensive use in image compression, where the encoder compresses images into a compact latent representation. This representation retains essential visual features, allowing for efficient storage and transmission. Notable examples include JPEG compression techniques leveraging autoencoder principles.

- **Unsupervised learning and dimensionality reduction**: Autoencoders excel in unsupervised learning scenarios, especially in reducing the dimensionality of input data. By capturing essential features in the latent space, autoencoders facilitate efficient representation learning without relying on labeled data.

- **Generative modeling with VAEs**: VAEs extend the basic autoencoder concept by introducing probabilistic modeling. They not only encode input data but also generate new samples by sampling from the learned distribution in the latent space. This makes VAEs potent tools for generative modeling in diverse domains.

- **Anomaly detection and denoising**: Autoencoders are effective in anomaly detection by learning to reconstruct normal instances and identifying deviations. Denoising autoencoders, trained to reconstruct from noisy inputs, are adept at filtering out irrelevant information, contributing to robust feature extraction.

- **Representation learning in natural language processing**: Autoencoders extend their utility to NLP tasks by learning meaningful representations of textual data. By encoding and decoding sequences of words, autoencoders contribute to feature extraction in language understanding and generation tasks.

- **Transfer learning and pre-training**: Autoencoders play a crucial role in transfer learning. Pre-training an autoencoder on a large dataset allows the network to learn general features that can be fine-tuned for specific tasks with limited labeled data. This transferable knowledge enhances the performance of downstream tasks.

- **Limitations and challenges**: Despite their versatility, autoencoders face challenges such as sensitivity to noise, difficulty in capturing long-range dependencies, and the risk of learning trivial solutions. Addressing these challenges requires careful design choices and augmentation with techniques like regularization.

- **Future directions and research trends**: Ongoing research explores advanced autoencoder architectures, improved regularization techniques, and the integration of autoencoders with other deep learning paradigms. The pursuit of more robust and efficient unsupervised learning remains a central theme.

Autoencoders stand as foundational components in neural network architectures, showcasing their adaptability across diverse applications. As research continues to unveil novel variants and address challenges, autoencoders remain at the forefront of self-learning neural networks, contributing to advancements in artificial intelligence and machine learning.

Autoencoders have found practical applications across various industries, showcasing their versatility in solving complex problems. Several tech companies and vendors have embraced autoencoders for tasks ranging from image compression to anomaly detection. Here are some examples:

- **Image compression with JPEG**: Joint Photographic Experts Group (JPEG) compression utilizes a form of autoencoder for image compression. The encoding phase reduces the dimensionality of the image, and the decoding phase reconstructs the compressed image. This widely-used compression standard has become a de facto application of autoencoder principles.

- **Fraud detection in finance**: In the finance sector, autoencoders are employed for anomaly detection in transaction data. Companies like PayPal and Square leverage autoencoders to identify unusual patterns or outliers in financial transactions, helping detect potential fraud.

- **Healthcare and medical imaging**: Siemens Healthineers, a leading medical technology company, applies autoencoders for medical image denoising and reconstruction. Autoencoders assist in enhancing the quality of medical images, contributing to more accurate diagnoses.

- **Speech processing in virtual assistants**: Companies like Amazon, with its virtual assistant Alexa, utilize autoencoders for speech processing. Autoencoders can capture essential features in speech signals, aiding in tasks such as speaker identification and voice command recognition.

- **Manufacturing quality control**: General Electric (GE) employs autoencoders for quality control in manufacturing processes. By analyzing sensor data from production lines, autoencoders help identify anomalies or defects, contributing to improved product quality.

- **Retail and recommendation systems**: Retail giants like Amazon leverage autoencoders in recommendation systems. Autoencoders can learn representations of user preferences and product features, enabling personalized recommendations for users based on their historical interactions.

Autoencoders implementation framework

In this section, we will discuss in detail the Autoencoders implementation framework. This framework will give step by step guidance on how to use autoencoders for various use cases:

1. **Data preprocessing**: Prepare and preprocess the input data, ensuring it is suitable for training the autoencoder. This may involve normalization, scaling, or other data-specific preprocessing steps.

2. **Choosing an autoencoder architecture**: Select an appropriate type of autoencoder based on the nature of the data and the task. Options include vanilla autoencoders, convolutional autoencoders for image data, and variational autoencoders for generative tasks.

3. **Defining the model architecture**: Specify the architecture of the autoencoder, including the number of layers, neurons in each layer, and the activation functions. For convolutional autoencoders, design the encoder and decoder layers to handle spatial features.

4. **Loss function and optimization**: Choose a suitable loss function, often mean squared error for reconstruction tasks, and an optimization algorithm such as **stochastic gradient descent (SGD)** or Adam. The loss function guides the training process to minimize the difference between input and reconstructed output.

5. **Training the model**: Train the autoencoder using the prepared dataset. During training, the network learns to encode essential features in the latent space and reconstruct the input data during decoding. Adjust hyperparameters and monitor training metrics for convergence.

6. **Evaluating performance**: Assess the performance of the trained autoencoder on validation or test datasets. Evaluate metrics such as reconstruction accuracy, anomaly detection capability, or other task-specific criteria.

7. **Fine-tuning or transfer learning (optional)**: Depending on the task, fine-tune the autoencoder on specific data or apply transfer learning if pre-training on a related task is beneficial.

8. **Deployment**: Once satisfied with the performance, deploy the trained autoencoder for inference on new, unseen data. Integrate it into applications or systems where its learned representations can be leveraged for various tasks.

Autoencoders, with their ability to learn meaningful representations from data, have become integral tools in machine learning and artificial intelligence applications. Implementing them involves understanding the specific requirements of the task and tailoring the architecture accordingly.

CycleGAN

CycleGAN is designed for image-to-image translation without paired training data. It employs cycle consistency to ensure that the translated image can be faithfully converted back to the original domain. CycleGAN has been used for artistic style transfer in images, allowing the transformation of photographs into the style of famous paintings. CycleGAN stands as a groundbreaking development in generative models. Unlike traditional GANs that focus on generating realistic images from random noise, CycleGAN excels in unpaired image-to-image translation across different domains. This innovative approach has found applications in various fields, offering a versatile solution for tasks like style transfer, artistic rendering, and domain adaptation.

Key concepts

Let us discuss some key concepts and applications of CycleGANs:

- **Unpaired image-to-image translation**: CycleGAN addresses the challenge of unpaired image translation, where corresponding images in source and target domains are not explicitly paired during training. This is particularly valuable in scenarios where obtaining paired data is impractical or expensive.

- **Dual generators and adversarial training**: CycleGAN employs two generators and two discriminators in a cyclical adversarial training process. The generators aim to translate images from one domain to another and back, while the discriminators assess the realism of the translated images. This cyclical process enforces consistency and realism in the generated images.

- **Cycle-consistency loss**: The cycle-consistency loss is a key component of CycleGAN. It ensures that the translated image, when converted back to the original domain, closely resembles the input image. This loss term enforces a mapping that is reversible, contributing to the model's stability and the fidelity of the generated images.

- **Applications in artistic rendering**: CycleGAN has gained popularity in the field of artistic rendering. Artists and designers use it to transform images in the style of famous paintings, creating unique and visually appealing results. For example, transforming a photograph into the style of *Van Gogh*'s *Starry Night*.

- **Style transfer and domain adaptation**: CycleGAN is effective in style transfer, enabling the transformation of images to match the artistic style of a reference image. Additionally, it finds applications in domain adaptation, where the model learns to adapt the style of images from one domain to another without requiring paired data.

- **Semantic segmentation and object transfiguration**: Beyond mere style transfer, CycleGAN demonstrates proficiency in semantic segmentation. It can transform images to resemble a particular artistic style while preserving the semantic content. Moreover, the model can transfigure objects in images, turning horses into zebras or summer landscapes into winter scenes.

- **Data augmentation and image synthesis**: CycleGAN is employed for data augmentation in scenarios with limited labeled data. By transforming existing images, it generates additional diverse samples for training models. Furthermore, it serves as a tool for image synthesis, creating realistic images in domains where capturing real data is challenging.

- **Challenges and limitations**: While CycleGAN presents a powerful solution for unpaired image translation, it is not without challenges. Ensuring the preservation of content and avoiding distortions in translated images can be intricate. Additionally, achieving photorealistic results in certain applications remains an ongoing research focus.

- **Future directions and research trends**: Ongoing research in the field explores enhancements to CycleGAN, addressing limitations and extending its capabilities. This includes improving the model's ability to handle diverse styles, refining the cycle-consistency loss, and exploring applications in new domains.

CycleGAN has ushered in a new era in image translation, enabling the seamless transformation of visual content across diverse domains without the need for paired training data. Its applications span artistic expression, domain adaptation, and data augmentation, showcasing its versatility and impact on the intersection of computer vision and generative modeling. As research continues, CycleGAN is poised to contribute to even more sophisticated and practical applications in the world of visual synthesis and interpretation.

Examples of CycleGAN implementations

The following are some examples of CycleGAN implementations.

ZooGAN

ZooGAN is a project that leverages CycleGAN for animal image translation. It can transform images of one animal species into another while maintaining the background and surroundings.

CycleGAN for art style transfer

Various artists and developers have implemented CycleGAN for artistic style transfer. This involves transforming photographs or images into the distinct styles of famous artists, such as Van Gogh, Picasso, or Monet.

CycleGAN for object transfiguration

Implementations of CycleGAN have been explored for object transfiguration, where images of one type of object are transformed into another type. For example, turning images of horses into zebras or apples into oranges.

Pix2PixHD

Although not the same as CycleGAN, Pix2PixHD is a related model for high-resolution image-to-image translation. It incorporates ideas from CycleGAN and is particularly effective for tasks like translating satellite images to maps.

DeepArt.io

DeepArt.io is an online platform that utilizes neural networks, potentially including CycleGAN-like architectures, for artistic style transfer. Users can upload their photos and apply the style of famous artists to them.

Using CycleGAN

Using CycleGAN typically involves the following steps:

1. **Data collection**: Collect datasets for the source and target domains. It is important that the datasets are diverse and representative of the variability in the domains.

2. **Data preprocessing**: Preprocess the data, ensuring that images are normalized, resized, and prepared for training. Consideration of data augmentation techniques may also be beneficial.

3. **Model architecture selection**: Choose the appropriate architecture for the generator and discriminator networks. For CycleGAN, this involves using dual generators for both forward and backward transformations.

4. **Loss function specification**: Define the adversarial loss, cycle-consistency loss, and any other relevant losses. These losses guide the training process to ensure the generated images are realistic and consistent.

5. **Training the model**: Train the CycleGAN model using the prepared datasets. Monitor the training process, evaluate performance on validation sets, and adjust hyperparameters as needed.

6. **Model evaluation**: Evaluate the model on a test dataset to assess its performance. This involves visually inspecting the translated images, calculating metrics, and ensuring the model generalizes well to unseen data.

7. **Application deployment (optional)**: Depending on the use case, deploy the trained CycleGAN model for image translation in real-world applications. This

might involve integrating the model into an image processing pipeline or an interactive application.

It is essential to note that the success of CycleGAN depends on the quality and diversity of the training data, the choice of hyperparameters, and the specific task at hand. Experimentation and fine-tuning are often necessary to achieve desired results. Additionally, various open-source implementations and pre-trained models are available, making it accessible for researchers and developers to apply CycleGAN to their specific use cases.

Bidirectional Encoder Representations from Transformers

While traditionally used for natural language processing, **Bidirectional Encoder Representations from Transformers (BERT)**'s contextual embedding capabilities have found applications in generating coherent and context-aware text.

BERT-based models can generate contextually relevant and grammatically sound text responses in conversational AI applications.

BERT stands as a watershed moment in the field of NLP. Introduced by Google in 2018, BERT represents a groundbreaking approach to pre-training language representations. Unlike its predecessors, BERT's bidirectional nature allows it to consider the entire context of a word within a sentence, ushering in a new era of contextualized word embeddings and significantly improving the performance of a wide range of NLP tasks.

Key concepts

Following are the key concepts with respect to BERT:

- **Bidirectional contextualization**: BERT's distinguishing feature is its ability to understand the context of a word by considering both the preceding and following words in a sentence. Traditional models, in contrast, often only consider one direction, limiting their understanding of context.

- **Transformer architecture**: BERT is built upon the Transformer architecture, initially proposed by *Vaswani et al.* in 2017. The Transformer's self-attention mechanism allows BERT to weigh the importance of different words in a sentence dynamically, capturing intricate dependencies.

- **Pre-training and fine-tuning**: BERT undergoes a two-step process - pre-training and fine-tuning. During pre-training, the model learns contextualized embeddings by predicting missing words in sentences. Fine-tuning adapts the pre-trained model to specific downstream tasks, such as text classification, named entity recognition, and question-answering.

- **Contextual word embeddings**: BERT produces contextualized word embeddings, meaning the representation of a word varies based on its context in a sentence. This leads to richer, more informative embeddings compared to static word embeddings like Word2Vec or GloVe.

- **Masked Language Model (MLM)**: BERT's pre-training involves training the model to predict masked-out words in sentences. This forces the model to understand the bidirectional context of each word, as it must infer the missing word based on its surroundings.

- **Applications in downstream tasks**: BERT has demonstrated remarkable success in a myriad of NLP tasks. In sentiment analysis, named entity recognition, machine translation, and question-answering, BERT consistently outperforms previous models, showcasing its versatility and generalizability.

- **Multilingual BERT**: Recognizing the importance of linguistic diversity, multilingual versions of BERT have been developed. These models can understand and generate text in multiple languages, contributing to the democratization of NLP advancements globally.

- **BERT's impact on search engines**: Google has integrated BERT into its search algorithm to enhance the understanding of user queries. This enables more accurate and context-aware search results, improving the overall user experience.

- **Challenges and considerations**: Despite its success, BERT is not without challenges. The model is computationally intensive, requiring substantial resources for training and inference. Additionally, fine-tuning BERT for specific tasks often involves task-specific architectures and datasets.

- **Open-source availability**: BERT's pre-trained models and code have been made open-source, fostering a collaborative environment for researchers and practitioners. This accessibility has spurred innovations and improvements in NLP across the community.

Examples of Bidirectional Encoder Representations from Transformers implementations

Here are some examples of BERT implementation that we will discuss in the section below:

Hugging Face Transformers library

Hugging Face provides a comprehensive Transformers library, offering pre-trained BERT models along with a user-friendly API for fine-tuning and inference.

Transformers is backed by the three most popular deep learning libraries: Jax, PyTorch and TensorFlow — with a seamless integration between them. It is straightforward to train your models with one before loading them for inference with the other.

Google's Bidirectional Encoder Representations from Transformers GitHub repository

Google has released the official BERT GitHub repository, providing the original implementation, pre-trained models, and resources for the research community.

Bidirectional Encoder Representations from Transformers for TensorFlow 2.0

TensorFlow 2.0 users can leverage the official BERT implementation for TensorFlow, facilitating integration into TensorFlow-based projects.

Future directions and ongoing research

Ongoing research is focused on refining BERT and addressing its limitations, such as computational efficiency. Researchers are exploring methods for distilling BERT's knowledge into smaller models, making it more accessible for resource-constrained environments.

BERT's impact on NLP has been transformative, setting new benchmarks and establishing a foundation for contextualized language understanding. As research progresses, BERT continues to influence the development of more sophisticated language models, paving the way for advancements in natural language understanding and interaction.

DeepDream

DeepDream is a neural network visualization technique that enhances patterns in images. While not a traditional generative model, it exemplifies the creative potential of neural networks. DeepDream has been applied in art, transforming photographs into intricate and surreal dream-like images. It stands at the intersection of art and artificial intelligence, offering a fascinating glimpse into the creative capabilities of neural networks. Developed by Google, DeepDream utilizes the neural network's ability to recognize and enhance patterns, transforming ordinary images into intricate, dreamlike artworks. This section explores the origins, workings, and artistic applications of DeepDream, shedding light on its impact on the intersection of AI and the visual arts.

Origins and working principle

DeepDream emerged from Google's research on **convolutional neural networks (CNNs)**, particularly those trained for image recognition. It is based on a deep neural network architecture called GoogLeNet, trained on a vast dataset of images. The primary idea behind DeepDream is to reverse the process of image classification, transforming the network from a detector of objects to a generator of imaginative patterns.

The working principle involves injecting feedback loops into the neural network. DeepDream introduces the concept of *dreaming* by iteratively enhancing patterns detected by the neural network. When the network recognizes a feature, it amplifies it, creating a hallucinatory effect in the image. This iterative process allows the network to emphasize patterns that trigger specific neurons, resulting in visually stunning and often surreal outcomes.

Artistic applications

This section discusses some of the artistic applications of DeepDream:

- **Dreamlike creations**: DeepDream's most immediate impact is in generating dreamlike and hallucinogenic images. Ordinary scenes are transformed into vibrant, intricate tapestries of patterns and textures. This artistic application showcases the neural network's ability to reinterpret visual stimuli in a uniquely creative manner.
- **Style transfer**: Beyond hallucinogenic visuals, DeepDream has been adapted for style transfer. By merging the neural network's patterns with famous artworks, the algorithm can imbue photographs with the artistic style of renowned painters. This fusion of AI and art results in images that harmonize the recognizable with the abstract.
- **Video transformations**: DeepDream is not limited to static images; it can be applied to videos, creating dynamic and evolving dreamscapes. The continuous transformation of frames introduces a temporal dimension to the artistic process, leading to mesmerizing visual experiences.
- **Interactive art**: Some implementations of DeepDream allow users to interactively guide the neural network's dreaming process. Users can influence the patterns generated by providing feedback, turning the creation of digital art into a collaborative and participatory experience.

Cultural impact

DeepDream has transcended its role as a mere algorithmic experiment, becoming a cultural phenomenon. It has sparked interest and discussions around the role of AI in creative processes. The juxtaposition of technology and artistic expression challenges traditional notions of creativity and authorship, prompting a reevaluation of the creative potential residing within machine intelligence.

Challenges and ethical considerations

While DeepDream offers a glimpse into the artistic capabilities of neural networks, it also raises ethical considerations. The algorithm's reliance on pre-trained datasets introduces biases. Moreover, the uncanny, hallucinatory nature of the generated images raises questions about the intersection of AI and human perception. Additionally, there are concerns about the potential misuse of such technology, prompting discussions about responsible AI use.

DeepDream represents more than an algorithm; it is a testament to the symbiotic relationship between technology and art. As we delve deeper in neural networks, their ability to reinterpret reality through a lens of creativity challenges conventional boundaries. DeepDream is not merely an experiment; it is an exploration of the untapped potential residing within the neural networks that power our AI systems. In this fusion of algorithms and imagination, we find a canvas where the digital and the artistic converge, offering new perspectives on the nature of creativity in the age of artificial intelligence.

So far, the chapter provided readers with a foundational understanding of various generative models, shedding light on their role in artificial intelligence. The section introduced prominent models like GANs, VAEs, and discussed the underlying principles that differentiate generative models from discriminative models. Readers gained insights into the diverse applications of generative models in creating new data instances, fostering creativity, and generating content in various domains. This overview laid the groundwork for a deeper exploration of these models, setting the stage for a more comprehensive understanding of their functionalities and real-world implications in subsequent chapters.

The upcoming section provides an in-depth exploration of the foundational principles that govern generative models. The section will delve into the mathematical and conceptual frameworks that underpin the functioning of models like GANs and VAEs. By elucidating the core principles, readers will gain a deeper comprehension of how these models generate novel content and learn to distinguish between different approaches. This understanding sets the stage for readers to engage more meaningfully with the subsequent chapters, fostering a solid grasp of the theoretical underpinnings of generative AI.

Understanding the underlying principles

The section serves as a crucial bridge to the intricate workings of generative models. Readers can anticipate a comprehensive exploration of the mathematical and conceptual foundations behind models like GANs and VAEs. This section aims to demystify the intricate algorithms, providing clarity on how these models generate data and exhibit creative capabilities. By grasping the underlying principles, readers will be better equipped to navigate subsequent discussions, fostering a more profound understanding of the theoretical aspects of generative AI. Topics covered will include the core mathematical concepts, training mechanisms, and the distinguishing features of various generative models, empowering readers with the knowledge necessary for a nuanced comprehension of generative AI.

Generative models stand at the forefront of artificial intelligence, breathing life into creative content generation, data synthesis, and beyond. To truly grasp their magic, one must embark on a journey into the intricate fabric that weaves these models into existence. This section opens the gateway to the profound understanding of generative models, peeling back the layers to reveal the mathematical foundations, the adversarial dance of GANs, the probabilistic beauty of VAEs, and the nuanced training mechanisms that mold these algorithms. We delve into the metrics that quantify their excellence, the ethical considerations that shadow their capabilities, and the transformative applications that unfold across real-world landscapes. Let us unravel the tapestry of principles underlying generative models, offering a profound insight into their inner workings and their impact on the ever-evolving landscape of artificial intelligence.

Generative models, the maestros of artificial intelligence, are poised to revolutionize how we perceive and interact with technology. As we embark on this intellectual journey, we encounter the foundational bedrock—mathematics. In this realm, probability distributions are integrated with linear algebra, orchestrating the symphony that underpins generative models' creation and training. Imagine probability distributions as the artists, shaping uncertainty, while linear algebra crafts the canvas, manipulating and transforming data into meaningful patterns.

The adversarial stage is set with GANs, where a generator and discriminator engage in a fierce duel. The generator strives to craft data indistinguishable from reality, and the discriminator hones its discernment. This adversarial tussle births realism, exemplified by the stunning creations of art generated by GANs. Consider *DeepArt* transforming photographs into mesmerizing artworks or the eerily realistic faces conjured by StyleGAN.

VAEs introduce a probabilistic twist, employing latent variables to navigate the intricate space of data representation. They are akin to a painter exploring a spectrum of colors to capture the essence of a scene. VAEs excel not just in reproduction but in generating diverse outputs. For example, picture an AI artist capable of morphing a cat into a spectrum of feline possibilities, how powerful and efficient the AI artist will be by availing this capability.

Training mechanisms unfold as iterative symphonies, where model parameters refine their performance to minimize defined objectives. This process, akin to sculpting, transforms raw data into refined art. The loss functions serve as the critical judges, quantifying the harmony between generated and actual outputs. In this critique, the models learn and evolve, akin to artists honing their craft through constructive criticism.

Generative Model Evaluation introduces metrics, the judges of this AI talent show. Inception Score and Frechet Inception Distance critique the quality and diversity of generated samples. It is akin to a competition where the contestants are not only judged on realism but also on the variety of their artistic expressions.

Yet, the rise of these generative talents brings ethical considerations. The power to create lifelike content necessitates responsible use. Consider the biases inherent in data and the ethical dilemmas in crafting convincing deepfakes. The ethical compass guides the responsible deployment of these generative marvels.

Comparing with their discriminative counterparts, generative models redefine the artist's role. While discriminative models classify, generative models birth new instances, opening avenues beyond mere recognition. The canvas broadens from identifying objects to creating entirely new ones.

Transfer learning introduces a twist to this artistic journey, where pre-trained models share their knowledge. It is akin to a master painter imparting techniques to an apprentice. This accelerates learning, vital in scenarios where training from scratch is impractical.

Underlying principles of generative models

In this section we will discuss foundational principles of generative models. These principles ensure authentic and responsible generative AI models. Let us discuss them one by one in detail.

Mathematical foundations

Generative models heavily rely on mathematical concepts. The mathematical concepts mostly used as foundation of models and their importance are explained as follows.

Among the major concepts, probability distributions, crucial for modeling uncertainty, are central to the generative process. Linear algebra facilitates the manipulation and transformation of data, playing a vital role in model design. A solid understanding of these mathematical foundations provides the necessary toolkit for designing and training generative models effectively.

At the heart of generative models lies a profound connection to mathematical abstractions, shaping the very essence of their creation and functionality. The canvas on which generative models paint their vivid creations is woven with intricate threads of probability theory and linear algebra. Let us elaborate a little more on each of these mathematical concepts in the section below.

Probability theory

Probability distributions play a pivotal role, orchestrating the uncertainty that is intrinsic to generative modeling. Imagine a scenario where a model must generate diverse outputs while encapsulating inherent variability. Probability distributions serve as the artists in this context, defining the likelihood of different outcomes. The Gaussian distribution, for instance, is often a fundamental choice, embodying the normalcy seen in many real-world phenomena.

In the context of GANs, probability distributions serve as the foundation for the adversarial dance. The generator aims to approximate the true data distribution, transforming random noise into realistic samples. This dance, expressed through probability distributions, ensures that the generated samples align with the underlying data.

Linear algebra

Linear algebra provides the tools for transforming and manipulating data. Consider a matrix as a palette of numbers, each contributing to the creation of patterns and structures. The generative process often involves transforming a latent space into a space that mimics the distribution of real data. This transformation, achieved through linear algebraic operations, is akin to shaping the raw materials into a coherent and meaningful form.

In VAEs, linear algebra becomes the brushstroke that navigates the latent space. The encoder transforms the input data into a distribution in this space, and the decoder reshapes it back into the data domain. Each operation, each matrix multiplication, is a calculated stroke that contributes to the generative process.

Generative modelling as mathematical composition

Generative models can be seen as compositions of mathematical functions. The generator and discriminator in GANs, the encoder and decoder in VAEs—all are mathematical functions that, when orchestrated harmoniously, bring forth the creation of new data instances. The training process, guided by loss functions, is a mathematical optimization task where parameters of these functions are refined iteratively.

Understanding the mathematical foundations demystifies the seemingly magical process of generative modeling. It is a symphony of probabilities and matrices, where each element contributes to the creation of art in the form of data. The generative models, in essence, are mathematicians at work, weaving elegant equations to transform randomness into meaningful patterns.

Generative adversarial networks

GANs introduce a novel training paradigm where a generator and discriminator engage in a competitive process. The generator aims to create realistic data, and the discriminator learns to distinguish between real and generated samples.

This adversarial framework allows GANs to generate high-quality, realistic outputs, making them invaluable for tasks such as image generation.

Variational autoencoders

VAEs approach generative modeling from a probabilistic perspective, introducing a latent variable that captures essential features of the data distribution.

The probabilistic nature of VAEs enables them to generate diverse outputs and provides a framework for learning meaningful representations of data.

Training mechanisms

The training process is iterative and involves adjusting model parameters to minimize a defined objective function. This refinement enhances the model's ability to generate desired outputs.

Understanding training mechanisms is crucial for practitioners to navigate the optimization landscape effectively and train models that generalize well to unseen data.

Loss functions

Loss functions guide the training process by quantifying the difference between predicted and actual outputs. Different models use distinct loss functions tailored to their objectives.

Designing appropriate loss functions is critical for training generative models effectively and aligning them with specific objectives such as image reconstruction or adversarial competition.

In the generative landscape, loss functions serve as the compass, guiding the training process to ensure that the generative models traverse the terrain of creativity with precision and purpose. These functions encapsulate the essence of what it means for a generated sample to be faithful to the original data, acting as the evaluative lens that shapes the learning journey.

Adversarial loss of generative adversarial networks

At the heart of GANs is the adversarial loss. This loss encapsulates the competitive spirit between the generator and the discriminator. The generator aims to generate samples that are indistinguishable from real data, while the discriminator strives to become an expert in telling real from fake. The adversarial loss reflects the success of the generator in fooling the discriminator and, simultaneously, the discriminator's adeptness in distinguishing genuine from synthetic. This adversarial dance, expressed through the loss function, propels the models toward equilibrium, where the generator produces realistic samples.

Reconstruction loss of variational autoencoders

VAEs embrace the concept of reconstruction loss. At its core, this loss measures the fidelity of the generated output to the original input. The encoder maps input data to a latent space, and the decoder reconstructs the input from this latent representation. The reconstruction loss evaluates how well this reconstruction aligns with the initial input. It compels the model to capture the essential features of the data in the latent space and ensures that the generative process retains the crucial characteristics of the original.

Perceptual loss for Style Transfer and Image Generation

In scenarios where the goal is not just faithful reproduction but also capturing perceptual similarity, perceptual loss takes center stage. This loss function evaluates the difference in high-level features between the generated and real samples. In image generation tasks, it ensures that the generated image not only looks similar pixel-wise but also captures the higher-level content and style of the reference. Perceptual loss adds an artistic touch to the generative process, emphasizing the importance of capturing the essence rather than pixel-by-pixel reproduction.

Cycle consistency loss for CycleGAN

For models like CycleGAN, which excel in domain translation tasks, cycle consistency loss is instrumental. This loss enforces the idea that translating from one domain to another and back should yield the original input. It ensures that the transformations are meaningful and reversible, maintaining consistency in the generative process. Cycle consistency loss fosters versatility in generative models, enabling them to perform bidirectional translations while preserving the inherent characteristics of the data.

Balancing act of loss functions

Generative models often involve a delicate balancing act of multiple loss functions. The art lies in crafting a combination that encourages the desired characteristics—realism, fidelity, style, and so on—while discouraging undesirable artifacts. The tuning of these loss functions is akin to orchestrating a symphony, where each instrument (loss term) contributes to the overall harmony of the generative output.

In essence, loss functions in generative models are the evaluative guides that steer the models toward the creation of meaningful and aesthetically pleasing outputs. They encapsulate the objectives of the generative journey, translating abstract goals into quantifiable measures that propel the models toward mastery in their artistic endeavors.

Generative model evaluation

Evaluating generative models ensures the quality and diversity of generated samples. Metrics like Inception Score and FID provide quantitative assessments.

Robust evaluation metrics are essential for comparing models, selecting the most suitable architecture, and ensuring the generated content meets desired criteria.

Ethical considerations

Generative models, capable of producing realistic content, raise ethical concerns related to bias, fairness, and responsible use. Exploring the ethical dimensions ensures that practitioners and researchers are aware of potential biases and work towards responsible deployment of generative AI in real-world applications.

Comparison with discriminative models

Understanding the differences between generative and discriminative models clarifies their distinct roles in the broader landscape of machine learning. While discriminative models focus on classification tasks, generative models create new data instances, broadening their applications to tasks like data synthesis and creative content generation.

Transfer learning in generative models

Transfer learning techniques leverage pre-trained models or knowledge transfer to expedite training on specific tasks, especially in scenarios with limited data. This approach is crucial for practical applications where training from scratch may be impractical or resource intensive.

Case studies and real-world applications

Real-world applications showcase the versatility of generative models across domains, from computer vision to creative arts. Case studies provide concrete examples of how generative models are transforming industries, inspiring further exploration and innovation.

Understanding these underlying principles empowers practitioners and researchers to navigate the complexities of generative models. It lays the groundwork for informed decision-making, ethical considerations, and the application of generative AI in diverse and impactful ways.

In unraveling the intricate tapestry of generative models, we have delved into the foundational principles that orchestrate the artistic symphony of creation. From probability distributions shaping uncertainty to the brushstrokes of linear algebra transforming latent spaces, and from adversarial dances defining GANs to the harmony of loss functions guiding the way—each principle plays a crucial role. As we draw the curtain on this section, readers have acquired not just knowledge but a lens to perceive generative models as mathematical compositions. The canvas of generative art is demystified, and the mathematical orchestration that underlies the captivating creations of generative models is now within grasp. Armed with these principles, readers are poised to embark on the next phase of their generative journey, where the nuances of specific models and their applications will come vividly to life.

In machine learning, generative models and discriminative models tread distinct paths, each with its own narrative and purpose. The next section serves as a guide through the labyrinth of differences, unraveling the unique characteristics that set these models apart. Readers can anticipate an exploration of the fundamental dissimilarities in their objectives, training methodologies, and the rich tapestry of applications that make them indispensable components of the machine learning landscape. By the end, readers will not only comprehend the nuanced divergence between generative and discriminative models but will also gain insight into the specific scenarios where each shines with unparalleled brilliance. The journey into the heart of this comparison promises to illuminate the intricate dance between generation and discrimination, offering a profound understanding of their roles in the grand mosaic of machine learning.

Fundamental differences between generative and discriminative models

In this section, we embark on a journey to unravel the fundamental distinctions that carve a chasm between generative models and discriminative models. From their divergent objectives to the methodologies steering their training, we navigate the landscape of dissimilarity. Expect to delve into the essence of generative models, which strive to create new, meaningful data, and discriminative models, designed to differentiate between classes with acumen. The exploration extends to the rich tapestry of applications, illuminating when each model type takes the spotlight. As we traverse this comparative terrain, readers will gain a comprehensive understanding of the unique roles these models play in the intricate dance of machine learning.

Decoding the dichotomy

At the heart of machine learning lie two archetypes, generative models and discriminative models, each donning distinct roles and aspirations in the realm of data comprehension and creation. Let us embark on a detailed exploration of the multifaceted differences that define these two paradigms.

Generative models are a type of machine learning model that can be used to create new data that resembles the training data. They are often used for tasks such as image generation, text generation, and music composition.

Discriminative models are a type of machine learning model that can be used to classify data into pre-defined categories. They are often used for tasks such as image classification, natural language processing, and sentiment analysis.

The objective of a generative model is to understand the underlying structure of the data and create new samples that resemble the training data. This can be done by learning the distribution of the data, or by learning a function that can map from a latent space to the data space.

The objective of a discriminative model is to classify data into pre-defined categories. This can be done by learning a function that maps from the data space to the label space.

Training methodology

Generative models are typically trained using unsupervised learning methods, such as maximum likelihood estimation or variational inference. Discriminative models are typically trained using supervised learning methods, such as logistic regression or support vector machines.

Applications

Generative models have been used for a variety of applications, including:

- **Image generation**: Generative models can be used to create new images that resemble the training data. This can be used for tasks such as image editing, image restoration, and image synthesis.
- **Text generation**: Generative models can be used to generate new text that resembles the training data. This can be used for tasks such as machine translation, summarization, and creative writing.
- **Music composition**: Generative models can be used to compose new music that resembles the training data. This can be used for tasks such as music generation, music editing, and music arrangement.

Discriminative models have been used for a variety of applications, including:

- **Image classification**: Discriminative models can be used to classify images into pre-defined categories. This can be used for tasks such as object detection, facial recognition, and medical imaging.

- **Natural language processing**: Discriminative models can be used for natural language processing tasks such as sentiment analysis, machine translation, and question answering.

- **Sentiment analysis**: Discriminative models can be used to classify text into pre-defined categories, such as positive, negative, or neutral.

Uncertainty handling

Generative models are often able to handle uncertainty better than discriminative models. This is because generative models are able to learn the distribution of the data, which allows them to generate new samples that are more likely to be realistic. Discriminative models, on the other hand, are only able to learn the relationship between the data and the labels, which does not give them any information about the distribution of the data.

Trade-offs and synergy

Generative models often sacrifice precision for diversity. This means that they are able to generate a wider range of new samples, but the individual samples may not be as accurate as the samples generated by a discriminative model. Discriminative models, on the other hand, shine in precision but might lack the creativity to generate entirely new content.

Generative and discriminative models can be used together to achieve better results than either model can achieve on its own. For example, a generative model can be used to generate many new samples, and then a discriminative model can be used to classify the samples into pre-defined categories. This can help to improve the accuracy of the discriminative model, and it can also help to reduce the amount of bias in the model.

Context in ummary

Generative and discriminative models are powerful tools for machine learning. Each paradigm has its own strengths and weaknesses, and the best choice for a given task will depend on the specific requirements. By understanding the differences between these two paradigms, you can make informed decisions about which approach to use for your next machine learning project. Understanding these nuanced distinctions between generative and discriminative models offers a profound insight into their unique roles and contributions to the expansive canvas of machine learning. Whether one is an artist seeking inspiration from the data or a detective discerning patterns, both paradigms weave a rich tapestry in the ever-evolving narrative of artificial intelligence.

In conclusion, this section has provided a comprehensive understanding of the fundamental distinctions between generative and discriminative models. Readers have delved into the varied applications, trade-offs, and synergies inherent in each approach. By grasping these nuances, readers are equipped to navigate the landscape of artificial intelligence, making informed choices about model selection based on the specific requirements of their tasks. Whether aiming for creative content generation or precise classification, the comprehension gained here serves as a solid foundation for further exploration into the realm of generative and discriminative models.

Conclusion

The chapter on the *Fundamentals of Generative Models* has provided readers with a robust foundation in the realm of generative AI. Beginning with an insightful overview that included prominent models like GANs and VAEs, readers delved into the underlying principles, encompassing mathematical foundations and critical aspects such as loss functions. The chapter culminated in a deep understanding of the distinctions between generative and discriminative models, elucidating their applications and trade-offs. Readers have gained a comprehensive knowledge base, empowering them to navigate the complexities of generative models with confidence. Whether readers are aspiring data scientists, machine learning practitioners, or enthusiasts, this chapter equips them with essential insights into the core principles and applications of generative AI, setting the stage for further exploration and mastery.

The upcoming chapter, *Applications Across Industries* promises a comprehensive exploration of how generative AI transcends various sectors. Readers can anticipate a deep dive into real-world applications in healthcare, finance, entertainment, and beyond. The chapter will feature enlightening case studies, offering tangible insights into the transformative impact of generative AI in diverse industries. As readers navigate through these practical examples, they will gain a nuanced understanding of the technology's versatility and its potential to disrupt traditional paradigms. Furthermore, the chapter will conclude with a forward-looking lens, discussing emerging trends and the anticipated evolution of generative AI, providing readers with a holistic perspective on the technology's role in shaping the future.

Join our book's Discord space

Join the book's Discord Workspace for Latest updates, Offers, Tech happenings around the world, New Release and Sessions with the Authors:

https://discord.bpbonline.com

CHAPTER 4
Applications Across Industries

Introduction

The chapter embarks on a comprehensive journey through the multifaceted landscape of generative AI. It will delve into the intricate applications of this transformative technology in pivotal sectors such as healthcare, finance, entertainment, and beyond. Through compelling case studies, readers will gain invaluable insights into real-world scenarios where generative AI has substantially impacted. By the end of this chapter, readers can expect to not only comprehend the practical applications but also envision the potential disruptions and future trends that generative AI holds for diverse industries. The exploration within this chapter is poised to equip readers with a nuanced understanding of how generative AI is shaping the present and future landscape of various sectors.

Structure

This chapter will cover the following topics:

- Exploring generative AI in healthcare, finance, entertainment, and more
- Generative AI in healthcare
- Generative AI in the financial sector
- Generative AI in the entertainment sector

- Ethical considerations in AI-generated art
- Case studies showcasing real-world applications
- Future trends and potential disruptions

Objectives

This chapter will provide readers with a comprehensive understanding of generative AI and its transformative potential across various industries. By delving into the intricacies of generative AI applications in pivotal sectors like healthcare, finance, and entertainment, readers will gain insights into the practical applications of this technology. In the healthcare sector, readers will explore how generative AI is revolutionizing personalized treatment plans, developing new drugs, and enhancing medical imaging. In the financial sector, they will discover applications in fraud detection, risk management, and financial reporting. Additionally, the chapter will examine the creative applications of generative AI in the entertainment industry, where it is used to create new music, generate art, and develop immersive virtual experiences.

Looking towards the future, readers will gain insights into emerging trends in generative AI research, such as the development of more powerful generative models and its integration with other AI technologies. They will also examine the potential impact of generative AI on society, considering both its benefits and challenges.

To bring the concepts to life, the chapter will present real-world case studies that illustrate how generative AI is solving real-world problems and improving people's lives. These case studies will cover a wide range of industries and applications, providing concrete examples of the transformative potential of generative AI.

By the end of the chapter, readers will have a holistic understanding of generative AI, its impact on society, and the ethical considerations surrounding its development and use.

Exploring generative AI in healthcare, finance, entertainment, and more

This section is a thorough investigation into the transformative impact of generative AI across diverse industries. Readers can anticipate an in-depth exploration of the specific applications within healthcare, finance, entertainment, and other sectors, unveiling how generative AI has become a catalyst for innovation. Through real-world examples and use cases, readers will gain a profound understanding of how generative AI is being leveraged to address complex challenges and foster advancements in each industry. This section aims to provide readers with practical insights, inspiring them to envision the extensive possibilities and potential advancements that generative AI brings to various domains.

Generative AI has emerged as a transformative force across diverse industries, offering innovative solutions and driving unprecedented advancements. In healthcare, generative AI is pivotal in medical imaging, aiding diagnostics, and even contributing to drug discovery. By leveraging generative models, researchers can simulate molecular structures, accelerating the identification of potential drugs and treatments.

The financial sector benefits from generative AI's ability to analyze vast datasets, enhance fraud detection, and optimize trading strategies. Generative models can simulate market scenarios, enabling financial institutions to make more informed decisions and mitigate risks.

In the entertainment industry, generative AI is revolutionizing content creation. From generating lifelike characters and scenes in movies to composing music and crafting virtual worlds in gaming, the applications are boundless. Creativity augmented by generative models is reshaping the artistic landscape.

Beyond these sectors, generative AI finds applications in fields such as manufacturing, design, and more. It is streamlining the design process, optimizing production workflows, and fostering innovation. Through a series of case studies, this section provides a detailed exploration of generative AI's impact on each industry, showcasing the tangible benefits and transformative potential. As readers delve into these real-world examples, they gain a profound understanding of how generative AI is not just a technological tool but a catalyst for positive change across the spectrum of human endeavors.

Generative AI in healthcare

Generative AI has revolutionized the healthcare sector by introducing innovative solutions and enhancing various facets of medical practice. *Figure 4.1* below is a representational image of using generative AI in healthcare:

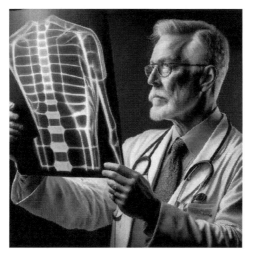

Figure 4.1: *Representational image of Gen AI in healthcare*

Here are some notable use cases and examples.

Medical imaging enhancement

Generative models, particularly **generative adversarial networks (GANs)**, are used to enhance medical imaging data.

Example: AI algorithms can generate high-resolution images from low-resolution inputs, aiding in the detailed analysis of medical scans such as MRIs and CT scans.

Generative AI, particularly GANs, plays a pivotal role in revolutionizing medical imaging by addressing challenges related to data resolution and quality. Here is a more detailed exploration of the application.

Application in medical imaging

Medical imaging often involves working with images that may have limitations in resolution due to factors such as hardware constraints or the need for faster processing.

Let us see how GAN's address above mentioned challenges:

- **Super-resolution enhancement**: GANs, known for their ability to generate high-quality images, are employed in the super-resolution domain of medical imaging.
- **Generating realistic details**: GANs are trained on large datasets of high-resolution medical images. Once trained, they can take a low-resolution image as input and generate a corresponding high-resolution version with realistic details.

Real-world impact

Let us explore some real-world impact of medical imaging:

- **Improved diagnostic accuracy**: Enhanced resolution improves diagnostic accuracy, allowing medical professionals to identify subtle details in images that might be crucial for accurate diagnoses.
- **Advancing research**: Higher-resolution images aid researchers in conducting more detailed studies, contributing to advancements in medical knowledge and treatment strategies.

Example use case

GANs can be applied to enhance the resolution of **Magnetic Resonance Imaging (MRI)** scans. A low-resolution MRI scan of a particular organ, when processed through a trained GAN, can yield a high-resolution image, providing clearer insights for medical interpretation.

Industry adoption

Enlisted below are some industry adoptions of medical imaging:

- **Research institutions**: Leading research institutions and medical centers collaborate with AI researchers to implement GANs for medical imaging enhancement.

- **Commercial solutions**: Companies specializing in medical imaging equipment and software integrate GAN-based enhancement features into their products.

Generative AI's role in medical imaging enhancement goes beyond mere upscaling; it involves the creation of realistic details that can significantly impact diagnostic precision and contribute to advancements in medical research and patient care.

Drug discovery and molecular design

Generative models simulate molecular structures and aid in drug discovery.

Example: AI algorithms analyze chemical properties and simulate interactions, accelerating the identification of potential drug candidates. Atomwise and BenevolentAI are companies using generative models for drug discovery.

Generative AI, particularly in the forms of generative models and reinforcement learning, has brought transformative capabilities to drug discovery and molecular design. Here is a detailed exploration.

Application in drug discovery

The process of drug discovery is intricate and time-consuming, involving the exploration of vast chemical spaces to find compounds with desired therapeutic properties.

Let us see how generative AI addresses challenges mentioned above in drug discovery:

- **Virtual compound generation**: Generative models, including GANs and **variational autoencoders (VAEs)**, are employed to generate virtual compounds based on known chemical structures.

- **Reinforcement learning**: Reinforcement learning algorithms guide the generation process, optimizing for specific molecular properties or interactions.

Real-world impact

Let us explore the real-world impact of Gen AI in drug discovery:

- **Accelerated drug development**: Generative AI expedites the exploration of chemical spaces, potentially reducing the time required for drug discovery from years to months.

- **Targeted drug design**: The precision of generative models allows for the design of molecules tailored to interact with specific biological targets, enhancing the effectiveness of drugs.

Example use case

Generative AI has been utilized to design novel antibiotics with unique chemical structures, addressing the challenge of antibiotic resistance. Virtual compounds generated by AI models undergo further validation in the laboratory.

Industry adoption

Enlisted below are some examples of industry adoptions of Gen AI in drug discovery:

- **Pharmaceutical companies**: Major pharmaceutical companies integrate generative AI into their drug discovery pipelines to identify promising compounds.
- **Collaborative research**: Interdisciplinary collaborations between AI researchers, chemists, and biologists contribute to the development and application of generative models in drug discovery.

Generative AI's impact on drug discovery extends beyond computational predictions, actively contributing to the identification of novel therapeutic compounds with the potential to address pressing health challenges.

Personalized treatment plans

Generative models analyze patient data to tailor treatment plans. AI algorithms can predict how individual patients will respond to specific treatments, enabling personalized and more effective healthcare interventions.

Generative AI plays a pivotal role in revolutionizing healthcare by tailoring treatment plans to individual patients. Here is an in-depth exploration of how generative AI does that customization:

Context and challenges

The customization begins with understanding the context and challenges as detailed below:

- **Individual variability**: Healthcare treatments that account for the unique genetic, environmental, and lifestyle factors of each patient are increasingly recognized as essential for optimal outcomes.
- **Data complexity**: Personalized medicine relies on extensive and diverse datasets, including genomics, medical history, and lifestyle information.

Generative AI's role

Next step in customization is to understand generative AI's role as detailed below

- **Data integration**: Generative models integrate diverse datasets, allowing for a comprehensive understanding of each patient's health profile.

- **Predictive analytics**: AI models predict individual responses to treatments based on genetic markers, past treatment outcomes, and other relevant factors.

Real-world impact

Let us get some details around real-world impact of generative AI in customization for patients:

- **Tailored therapies**: Generative AI contributes to the development of personalized treatment plans, guiding healthcare professionals in selecting interventions that are more likely to be effective for a specific patient.

- **Preventive strategies**: By analyzing individual risk factors, AI models assist in identifying preventive measures and interventions to reduce the likelihood of future health issues.

Example use case

In cancer care, generative AI analyzes genomic data to predict the efficacy of different treatment options for specific cancer subtypes. This enables oncologists to choose targeted therapies with higher success rates.

Industry adoption

Some of the examples of Industry adoption of customization in treatment for patients using generative AI are enlisted below:

- **Clinical decision support**: Hospitals and healthcare providers integrate generative AI into their clinical decision support systems to enhance the precision of treatment planning.

- **Research collaborations**: Research institutions and pharmaceutical companies collaborate to leverage AI in developing personalized therapies for conditions like cancer, cardiovascular diseases, and neurodegenerative disorders.

Generative AI's ability to analyze complex datasets and generate personalized insights contributes significantly to the paradigm shift towards precision medicine, offering patients treatments that are not only effective but also tailored to their unique biology and health characteristics.

Medical text generation

Generative AI, particularly models like OpenAI's GPT, holds immense potential to revolutionize the way healthcare professionals generate medical text. This technology offers a powerful tool to address the challenges of time-consuming documentation, inconsistent formatting, and limited personalization, ultimately improving efficiency, communication, and patient care. **Natural language processing (NLP)** models generate medical documentation and reports.

Example: OpenAI's GPT models can assist healthcare professionals by generating detailed medical notes, reducing administrative burden.

Generative AI, particularly in NLP models, has shown remarkable capabilities in generating medical text.

Context and challenges

Let us get some context and challenges around medical text generation using generative AI:

- **Documentation burden**: Healthcare professionals often face the challenge of extensive documentation, including medical reports, patient notes, and research papers.
- **Accuracy requirements**: Medical texts demand a high level of accuracy, clarity, and adherence to medical terminology and standards.

Generative AI's role

As next step in the process of applying of generative AI, we need to identify its role. These roles are enlisted below

- **Automated report generation**: Generative models can automate the creation of medical reports, reducing the burden on healthcare professionals and ensuring standardized documentation.
- **Assistance in note-taking**: AI-powered assistants help physicians by summarizing patient interactions and generating concise notes for medical records.

Real-world impact

Let us explore some real-world impact of generative AI on medical text generation:

- **Time efficiency**: By automating the generation of medical texts, AI enables healthcare professionals to focus more on patient care and less on administrative tasks.

- **Consistency and standardization**: AI-generated medical texts adhere to standardized terminology and formats, ensuring consistency across healthcare documentation.

Example use case

Radiology reporting: Generative models are employed to automatically generate radiology reports based on imaging data. These reports include detailed findings, interpretations, and recommendations.

Industry adoption

Enlisted below are some industry adoptions of medical text generation using generative AI:

- **Health information systems**: Hospitals and healthcare institutions integrate generative AI into their health information systems to streamline the generation of medical texts.
- **Research publications**: AI-powered tools assist researchers in drafting manuscripts, abstracts, and summaries, contributing to the efficient dissemination of medical knowledge.

Generative AI's role in medical text generation not only addresses the practical challenges faced by healthcare professionals but also enhances the overall efficiency and accuracy of medical documentation processes. This application is poised to revolutionize how information is documented and communicated within the healthcare ecosystem.

Predictive analytics for patient outcomes

Generative models analyze patient data to predict outcomes and potential complications. AI algorithms can identify patterns in patient data to predict the likelihood of readmission, allowing for proactive interventions.

Generative AI plays a pivotal role in healthcare by enabling predictive analytics for patient outcomes. Here is a comprehensive exploration of predictive analytics for patient outcomes.

Context and challenges

Let us explore some context and challenges around predicting patient outcomes:

- **Clinical decision-making**: Healthcare providers face challenges in predicting patient outcomes accurately, which is crucial for effective clinical decision-making.
- **Data complexity**: Healthcare data is diverse, ranging from **electronic health records** (**EHRs**) to medical imaging, making it challenging to extract meaningful insights.

Generative AI's role

Here we discuss generative AI's role in helping create predictions for patient outcomes:

- **Risk prediction models**: Generative models, particularly those employing deep learning techniques, are utilized to develop risk prediction models for various medical conditions.

- **Personalized treatment plans**: By analyzing historical patient data, generative models assist in creating personalized treatment plans based on the predicted likelihood of different outcomes.

Real-world impact

Generative AI has been creating some real-world impact in the area of predictive analytics for patient outcomes. Below are some examples to elaborate on it:

- **Early disease detection**: Predictive analytics powered by generative AI contribute to the early detection of diseases by identifying subtle patterns and trends in patient data.

- **Resource optimization**: Hospitals and healthcare systems leverage predictive models to optimize resource allocation, ensuring that critical interventions are prioritized for patients at higher risk.

Example use case

Enlisted below is an example use case for this application of generative AI:

Heart disease prediction: Generative AI models analyze a combination of patient demographics, lifestyle factors, and historical health data to predict the likelihood of developing cardiovascular diseases.

Industry adoption

This section discusses how generative AI is being adopted by healthcare for predictive analytics:

- **Clinical decision support systems**: Healthcare providers integrate generative AI into their decision support systems to enhance the accuracy of prognosis and treatment planning.

- **Population health management**: Predictive analytics assists healthcare organizations in managing population health by identifying high-risk individuals and implementing preventive measures.

Generative AI's application in predictive analytics for patient outcomes marks a transformative shift in healthcare, empowering clinicians with data-driven insights to make informed decisions and ultimately improve patient care. This approach holds immense potential for shaping the future landscape of personalized medicine and healthcare delivery.

Synthetic data generation for research

Generative models create synthetic datasets for medical research. AI-generated datasets can help researchers overcome limitations related to privacy concerns and data scarcity, facilitating more robust studies.

The integration of generative AI in healthcare not only improves diagnostic capabilities but also opens avenues for personalized medicine, accelerates drug discovery, and enhances overall patient care.

Generative AI serves a crucial role in healthcare research by facilitating the creation of synthetic data sets. Here is a comprehensive exploration on synthetics data generating for research using generative AI.

Context and challenges

Let us get some context on challenges in synthetics data generation:

- **Data privacy concerns**: Healthcare research often involves sensitive patient data, posing challenges related to privacy regulations and ethical considerations.
- **Data diversity**: Researchers require diverse datasets to ensure the representativeness of their studies, which may be limited by the availability of real-world data.

Generative AI's role

Elaborated below are details on how generative AI has been playing a pivotal role in synthetics data generation:

- **Privacy-preserving research**: Generative models can generate synthetic data that mimics the statistical characteristics of real patient data without containing personally identifiable information (PII).
- **Data augmentation**: Researchers use synthetic data to augment existing datasets, enhancing the diversity and volume of data available for analysis.

Real-world impact

Let us discuss some real-world impact on generative AI in this space:

- **Enabling collaboration**: Synthetic data generation enables researchers to share datasets more freely, fostering collaboration across institutions and research groups.

- **Overcoming data scarcity**: In situations where real patient data is scarce or restricted, generative models provide a valuable solution for expanding the pool of available data for analysis.

Example use case

Here is an example use case of leveraging generative AI in synthetics data generation:

Clinical trial simulations: Generative AI is employed to generate synthetic datasets simulating patient responses in clinical trials, allowing researchers to conduct virtual experiments and optimize trial designs.

Industry adoption

Let us see how industries are adopting generative AI for synthetic data generation:

- **Cross-institutional research**: Healthcare institutions and research organizations leverage generative models to generate synthetic data that can be shared securely for joint research initiatives.

- **Training machine learning models**: Synthetic data is used to train machine learning models when real-world data is limited, ensuring the models' robustness and generalizability.

Generative AI's role in synthetic data generation for research addresses the ethical and privacy challenges associated with healthcare data, opening new avenues for collaborative and impactful research endeavors in the medical field.

Generative AI in the financial sector

In the dynamic landscape of the financial sector, the integration of generative AI has sparked a transformative wave, revolutionized traditional practices and introduced unprecedented opportunities. From fortifying cybersecurity measures to enhancing algorithmic trading strategies, generative AI stands as a catalyst for innovation. This section delves into the profound impact of generative AI on the financial domain, exploring its multifaceted applications, real-world use cases, and the tangible benefits it brings to fraud detection, algorithmic trading, customer service, and risk management. Let us navigate through synthetic data, algorithmic advancements, and heightened customer experiences, witnessing how generative AI is reshaping the future of finance. Generative AI plays a significant role in the financial sector, offering innovative solutions and improvements in various areas. *Figure 4.2* is a representational image of generative AI in the financial sector:

Figure 4.2: *Representational image depicting use of generative AI in financial sector*

Fraud detection and prevention

Generative AI has emerged as a formidable ally in the ongoing battle against financial fraud. Its ability to analyze patterns and anomalies within vast datasets in real time enhances the efficiency of fraud detection systems. By learning from historical data, generative AI models can identify irregularities, recognize new types of fraudulent activities, and adapt to evolving tactics employed by malicious actors. This proactive approach significantly strengthens a financial institution's defense mechanisms, reducing false positives and providing a more accurate and agile response to emerging threats. Whether detecting unusual transaction patterns, identifying potentially compromised accounts, or recognizing fraudulent login attempts, generative AI plays a pivotal role in fortifying the cybersecurity posture of financial organizations. The synergy between advanced machine learning algorithms and real-time data analysis empowers financial institutions to stay one step ahead in the ongoing cat-and-mouse game with fraudsters.

Context and importance

Financial institutions face constant threats of fraud and cyber-attacks, requiring advanced methods for detection and prevention.

Generative AI's role

Generative models can analyze patterns in historical transaction data to identify anomalies or potentially fraudulent activities. They contribute to the creation of synthetic datasets that simulate diverse fraudulent scenarios, enhancing the robustness of fraud detection algorithms.

Real-world impact

Improved accuracy in detecting previously unseen fraud patterns, reducing false positives and negatives. Enhanced adaptability to evolving fraud tactics by training on synthetic data that covers a wide range of scenarios.

Generative AI plays a crucial role in fortifying financial institutions against fraudulent activities, providing advanced tools for detection and prevention tailored to the unique challenges of the financial sector. The following is a breakdown:

Anomaly detection

Generative AI excels at recognizing anomalies within vast financial datasets, detecting irregularities that might indicate fraudulent transactions. Traditional rule-based systems may struggle to keep pace with evolving fraud patterns, making them susceptible to sophisticated attacks.

Real-time monitoring

Generative AI models analyze historical transaction data and flag potentially fraudulent activities in real time. Continuous training of these models ensures they stay ahead of emerging threats, contributing to a more proactive defense against fraud.

Machine learning algorithms

Machine learning algorithms within generative AI understand normal spending behavior, detect anomalies, and trigger alerts for further investigation. Factors analyzed may include transaction frequency, location, and user behavior, allowing for a more nuanced and adaptive approach.

Adaptability to new patterns

Generative AI models can swiftly adapt to new patterns and trends, making them invaluable in combating ever-evolving fraud schemes. This adaptability ensures that the system remains effective, even as fraud tactics change, providing a resilient defense against emerging threats.

Predictive models

Predictive models created by generative AI understand normal spending behavior and detect anomalies, contributing to the prevention of fraudulent activities. These models enhance security measures by identifying irregularities and potential fraud risks before they escalate.

Maintaining trust in financial systems

The integration of generative AI in fraud detection and prevention not only enhances security measures but also contributes to maintaining trust and confidence in financial systems. The proactive nature of generative AI in identifying and preventing fraud supports a robust and trustworthy financial ecosystem.

Algorithmic trading strategies

Generative AI has emerged as a formidable ally in the ongoing battle against financial fraud. Its ability to analyze patterns and anomalies within vast datasets in real time enhances the efficiency of fraud detection systems. By learning from historical data, generative AI models can identify irregularities, recognize new types of fraudulent activities, and adapt to evolving tactics employed by malicious actors. This proactive approach significantly strengthens a financial institution's defense mechanisms, reducing false positives and providing a more accurate and agile response to emerging threats. Whether it is detecting unusual transaction patterns, identifying potentially compromised accounts, or recognizing fraudulent login attempts, generative AI plays a pivotal role in fortifying the cybersecurity posture of financial organizations. The synergy between advanced machine learning algorithms and real-time data analysis empowers financial institutions to stay one step ahead in the ongoing cat-and-mouse game with fraudsters.

Context and importance

Financial markets operate at high speeds, and developing effective algorithmic trading strategies is crucial for success.

Generative AI's role

Generative models can simulate market conditions and generate synthetic financial data for backtesting trading algorithms. They contribute to the generation of diverse scenarios, aiding in the creation of robust trading models.

Real-world impact

One of the major impacts of generative AI is that it has improved algorithmic trading strategies by training on synthetic data that captures a broader range of market conditions.

It also has enhanced risk management through the exploration of various market scenarios in a controlled environment.

Generative AI is revolutionizing algorithmic trading strategies in the financial sector, providing sophisticated tools that leverage data-driven insights for more informed decision-making. Here is an in-depth exploration:

Data-driven decision-making

Generative AI analyzes vast datasets to identify patterns, trends, and correlations that may not be apparent through traditional analysis. By leveraging this data-driven approach, algorithmic trading strategies powered by generative AI can make more informed and timely decisions.

Market sentiment analysis

Generative AI models excel in analyzing market sentiments by processing and understanding textual data from news articles, social media, and financial reports. This analysis contributes to a comprehensive understanding of market dynamics, helping traders anticipate shifts in sentiment and adjust strategies accordingly.

Dynamic portfolio optimization

Generative AI algorithms optimize investment portfolios dynamically based on real-time market data and predefined risk parameters. These algorithms ensure that portfolios are continuously adjusted to align with changing market conditions, optimizing returns while managing risks.

Risk management strategies

Generative AI contributes to the development of sophisticated risk management models, helping traders identify potential risks and implement strategies to mitigate them. The adaptive nature of generative AI allows for real-time adjustments in risk management approaches, enhancing overall portfolio resilience.

Predictive analytics for market trends

Generative AI models predict market trends by analyzing historical data, economic indicators, and external factors influencing financial markets. Traders can leverage these predictions to formulate strategies that capitalize on emerging opportunities and navigate potential downturns.

Backtesting and continuous improvement

Generative AI enables extensive backtesting of trading strategies using historical data, allowing traders to assess the viability of strategies in different market scenarios.

Continuous learning from past performance facilitates the refinement and improvement of algorithmic trading strategies over time.

Adaptability to market changes

Generative AI-powered algorithms are designed to adapt to evolving market conditions, ensuring resilience in the face of unforeseen events or sudden shifts in financial landscapes. This adaptability enhances the agility of algorithmic trading strategies, making them well-suited for dynamic and unpredictable markets.

In summary, generative AI is transforming algorithmic trading in the financial sector by introducing advanced analytics, predictive capabilities, and adaptability, ultimately enhancing decision-making processes and improving overall trading performance.

Customer service chatbots

In the era of generative AI, customer service chatbots are evolving into sophisticated conversational AI systems capable of providing personalized, empathetic, and efficient support.

Context and importance

Financial institutions handle a large volume of customer inquiries, necessitating efficient and responsive customer service.

Generative AI's role

Generative models contribute to the development of conversational AI and chatbots that can understand and respond to customer queries. They aid in generating realistic and contextually relevant responses, improving the overall customer experience.

Real-world impact

AI-powered chatbots for enhanced customer service: Leveraging AI, chatbots efficiently resolve customer queries, expedite response times, and elevate customer satisfaction. Their scalability ensures they can handle a high volume of inquiries simultaneously.

Improving customer service efficiency: AI-powered chatbots can swiftly address customer inquiries, minimizing response times and boosting customer satisfaction. Their ability to handle multiple inquiries simultaneously enhances scalability, ensuring timely and effective support.

Elevating customer service with AI: AI-driven chatbots streamline customer interactions, reducing response times and fostering customer satisfaction. Their scalability allows them to handle a surge in inquiries, maintaining seamless support.

Generative AI has found significant applications in the financial sector, particularly in customer service. The integration of chatbots powered by generative AI brings about a transformative impact on customer interactions. Here is a detailed exploration on the real-world impact of generative AI:

- **24X7 accessibility**: Generative AI-powered chatbots offer round-the-clock customer service, ensuring accessibility at any time. This is crucial in the financial sector where customers may require assistance beyond traditional office hours.

- **Instant query resolution**: Chatbots equipped with generative AI can instantly understand and respond to customer queries. They are trained on vast datasets, enabling them to provide quick and accurate information about account details, transaction history, and financial products.

- **Personalized customer interactions**: Generative AI allows chatbots to analyze customer preferences and behaviors. This information is then utilized to personalize interactions, offering tailored recommendations, and addressing individual needs effectively.

- **Transaction support and guidance**: Customers often seek assistance with transactions, account management, or product information. Generative AI-powered chatbots can guide users through these processes, offering step-by-step assistance and ensuring a seamless experience.

- **Fraud detection and prevention**: Chatbots can play a crucial role in fraud detection by monitoring user activities and identifying potential irregularities. Generative AI algorithms enhance their capability to recognize patterns associated with fraudulent behavior.

- **Educational support**: Financial literacy is a key aspect of customer service. Generative AI-powered chatbots can provide educational support by explaining complex financial concepts, investment strategies, or the functionalities of different financial products.

- **Language understanding and contextual responses**: Generative AI enables chatbots to understand natural language and respond contextually. This enhances the quality of interactions, making the conversation more human-like and intuitive for users.

- **Feedback collection and improvement**: Chatbots can collect user feedback and interactions data, contributing to continuous improvement. Generative AI algorithms analyze this feedback to enhance the chatbot's performance, making it more effective in addressing customer queries.

- **Compliance and security**: Generative AI ensures that chatbots adhere to regulatory compliance and security standards in the financial sector. This includes handling sensitive information securely and providing responses in accordance with privacy regulations.

- **Integration with other systems**: Generative AI-powered chatbots seamlessly integrate with other systems in the financial ecosystem. This enables them to fetch real-time data, such as account balances or recent transactions, providing customers with the latest information.

In summary, generative AI-powered chatbots are revolutionizing customer service in the financial sector by offering instant, personalized, and efficient interactions. Their ability to understand natural language, provide educational support, and contribute to fraud prevention makes them invaluable tools in enhancing overall customer satisfaction and operational efficiency.

Credit scoring and risk assessment

Generative AI is revolutionizing credit scoring and risk assessment by enabling more accurate, predictive, and personalized evaluations of creditworthiness.

It emphasizes the ability of generative AI to analyze vast amounts of data, identify subtle patterns, and make predictions that go beyond traditional credit scoring models. This leads to more accurate assessments of creditworthiness, enabling lenders to make informed decisions while also reducing biases and promoting financial inclusion.

Context and importance

Accurate credit scoring is essential for evaluating an individual's creditworthiness and managing lending risks.

Generative AI's role

Generative models assist in creating synthetic datasets that represent diverse financial profiles, contributing to more robust credit scoring models. They enable the simulation of various economic scenarios, aiding in stress testing risk management strategies.

Real-world impact

Gen AI has enhanced credit scoring methodologies to promote data-driven lending decisions, reducing the risk of default and improving financial stability. It has amplified risk management through synthetic data analysis, covering a broad spectrum of economic scenarios.

Generative AI has emerged as a powerful tool in reshaping how credit scoring and risk assessment are conducted in the financial sector. Its application in this domain brings about advancements that enhance accuracy, efficiency, and inclusivity. Here is a comprehensive exploration on the real-world impact of generative AI.

- **Holistic data analysis**: Generative AI facilitates the analysis of a diverse range of data points beyond traditional credit scores. It considers non-traditional variables, such as social media behavior, online transactions, and other alternative data sources, providing a more holistic view of an individual's financial behavior.

- **Predictive modeling**: Utilizing advanced machine learning algorithms, generative AI aids in building predictive models that can assess the likelihood of default or delinquency. These models go beyond historical data, incorporating real-time information to make more accurate predictions.

- **Incorporating behavioral analysis**: Generative AI enables the incorporation of behavioral analysis into credit scoring. By understanding patterns of financial behavior, spending habits, and transaction histories, the system can make more nuanced predictions about an individual's creditworthiness.

- **Real-time risk monitoring**: Traditional credit scoring models often operate on static data. Generative AI allows for real-time risk monitoring by continuously analyzing ongoing financial activities. This ensures that credit scores dynamically adapt to changing financial behaviors, offering a more accurate representation of risk.

- **Reducing bias and enhancing fairness**: Generative AI models can be designed to reduce bias in credit scoring. Traditional models might exhibit biases based on demographic factors. Generative AI algorithms, if carefully trained and monitored, can contribute to fairer assessments by focusing on relevant financial behaviors.

- **Enhancing fraud detection in credit applications**: Generative AI algorithms excel in detecting anomalies and patterns indicative of fraudulent activities. When applied to credit applications, these algorithms can contribute significantly to fraud prevention by identifying suspicious patterns or inconsistencies.

- **Improved credit access for the unbanked**: Traditional credit scoring models often struggle to assess the creditworthiness of individuals with limited credit histories. Generative AI, with its ability to analyze alternative data sources, opens avenues for assessing creditworthiness for the unbanked or those with thin credit files.

- **Customized risk models for different products**: Generative AI allows financial institutions to create customized risk models for different financial products. Whether assessing credit for a mortgage, credit card, or personal loan, the system can adapt its evaluation criteria to match the specific risk factors associated with each product.

- **Explainability and transparency**: Generative AI models can be designed to provide explanations for their credit scoring decisions. This transparency is crucial in gaining the trust of consumers and regulators, ensuring that individuals understand the factors influencing their credit assessments.

- **Adaptation to economic changes**: Generative AI-powered credit scoring systems can be designed to adapt quickly to economic changes. During periods of economic volatility, these systems can dynamically adjust risk assessments based on the current economic conditions, providing more accurate predictions.

In conclusion, generative AI is reshaping credit scoring and risk assessment by incorporating advanced analytics, reducing biases, and adapting to the complexities of the modern financial landscape. The application of generative AI in this context promises not only more accurate risk evaluations but also increased financial inclusion and fairness in credit access.

Generative AI's applications in the financial sector showcase its versatility in addressing critical challenges, from fraud detection to algorithmic trading and customer service. These innovations contribute to more resilient and adaptive financial systems.

Generative AI in the entertainment sector

In dynamic entertainment, generative AI is fostering groundbreaking advancements, shaping content creation, and elevating user engagement. It is at the forefront of revolutionizing the entertainment sector, introducing innovative capabilities that redefine content creation, user experiences, and artistic expression. In an era where creativity meets advanced technology, the application of generative AI has far-reaching implications for how we consume and interact with entertainment content. *Figure 4.3* is a representational image of using generative AI in the entertainment sector:

Figure 4.3: *Representational image depicting use of generative AI in entertainment sector*

Let us delve into the exciting realms where generative AI is leaving an indelible mark on the entertainment landscape.

Generative art and design

Generative AI is being used in several ways in the area of art and design. Let us get into some details of it. Following are the ways artists and designers are using generative AI to create unique visual content:

- **New styles and forms**: Generative AI can be used to create new and innovative visual styles and forms that would be difficult or impossible to create by hand. For example, generative AI can be used to create realistic-looking images of objects that do not exist in the real world, such as fantastical creatures or imaginary landscapes.

- **Interactive installations**: Generative AI can be used to create interactive installations that allow users to interact with and manipulate the visual content. For example, generative AI can be used to create a virtual reality experience where users can explore a simulated environment and interact with objects in the environment.

- **Dynamic visual content**: Generative AI can be used to create dynamic visual content that changes over time. For example, generative AI can be used to create a video game where the environment changes as the player progresses through the game.

- **Transforming the visual style of a scene**: Generative AI can be used to transform the visual style of a scene. For example, generative AI can be used to create a photorealistic image of a scene that has been rendered in a cartoon style.

- **Interactive and evolving storylines**: Generative AI can be used to create interactive and evolving storylines in games, films, and other forms of entertainment. For example, generative AI can be used to create a game where the storyline changes based on the player's actions.

- **Innovative and immersive attractions**: Generative AI can be used to create innovative and immersive attractions for theme parks and other entertainment venues. For example, generative AI can be used to create a virtual reality experience where users can interact with characters and objects in a simulated environment.

Here are some of the concerns raised by the integration of generative AI in entertainment:

- **Ownership of copyright to content**: This is a complex concern that has not yet been definitively answered. Some experts argue that the copyright belongs to the person who created the generative AI model, while others argue that the copyright belongs to the person who uses the model to create the content.

- **Ethical implications**: This is another complex concern that has not yet been definitively answered. Some experts argue that it is unethical to use generative AI to create content that could be seen as offensive or harmful, while others argue that it is up to the individual artist or designer to decide what content they create.

It is important to strike a balance between creative exploration and responsible use. As technology continues to influence artistic creation, it is important to strike a balance between creative exploration and responsible use. On the one hand, generative AI can be used to create amazing new forms of visual content that would be difficult or impossible to create by hand. On the other hand, it is important to use generative AI responsibly and to avoid creating content that could be seen as offensive or harmful.

The synergy between human creativity and algorithmic innovation is not only reshaping entertainment but also pushing the frontiers of what is artistically conceivable. As generative AI continues to develop, it will be exciting to see how artists and designers use it to create new and innovative visual content.

Interactive and immersive experiences

Virtual and augmented reality (VR/AR) applications are increasingly using generative models to enhance the immersive experience. Generative AI has ushered in a new era of interactive and immersive experiences within the entertainment sector, with applications in virtual worlds, immersive storytelling, interactive gaming experiences, virtual and augmented reality concerts, and immersive art installations. Let us explore each of these applications of generative AI.

- **Virtual worlds and augmented reality**: Generative AI algorithms can be used to create dynamic virtual worlds that respond to user interactions.
    - For example, Pokémon GO uses generative AI to place virtual Pokémon in real-world locations.
    - As users move around, the game generates new Pokémon that appear in their vicinity. This creates a sense of immersion and encourages users to explore their surroundings.
- **Immersive storytelling**: Generative AI can also be used to create personalized narratives that adapt to user choices and interactions.
    - For example, Netflix's interactive content allows viewers to make choices that influence the storyline.
    - This creates a more engaging and immersive experience for viewers, who feel like they are actively participating in the story.
- **Interactive gaming experiences**: Generative AI is also being used to create unique gaming content, such as landscapes, characters, and quests.

- For example, No Man's Sky uses a procedural generation algorithm to create a vast, procedurally generated universe.
- This means that no two planets in the game are exactly alike, which gives players a sense of exploration and discovery.

- **Virtual and augmented reality concerts**: Generative AI can also be used to create responsive and interactive environments for virtual and AR concerts.
  - For example, *Travis Scott's* virtual concert in Fortnite featured dynamic visuals that responded to the music and the actions of the audience.
  - This created a truly immersive experience for concertgoers, who felt like they were right there in the middle of the action.

- **Immersive art installations**: Generative AI is also being used to create interactive art installations that respond to the presence and actions of viewers.
  - For example, TeamLab Borderless uses generative algorithms to create interactive, borderless artworks.
  - These artworks change and evolve as viewers interact with them, creating a unique and immersive experience for each visitor.

- **Challenges and ethical considerations**: The implementation of generative AI in interactive and immersive experiences raises a number of technical challenges and ethical considerations.
  - For example, generative AI models can be biased, which can lead to the creation of inaccurate or harmful content.
  - Additionally, generative AI models can be used to create deepfakes, which are realistic-looking videos or images that have been manipulated to deceive viewers. It is important to be aware of these challenges and considerations when using generative AI to create interactive and immersive experiences.

Generative AI is a powerful tool that is being used to create new and innovative interactive and immersive experiences. As these technologies continue to evolve, the boundary between the virtual and physical worlds will become increasingly blurred. This will create new opportunities for entertainment, education, and communication.

AI-generated music and composition

Platforms like Jukedeck use generative AI to compose music tailored to specific moods, genres, or video content. Generative AI has revolutionized the music industry by introducing novel approaches to music creation and composition. AI systems can analyze patterns, styles, and emotions in existing music, leading to the generation of entirely new compositions.

Generative AI is used in music creation in three ways:

- **Algorithmic composition**: AI systems analyze vast datasets of musical compositions to learn the intricacies of different genres and artists. They can then use this knowledge to generate new compositions that are stylistically consistent with the target genre. This approach has been used to create music in a variety of genres, including pop, rock, electronic, and classical.

- **Collaboration with human musicians**: AI can also be used to assist human musicians in the creative process. For example, AI can be used to generate melodies, harmonies, or even entire sections of music. This can help human musicians to be more productive and to come up with new and innovative ideas.

- **Exploration of novel genres and styles**: AI can also be used to explore new and experimental genres of music. AI systems can be used to experiment with different combinations of sounds and rhythms, and to create new and unique musical experiences. This can help to push the boundaries of musical expression and to create new forms of art.

Generative AI is also being used to create personalized music experiences for listeners. AI systems can understand individual preferences and generate playlists, compositions, or even entire albums tailored to specific tastes. This can help listeners to discover new music that they would not have found otherwise, and to create a more personalized and enjoyable listening experience.

One challenge with AI-generated music is preserving the emotional depth and human touch in compositions. AI systems are still learning how to create music that is emotionally engaging and relatable to humans. Striking a balance between AI assistance and human creativity remains a key challenge.

Generative AI is a powerful tool that is reshaping the landscape of music. As the technology advances, the synergy between human intuition and AI innovation will continue to redefine the boundaries of musical expression.

Visual arts and style transfer

Generative AI is rapidly transforming the visual arts landscape. Let us see how AI is being used in this space.

- **Style transfer**: Through techniques like style transfer, AI is being used to create visually captivating images and videos that would be impossible for humans to create on their own.
    - One of the most exciting applications of generative AI in the visual arts is style transfer. Style transfer allows artists to take an image or video and apply the style of another image or video to it.

- o This can create stunning new visual effects that are impossible to achieve with traditional art techniques.
- o For example, an artist could use style transfer to take a photo of a cityscape and apply the style of a *Van Gogh* painting to it, creating a new image that looks like it was painted by Van Gogh.

- **Augmented and virtual reality**: AI is also being used in digital art generation, augmented reality and interactive installations, fashion and design, and GANs.
- **Digital art**: AI is also being used to create entirely new digital art.
  - o These artworks are often created by training a neural network on a large dataset of images, and then using the neural network to generate new images that are similar to the training data.
  - o This can create incredibly realistic and detailed images that would be impossible for a human artist to create on their own.
- **Interactive art installations**: In addition to creating new images, AI is also being used to create interactive art installations:
  - o These installations use AI to respond to the user's input, creating a unique and personalized experience for each visitor.
  - o For example, an installation could use AI to track the user's movement and create a real-time animation that responds to the user's movements.
- **Fashion and design**: AI is also being used in fashion and design. For example, AI can be used to create new designs for clothing, furniture, and other products. AI can also be used to help designers create more efficient and sustainable products.
- **Realistic images and videos**: GANs are a type of AI that can be used to create realistic images and videos.
  - o GANs work by training two neural networks against each other. One neural network, the generator, is responsible for creating new images. The other neural network, the discriminator, is responsible for distinguishing between real images and images created by the generator.
  - o The generator and discriminator are trained together, and over time, the generator learns to create more and more realistic images.
- **Photorealistic images and videos**: GANs are still in their early stages of development, but they have the potential to revolutionize the way we create visual art.
  - o GANs could be used to create photorealistic images and videos that are indistinguishable from real-world images.

- o GANs could also be used to create new and innovative art styles that would be impossible for humans to create on their own.
- **Ethical concerns**: As generative AI becomes more sophisticated; it is raising a number of ethical concerns.
  - o **Ownership and authorship**: One of the biggest concerns is the issue of ownership and authorship. When an AI creates an artwork, who owns the copyright to that artwork? And who is the author of the artwork? These are complex questions that do not have easy answers.
  - o **Fake news propaganda**: Another ethical concern is the potential for generative AI to be used to create fake news and propaganda. AI could be used to create realistic-looking images and videos that are designed to deceive people. This could have a significant impact on our democracy and our ability to make informed decisions.

Generative AI is a powerful new tool that has the potential to revolutionize the visual arts. However, it is important to be aware of the ethical implications of this technology and to take steps to mitigate the risks.

Generative AI's impact on visual arts transcends traditional boundaries, fostering a convergence of technology and creativity. From transforming styles to shaping augmented realities, the interplay between generative algorithms and artistic expression continues to redefine the possibilities in the visual arts landscape.

AI-enhanced filmmaking and animation

Generative AI is revolutionizing the entertainment sector by automating tasks, enhancing the storytelling process, and introducing novel visual elements. Let us see how generative AI is improving filmmaking and animation:

- **Script and storyline generation**: AI can suggest plot twists, character arcs, and dialogue, collaborating with human writers to enhance the narrative. For example, AI-powered writing tools like Botnik Studio can generate scripts, dialogue, and even entire stories based on a user's input. This can save writers time and help them to come up with new and innovative ideas.
- **Character design and animation**: AI can create lifelike, diverse, and visually compelling characters. For example, the Disney animated film *The Lion King* (2019) used AI to create photorealistic lions. This was a major technical achievement, and it helped to bring the characters to life in a way that was never before possible.
- **Scene composition and visual effects**: AI can create and optimize scenes, determining the placement of characters, props, and visual elements. This can help to create more visually appealing and cohesive scenes. For example, the AI-powered VFX tool Unreal Engine 5 can create photorealistic environments and

characters. This can help filmmakers to create more immersive and believable worlds.

- **Voice synthesis and dubbing**: AI can synthesize natural-sounding voices in various languages. This can be used for dubbing films and TV shows into other languages, or for creating entirely new voices for characters. For example, the AI-powered voice cloning tool Lyrebird can create a realistic voice for any person, even if there is no existing audio of them.

- **AI-driven editing and post-production**: AI can automate tasks such as color correction, pacing adjustments, and even suggesting edits based on cinematic conventions. This can save filmmakers time and help them to create more polished and professional films. For example, the AI-powered editing tool Wombo can automatically edit videos to match a specific genre or mood.

- **Interactive and personalized experience**: AI can create interactive films where viewers can influence the storyline's progression. This can create a more immersive and engaging experience for viewers. For example, the AI-powered interactive film *Black Mirror: Bandersnatch (2018)* allowed viewers to choose their own path through the story.

Generative AI's impact on filmmaking and animation extends beyond efficiency improvements, ushering in a new era of creativity and possibilities. By automating tasks, enhancing the storytelling process, and introducing novel visual elements, AI is helping to create more immersive, engaging, and visually stunning films and animations.

Creative chatbots and interactive storytelling

Generative AI is used to power chatbots that engage users in interactive storytelling, creating dynamic narratives based on user input. This technology is transforming how audiences engage with content, enabling them to:

- **Participate in interactive narrative experiences**: Chatbots can be used to create immersive and engaging stories that allow users to make choices that affect the outcome. This can be a great way to engage users and keep them coming back for more.

- **Have character-driven conversations**: Chatbots can be used to create characters that users can interact with. This can be a great way to build rapport with users and make them feel like they are part of the story.

- **Influence plot twists**: Chatbots can be used to give users the power to change the course of the story. This can be a great way to keep users engaged and guessing what will happen next.

- **Gamify storytelling**: Chatbots can be used to create games that are based on stories. This can be a great way to make storytelling more fun and engaging for users.

- **Receive personalized content recommendations**: Chatbots can be used to collect data about users' preferences and interests. This data can then be used to make personalized content recommendations.

- **Learn and adapt from user interactions**: Chatbots can be programmed to learn and adapt from user interactions. This means that the chatbot can become more intelligent and engaging over time.

These applications are creating immersive and participatory experiences that redefine traditional storytelling conventions, fostering a new era of audience engagement.

Ethical considerations in AI-generated art

As generative AI expands into the realm of art, ethical considerations become crucial. These include:

- **Authorship and attribution**: Who owns the generated artwork? This is a complex question with no easy answer. Some argue that the artist is the person who creates the algorithm, while others believe that the artist is the person who generates the artwork. There is also the question of whether the artist should be compensated for the use of their work.

- **Bias and cultural representation**: How can AI-generated art promote fair and culturally sensitive representations? AI models are trained on data that reflects the biases of the real world. This can lead to AI-generated art that perpetuates stereotypes and harmful representations. It is important to be aware of these biases and to take steps to mitigate them.

- **Commercialization and accessibility**: How can the benefits of AI creativity be distributed more broadly? AI-generated art can be used for commercial purposes, such as creating advertising campaigns or generating product images. However, it is important to ensure that the benefits of AI creativity are not limited to those who can afford to pay for it.

- **Originality and reproducibility**: How can we recognize and value the uniqueness of AI-generated creations? AI-generated art can be highly original, but it can also be reproducible. This raises the question of how we can value AI-generated art in a way that is fair to both the artist and the consumer.

- **Consent and privacy in data usage**: How can we respect user consent and ensure privacy in the creation of AI-generated art? AI models are trained on data that may include personal information. It is important to ensure that users' privacy is protected when their data is used to create AI-generated art.

- **Environmental impact of AI training**: How can we balance creative advancements with environmental responsibility? The training of AI models can have a significant environmental impact. It is important to be aware of this impact and to take steps to mitigate it.

These are just some of the ethical considerations that need to be addressed as generative AI expands into the realm of art. It is important to have a conversation about these issues and to develop policies that ensure that AI-generated art is created in a responsible and ethical manner.

Navigating the ethical landscape of AI-generated art requires a collaborative effort from artists, technologists, policymakers, and the public. As generative AI continues to redefine the boundaries of artistic creation, thoughtful ethical considerations pave the way for a responsible and inclusive future in AI-driven artistry.

Generative AI is not only pushing the boundaries of creativity but also challenging traditional notions of authorship and human-machine collaboration in the ever-evolving landscape of entertainment.

This section gave reader the perspective on ethical standards and compliance that need to be considered throughout the lifecycle of generative AI.

In the next section, dedicated to case studies showcasing real-world applications of generative AI, readers will delve into tangible examples that bridge theory with practical implementation. These case studies serve as illuminating narratives, providing insights into the actual deployment of generative AI across industries. Users can expect to gain a nuanced understanding of how organizations have successfully integrated generative AI into their workflows, overcoming challenges and capitalizing on opportunities. Through these real-world scenarios, readers will acquire valuable insights into the diverse ways generative AI can be leveraged for innovation and problem-solving, fostering a deeper appreciation for its transformative potential in various domains.

Case studies showcasing real-world applications

In the section dedicated to case studies showcasing real-world applications of generative AI, readers will embark on a journey through practical implementations across diverse industries. Through these case studies, users will gain firsthand insights into how generative AI has been effectively deployed to address real challenges and drive meaningful outcomes. This section serves as a bridge between theoretical concepts and concrete, impactful applications, offering readers a comprehensive view of the technology's potential. By examining specific use cases and success stories, users will not only deepen their understanding of generative AI but also acquire practical knowledge applicable to their own professional contexts.

In the section dedicated to case studies showcasing real-world applications, we delve into several compelling examples that highlight the versatility and impact of generative AI across diverse industries.

Healthcare

This section elaborates on a case study in healthcare:

- **Case study**: Application of generative AI in medical imaging enhancement.
- **Outcomes**: Improved accuracy in diagnostics, enhanced visualization for medical professionals, and potential acceleration of treatment plans.

Case study: Medical imaging enhancement in oncology

In the field of oncology, accurate and timely diagnosis is crucial for effective treatment planning. Medical imaging, such as MRIs and CT scans, plays a pivotal role in identifying and characterizing tumors. However, the clarity and precision of these images are vital for accurate diagnosis.

Application of generative AI: A healthcare institution integrated generative AI algorithms into its medical imaging process. Specifically, a GAN was employed to enhance the resolution and quality of oncological images.

How it works: The GAN analyzed a vast dataset of medical images, learning patterns and features specific to tumor structures. During the enhancement process, the generator network produced high-resolution versions of the input images, while the discriminator network ensured that the generated images closely resembled actual tumor structures.

Outcomes

The following were the outcomes of this case study:

- **Improved diagnostics**: The enhanced images provided radiologists with sharper and clearer views of tumors, enabling more accurate diagnosis and characterization.
- **Reduced false negatives**: The AI-driven enhancement reduced the likelihood of missing subtle or small lesions, minimizing false negatives in diagnostics.
- **Faster treatment planning**: With clearer images, oncologists could expedite treatment planning, leading to more prompt initiation of therapeutic interventions.

This case study exemplifies how generative AI applications in healthcare, specifically in medical imaging, can significantly contribute to enhanced diagnostic accuracy and improved patient outcomes in critical areas such as oncology.

Finance

This section elaborates on a case study in finance:

- **Case study**: Generative AI employed for fraud detection and prevention.

- **Outcomes**: Enhanced security measures, reduction in fraudulent activities, and increased trust in financial systems.

Case study: Fraud detection and prevention in financial transactions

Background: Financial institutions face constant challenges in detecting and preventing fraudulent activities in transactions. Traditional rule-based systems often struggle to adapt to evolving tactics used by fraudsters.

Application of generative AI: A leading bank implemented generative AI, particularly GANs, to enhance its fraud detection capabilities.

How it works: The GAN was trained on a diverse dataset of legitimate and fraudulent transactions. The generator learned patterns associated with both types of transactions, while the discriminator identified subtle anomalies that might indicate fraudulent behavior.

Outcomes

The following were the outcomes of the case study:

- **Increased accuracy**: The generative AI system significantly increased the accuracy of fraud detection by recognizing nuanced patterns that were challenging for traditional systems.
- **Adaptability to new tactics**: Unlike rule-based systems, the GAN could adapt to new fraud tactics and patterns, making it more resilient against emerging threats.
- **Reduced false positives**: By understanding the normal behavior of users, the system minimized false positives, ensuring legitimate transactions were not mistakenly flagged.

This case study demonstrates how generative AI, applied to fraud detection in financial transactions, can provide a dynamic and adaptive solution that outperforms traditional methods, enhancing security and trust in financial operations.

Entertainment

This section elaborates on a case study in entertainment:

- **Case study**: Creative content generation using generative AI in the entertainment industry.
- **Outcomes**: Accelerated content creation, novel artistic expressions, and innovative approaches to storytelling.

Case study: AI-enhanced filmmaking and animation

Background: The film industry constantly seeks innovative ways to enhance storytelling and visual experiences. Traditional filmmaking processes can be time-consuming and resource intensive.

Application of generative AI: A major film studio employed generative AI techniques to streamline and enhance the filmmaking and animation process.

How it works: Generative models were trained on vast datasets of existing films, animation sequences, and visual effects. These models could then generate new, realistic scenes, characters, and visual effects based on the learned patterns.

Outcomes

The following were the outcomes of the case study:

- **Efficient pre-visualization**: Generative AI allowed for quick pre-visualization of scenes, helping filmmakers visualize and plan complex shots before actual production.
- **Cost reduction**: By automating certain aspects of animation and visual effects, the studio experienced cost reductions in both time and resources.
- **Creative exploration**: Filmmakers could experiment with novel ideas and visual styles by leveraging the generative capabilities, leading to more creative and visually stunning productions.

This case study illustrates how generative AI can revolutionize the entertainment industry by offering tools that streamline creative processes, reduce costs, and open up new possibilities for storytelling and visual experiences.

Manufacturing and design

This section elaborates on a case study in manufacturing and design:

- **Case study**: Integration of generative AI in product design and optimization.
- **Outcomes**: Streamlined design processes, increased efficiency, and accelerated innovation.

Case study: Generative design in aerospace engineering

Background: A leading aerospace engineering firm faced challenges in optimizing complex designs for aircraft components. Traditional design processes were time-consuming and often did not exploit the full potential of innovative solutions.

Application of generative AI: Generative design algorithms were employed to optimize the structural design of aircraft components. These algorithms could iteratively generate and evaluate thousands of design variations based on specified criteria.

How it works: The generative AI system used a combination of computational modeling, simulation, and machine learning. It considered factors such as weight, material properties, and aerodynamics to evolve designs that met structural requirements while minimizing weight and maximizing performance.

Outcomes

The following were the outcomes of the case study:

- **Lightweight structures**: Generative design led to the creation of lightweight yet structurally efficient components, improving fuel efficiency and overall performance.
- **Reduced development time**: The iterative and automated nature of generative design significantly reduced the time required to arrive at an optimized solution.
- **Innovative solutions**: The system often proposed unconventional design solutions that human engineers might not have considered, pushing the boundaries of traditional aerospace design.

This case study showcases how generative AI can transform the manufacturing and design process in industries like aerospace, enabling engineers to explore innovative and optimized solutions more efficiently.

Urban planning and architecture

This section elaborates on a case study in urban planning and architecture:

- **Case study**: Leveraging generative AI for urban planning and architectural design.
- **Outcomes**: Optimized urban layouts, sustainable design solutions, and improved efficiency in the planning process.

Case study: Urban planning with generative AI

Background: A rapidly growing city faced challenges in urban planning, aiming to accommodate a rising population while ensuring sustainable, aesthetically pleasing, and functional urban spaces.

Application of generative AI: Generative AI was employed to assist urban planners in optimizing city layouts, designing public spaces, and ensuring efficient traffic flow. The goal was to create an environment that promotes both sustainability and a high quality of life.

How it works: Generative algorithms took into account various factors such as population density, traffic patterns, green spaces, and energy efficiency. The system iteratively generated and evaluated different urban designs, considering the input parameters and optimizing for multiple objectives.

Outcomes

The following were the outcomes of the case study:

- **Optimized traffic flow**: Generative AI suggested road layouts that minimized congestion and improved transportation efficiency.
- **Green and public spaces**: The system proposed designs that maximized the presence of parks, recreational areas, and green spaces, contributing to the residents' well-being.
- **Sustainable infrastructure**: Urban planners leveraged generative AI to incorporate sustainable practices, such as designing energy-efficient buildings and optimizing waste management.

This case study demonstrates how generative AI can be a valuable tool in urban planning, helping create smarter, more sustainable cities that cater to the needs of a growing population.

Human resources and recruitment

This section elaborates on a case study in human resources and recruitment:

- **Case study**: Application of generative AI in resume screening and candidate matching.
- **Outcomes**: Streamlined hiring processes, improved candidate-organization fit, and reduced bias in recruitment.

Case study: AI-enhanced recruitment in human resources

Background: A multinational company faced challenges in streamlining its recruitment process, aiming to identify top talent efficiently while minimizing biases and enhancing the overall candidate experience.

Application of generative AI: Generative AI was integrated into the recruitment process to automate and optimize various stages, from resume screening to candidate engagement.

How it works: Let us explore some of the applications of generative AI in the recruitment process:

- **Resume screening**: Generative algorithms were employed to analyze resumes, identifying relevant skills, experiences, and qualifications.

- **Chatbot interviews**: AI-driven chatbots conducted initial interviews, assessing candidates' communication skills and cultural fit.

- **Predictive analytics**: Generative models predicted candidates' future performance based on historical data, helping in shortlisting candidates likely to succeed in the role.

Outcomes: The outcomes of applying generative AI in the recruitment process affected various aspects positively as detailed below:

- **Efficiency**: The AI-driven process significantly reduced the time and effort required for initial screening, allowing recruiters to focus on higher-value tasks.

- **Diversity and inclusion**: By minimizing biases in the screening process, the company saw improved diversity in candidate pools.

- **Candidate experience**: The use of chatbots for initial interviews provided a seamless and standardized experience for candidates.

This case study illustrates how generative AI can revolutionize HR and recruitment processes, making them more efficient, fair, and aligned with the organization's goals.

Robotics and automation

This section elaborates on a case study in robotics and automation:

- **Case study**: Generative AI in optimizing robotic movements and automation processes.

- **Outcomes**: Increased efficiency, reduced errors, and enhanced adaptability in robotic systems.

Background: A manufacturing plant sought to enhance its production efficiency and safety by implementing robotics and automation. The goal was to optimize the assembly line, reduce manual labor, and improve overall productivity.

Application of generative AI: Generative AI was employed to design and optimize the robotics and automation systems, ensuring they could adapt to changing production requirements and environments.

How it works: Let us explore some of the applications of generative AI in robotics and automation:

- **Generative design**: AI algorithms generated multiple design options for robotic systems, considering factors like space constraints, production volume, and energy efficiency.

- **Simulation**: Generative models simulated different scenarios, predicting how the robotic systems would perform under various conditions and identifying potential bottlenecks.

- **Adaptive automation**: The implemented robotics systems utilized real-time data and machine learning to adapt to changes in production demands, minimizing downtime and maximizing efficiency.

Outcomes: The outcomes of applying generative AI in robotics and automation affected various aspects positively as detailed below:

- **Increased efficiency**: The AI-optimized robotics systems significantly improved production speed and efficiency.

- **Cost reduction**: By automating repetitive tasks, the company reduced labor costs and increased the overall cost-effectiveness of the manufacturing process.

- **Adaptability**: The generative AI-driven systems could adapt to fluctuations in demand and changes in the production environment, ensuring continuous operation.

This case study showcases the transformative impact of generative AI in the field of robotics and automation, enabling smarter, adaptive, and more efficient manufacturing processes.

These case studies provide concrete examples of how generative AI is making a substantial impact in various domains. Through the exploration of these applications, readers gain a nuanced understanding of the technology's transformative potential and its ability to address complex challenges in real-world scenarios.

Other sectors

Let us dive into more detailed case studies across various sectors where generative AI is making a significant impact:

- **Agriculture: Precision farming optimization**: With the growing demand for sustainable agriculture, a farming cooperative sought to optimize crop yields while minimizing environmental impact.

    Application of generative AI: Generative AI algorithms were employed to analyze various data sources, including satellite imagery, weather patterns, and soil conditions.

    Outcomes: The outcomes of applying generative AI in agriculture affected various aspects positively as detailed below:

    - **Precision farming**: AI-driven insights enabled precise and efficient use of resources like water and fertilizers.

- o **Increased yields**: Farmers experienced higher crop yields through optimized cultivation practices.
- **Energy: Renewable energy infrastructure planning**: A renewable energy company aimed to enhance the planning and implementation of solar and wind energy projects.

  Application of generative AI: Generative AI models were used to analyze geographical data, weather patterns, and energy consumption trends to design optimal renewable energy infrastructure.

  Outcomes: The outcomes of applying generative AI in renewable energy infrastructure planning affected various aspects positively as detailed below:
  - o **Optimized energy output**: AI-driven designs maximized energy capture from renewable sources.
  - o **Cost efficiency**: Efficient infrastructure planning led to reduced costs and increased competitiveness in the renewable energy market.
- **Education: Personalized learning paths**: A progressive education institution aimed to enhance student learning experiences by tailoring educational content to individual needs.

  Application of generative AI: Generative AI algorithms were employed to analyze students' learning styles, preferences, and performance to generate personalized learning paths.

  Outcomes: The outcomes of applying generative AI in education affected various aspects positively as detailed below:
  - o **Improved learning outcomes**: Personalized learning paths catered to individual strengths and weaknesses, improving overall academic performance.
  - o **Enhanced student engagement**: Tailored content increased student engagement and interest in learning.
- **Transportation: Traffic flow optimization**: A city faced challenges with traffic congestion, affecting both commuters and environmental quality.

  Application of generative AI: Generative AI models were used to analyze traffic patterns, historical data, and urban infrastructure to optimize traffic signal timings.

  Outcomes: The outcomes of applying generative AI in transportation affected various aspects positively as detailed below:
  - o **Reduced congestion**: AI-driven traffic signal optimization led to smoother traffic flow and reduced congestion.

- ○ **Environmental impact**: Improved traffic flow contributed to lower carbon emissions and improved air quality.
- **Retail: Personalized shopping experiences**: A retail chain aimed to enhance customer satisfaction by offering personalized shopping experiences.

    Application of generative AI: Generative AI algorithms analyzed customer preferences, purchase history, and real-time behavior to recommend personalized products and promotions.

    Outcomes: The outcomes of applying generative AI in retail affected various aspects positively as detailed below:
    - ○ **Increased sales**: Personalized recommendations led to higher conversion rates and increased customer loyalty.
    - ○ **Enhanced customer satisfaction**: Shoppers enjoyed a more tailored and comprehensive shopping experience.

These case studies underscore the transformative potential of generative AI across diverse sectors, showcasing its ability to drive innovation, efficiency, and positive outcomes tailored to the unique challenges and opportunities of each industry.

In this comprehensive exploration of case studies showcasing real-world applications of generative AI across diverse sectors, readers have gained a profound understanding of the tangible impacts and transformative potential of this technology. Through in-depth analyses of applications in healthcare, finance, entertainment, manufacturing, urban planning, human resources, and robotics, readers have developed a nuanced comprehension of the nuanced ways generative AI is revolutionizing industries. The case studies not only provide insights into the practical implementation of generative AI but also equip readers with the ability to identify opportunities and challenges unique to each sector. This section fosters a holistic appreciation for the adaptability and innovation that generative AI brings to real-world scenarios, empowering readers with the skills to navigate and contribute to the dynamic landscape of AI applications across various domains.

In the final section of this chapter, readers embark on a forward-looking journey into the evolving landscape of generative AI. This segment delves into emerging trends, technological advancements, and potential disruptions that are set to shape the future of this transformative technology. Readers will gain valuable insights into the trajectory of generative AI, enabling them to anticipate and adapt to upcoming innovations. The section not only highlights the ongoing advancements but also encourages readers to contemplate the broader societal and ethical implications of these trends. As a result, users will emerge with a strategic understanding of the future of generative AI, positioning them to stay at the forefront of this rapidly evolving field.

Future trends and potential disruptions

This segment is designed to illuminate the emerging trends, groundbreaking innovations, and potential disruptions that are poised to redefine the landscape of generative AI. Readers will gain a strategic foresight into the future developments and disruptive forces shaping this technology. From novel applications to evolving methodologies, this section serves as a compass, guiding readers through the exciting possibilities and challenges on the horizon. By the end of this exploration, readers will not only be informed about the imminent trends but will also be equipped with a forward-thinking perspective to navigate the future of generative AI.

Emerging from insights provided by leading think tanks and echoed in prominent reports, we identify key trends that are shaping the future landscape. One such trend revolves around the heightened integration of generative AI with edge computing, enabling real-time and decentralized processing. This shift not only enhances efficiency but also opens doors to innovative applications in sectors like IoT and autonomous systems.

Moreover, the evolution of **explainable AI** (**XAI**) is a noteworthy trend, responding to the increasing demand for transparency and interpretability in AI decision-making. As demonstrated in reports by organizations like Gartner and Forrester, the rise of XAI holds promise for addressing ethical concerns and fostering user trust.

Additionally, the growing synergy between generative AI and quantum computing emerges as a disruptive force. The potential to leverage quantum algorithms for complex generative tasks signals a paradigm shift in computational capabilities. Furthermore, industry-specific trends come to the forefront. For instance, in healthcare, the convergence of generative AI and precision medicine is creating personalized treatment pathways as corroborated by major strategy consulting firms. Similarly, in the financial sector, the integration of generative models for risk assessment aligns with predictions from financial analysts and institutions.

By navigating through these insights and examples, readers gain a comprehensive understanding of the imminent trends and potential disruptions that will shape the future of generative AI. The intersection of cutting-edge technologies, ethical considerations, and industry-specific applications paints a vivid picture of the transformative journey ahead.

Predicting future trends and potential disruptions involves a collaborative effort from various thought leaders, companies, and research institutions. Here are some key entities that contribute to shaping our understanding of the future landscape.

Gartner

Rationale: Gartner, a prominent research and advisory company, plays a pivotal role in forecasting technology trends. Their analysis often stems from extensive market research, expert insights, and evaluations of emerging technologies.

For example, Gartner's reports on edge computing and quantum computing provide valuable insights into their potential impact on the future of AI.

Gartner is a globally recognized research and advisory firm that plays a crucial role in shaping the landscape of technology and business trends. Known for its Magic Quadrant reports, Gartner provides strategic insights and analysis based on extensive research conducted by its team of experts. Here is a detailed exploration of Gartner's significance:

- **Research methodology**: Gartner employs a rigorous research methodology to assess technology trends and market players. Their analysts conduct thorough evaluations, leveraging a combination of primary research, expert interviews, client interactions, and quantitative assessments. The result is a comprehensive understanding of the technology landscape.

- **Magic quadrant**: One of Gartner's flagship tools is the Magic Quadrant, a graphical representation of a market's direction, maturity, and participants. It categorizes technology providers into quadrants—Leaders, Challengers, Visionaries, and Niche Players—providing a quick and visual assessment of a market's competitive landscape.

- **Hype cycles**: Gartner's Hype Cycles offer insights into the maturity, adoption, and business impact of specific technologies. These cycles track the journey of technologies from inception to widespread adoption and, in the process, help organizations identify opportunities and potential risks.

- **Strategic planning**: Businesses worldwide rely on Gartner's strategic planning insights. Through reports, webinars, and advisory services, Gartner guides organizations in making informed decisions about technology investments, digital transformation, and navigating the evolving business landscape.

- **Emerging technologies**: Gartner consistently explores emerging technologies and their potential impact on industries. From artificial intelligence and blockchain to edge computing and quantum computing, Gartner's research equips businesses with the knowledge needed to stay ahead in a rapidly changing technological environment.

- **Predictions and forecasts**: Gartner is known for its yearly predictions and forecasts that provide a glimpse into the future of technology. These predictions are based on a combination of ongoing research, industry insights, and a deep understanding of the factors shaping the business and technology ecosystem.

- **Advisory services**: Gartner's advisory services offer personalized guidance to organizations. Clients can engage with Gartner analysts for one-on-one consultations, gaining tailored advice to address specific challenges and capitalize on emerging opportunities.

In summary, Gartner's influence extends far beyond simple trend analysis. Its holistic approach to research, reliance on robust methodologies, and provision of actionable insights make it an indispensable resource for businesses navigating the complexities of the modern technological landscape.

Forrester

Forrester is known for its market research and analysis, particularly in the realm of technology and business. Their predictions often stem from a deep understanding of market dynamics and emerging technologies.

For example, Forrester's exploration of **explainable AI (XAI)** reflects their focus on the ethical and transparent use of AI, addressing concerns around bias and accountability.

Forrester Research is a prominent market research and advisory firm specializing in technology and its impact on business. Renowned for its in-depth analyses and forward-looking insights, Forrester contributes significantly to guiding organizations through digital transformation. Here is an elaborate exploration of Forrester's key attributes:

- **Customer-centric approach**: Forrester is distinguished by its customer-centric approach. The firm places a strong emphasis on understanding and analyzing technology trends from the perspective of end-users. This focus ensures that businesses receive insights aligned with customer expectations and market demands.

- **Research frameworks**: Forrester employs various research frameworks to delve into technology trends. These frameworks often include methodologies like the Forrester Wave, which evaluates and compares technology vendors based on specific criteria. Such assessments assist businesses in making informed decisions about technology adoption.

- **Total economic impact (TEI)**: Forrester's TEI methodology is a widely recognized tool for assessing the value of technology investments. TEI studies provide organizations with a comprehensive understanding of the potential **return on investment (ROI)** and the overall economic impact of adopting specific technologies.

- **Strategic guidance**: Businesses turn to Forrester for strategic guidance in navigating the complexities of the digital landscape. Forrester's advisory services offer personalized recommendations tailored to individual organizational needs, helping leaders make strategic decisions that align with their business objectives.

- **Thought leadership**: Forrester is a thought leader in the technology and business space. Through its reports, blogs, and events, the firm shares expert opinions on emerging trends, challenges, and opportunities. This thought leadership fosters a community of professionals and decision-makers seeking insights to drive innovation.

- **Cross-industry analysis**: Forrester's research spans various industries, allowing businesses to benefit from cross-industry insights. This broad perspective is particularly valuable as technology trends often have ripple effects across different sectors. Forrester's cross-industry analysis enables organizations to anticipate and prepare for such impacts.

- **Digital transformation guidance**: Forrester is instrumental in providing guidance on digital transformation strategies. Recognizing the pivotal role of technology in reshaping business models, Forrester's research helps organizations understand the evolving digital landscape and develop roadmaps for successful transformation.

- **Technology adoption profiles**: Forrester creates technology adoption profiles that offer a detailed understanding of how different organizations adopt and leverage specific technologies. These profiles assist businesses in benchmarking their own strategies against industry trends and best practices.

In conclusion, Forrester's impact on the tech industry is multifaceted. From its customer-centric approach to thought leadership and strategic guidance, the firm's contributions empower organizations to make informed decisions, stay ahead of industry shifts, and thrive in an era of rapid technological evolution.

Conclusion

The chapter provides a comprehensive exploration of the diverse applications of generative AI in various sectors. It commenced by delving into the healthcare domain, elucidating how generative AI is revolutionizing medical imaging, drug discovery, personalized treatment plans, medical text generation, and predictive analytics. The finance section uncovered the role of generative AI in fraud detection, algorithmic trading strategies, customer service chatbots, and credit scoring. The entertainment sector discussion unveiled insights into generative AI's impact on generative art, creative content generation, interactive and immersive experiences, AI-generated music and composition, visual arts and style transfer, AI-enhanced filmmaking, animation, creative chatbots, interactive storytelling, virtual fashion design, AI-generated literature, and ethical considerations in AI-generated art. Each sector was accompanied by real-world examples and use cases. The chapter culminated in case studies showcasing practical applications across healthcare, finance, entertainment, manufacturing, urban planning, human resources, and robotics. By integrating theoretical concepts with practical implementations, readers gained a nuanced understanding of the transformative potential of generative AI, equipped with insights and skills applicable across diverse industries. The upcoming chapter promises an exploration into the fascinating realms of art, music, and design powered by generative AI. Readers can anticipate a deep dive into the intersection of human creativity and artificial intelligence, examining the collaborations between humans and AI in the creative process. The chapter will not only showcase the impressive outputs of generative AI in creative domains but also delve into the ethical considerations inherent in deploying

AI in creative endeavors. Through this exploration, readers will gain insights into how generative AI is reshaping creative expression, the dynamics of human-AI collaboration, and the ethical implications of leveraging technology in the world of art and design.

Join our book's Discord space

Join the book's Discord Workspace for Latest updates, Offers, Tech happenings around the world, New Release and Sessions with the Authors:

https://discord.bpbonline.com

Chapter 5
Creative Expression with Generative AI

Introduction

In this captivating chapter, we embark on a journey through the dynamic intersections of generative AI, art, music, and design. This chapter unfolds the transformative impact of generative AI on the creative landscape, exploring how it manifests in diverse forms of artistic expression. We will delve into the exciting collaborations between humans and AI, witnessing the coalescence of human ingenuity and machine-generated creativity. Additionally, the chapter scrutinizes the ethical considerations that arise in the realm of creative AI, shedding light on the responsible and thoughtful deployment of these technologies. Brace yourself for an exploration that not only showcases the possibilities of generative AI in creative domains but also navigates the nuanced considerations that shape the future of artistic innovation.

Structure

This chapter will cover the following topics:

- Generative AI in art, music, and design
- Generative adversarial networks in visual arts
- Harmonies of code and melody

- Aesthetic revolution in design
- Collaborations between humans and AI
- Ethical considerations in creative AI

Objectives

The chapter will explore how generative AI is redefining the creative process and enabling the creation of new and innovative forms of art. It will examine the impact of generative AI on various creative domains, such as music, visual arts, and design. It will highlight the collaborative nature of human-AI partnerships in creative endeavors. It will showcase how human artists are harnessing the power of generative AI to expand their creative horizons and produce groundbreaking works of art.

The chapter will address the ethical considerations that arise in the use of generative AI for creative purposes. It will discuss issues such as attribution, copyright, and the potential for bias in AI-generated art. Further, we will conclude by examining the future trajectory of artistic innovation with generative AI. It will discuss emerging trends and advancements in generative AI technology and explore the potential for further collaboration between humans and AI in the creative realm.

Readers will gain a clear vision of the future trajectory of artistic innovation with generative AI. They will explore emerging trends and advancements in generative AI technology and gain an understanding of the potential for further collaboration between humans and AI in the creative realm.

In summary, readers will embark on a comprehensive journey through the transformative impact of generative AI on creative expression. They will gain a deep understanding of the technology, its applications, and the ethical considerations surrounding its use. This knowledge will empower them to appreciate the innovative and groundbreaking potential of generative AI in shaping the future of art and creativity.

Generative AI in art, music, and design

Embark on a mesmerizing voyage into the heart of creativity with this section. Here, we unveil the myriad ways in which generative AI converges with artistry, music composition, and design aesthetics. We will delve into the innovative applications and groundbreaking collaborations that redefine the boundaries of human expression. From algorithmic masterpieces in art to symphonies composed by machines, this section unveils the transformative potential of generative AI in shaping the future of artistic endeavors. Prepare to be captivated by the fusion of technology and creativity, exploring the unprecedented possibilities that emerge when algorithms become artists. This section delves into the following key areas.

Algorithmic artistry

We will explore the fusion of algorithms and artistic expression, witnessing the emergence of mesmerizing visual creations generated by artificial intelligence. We will also understand the role of generative models in redefining traditional artistic paradigms.

Algorithmic artistry is a testament to the harmonious convergence of code and creativity, unlocking new dimensions in the artistic domain. This section delves into its intricacies, exploring its significance, real-world examples, and transformative impact.

Significance: Algorithmic artistry represents a paradigm shift in artistic creation. By leveraging generative models, artists and programmers collaborate with algorithms to produce visually stunning and conceptually rich artworks. This approach challenges traditional notions of authorship, providing a canvas for the fusion of human intent and computational ingenuity.

Real-world examples and case studies

In this section we will discuss some of the real-world examples and case studies on algorithmic artistry.

- **The next Rembrandt**: In a groundbreaking project, generative algorithms analyzed *Rembrandt's* works to create a new painting in his distinctive style. This case study showcases how AI can channel the essence of renowned artists, sparking discussions about authenticity and creativity. *Figure 5.1* below is the image of the beautiful painting which is 3D printed and the result of analyzing data from Rembrandt's body of work. Please refer to the following figure:

Figure 5.1: *The Next Rembrandt painting*

- **Google's Magenta**: Magenta, an open-source research project by Google, explores the intersection of AI and the arts. It has produced compelling examples of algorithmically generated art and music, empowering creators to experiment with novel forms of expression. *Figure 5.2* showcases the expressive communication framework that magenta leverages. This brings together composers and listeners in comparing how well emotion is communicated through music made with different generative tools. Please refer to the following figure:

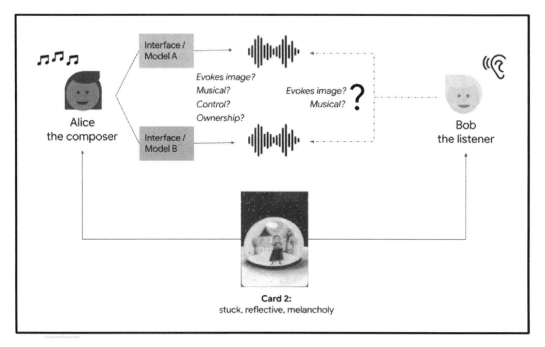

Figure 5.2: *The expressive communication framework, courtesy Magenta Tensorflow org*

- **DeepDream by Google**: Originally developed as an image classification tool, DeepDream has become a platform for artistic exploration. By enhancing and modifying images based on neural network patterns, it exemplifies the collaboration between human curators and AI algorithms. *Figure 5.3* shows The Mona Lisa with DeepDream effect using VGG16 network trained on ImageNet:

Figure 5.3: *The Mona Lisa with DeepDream effect, courtesy DeepDream wikipedia*

Impact and future trends

Algorithmic artistry not only redefines the creative process but also raises questions about the nature of art itself. As generative models become more sophisticated, we can anticipate an evolution in the way artists conceptualize and bring their ideas to life. The synergy between algorithms and artistic intuition promises an exciting future where the boundaries between creator and creation continue to blur.

In embracing algorithmic artistry, we witness the birth of a new era where art is co-authored by human imagination and artificial intelligence, expanding the horizons of what is conceivable in creative expression.

Algorithmic artistry represents a profound shift in the creation of visual expressions, where algorithms become the brushstrokes of innovation.

Generative adversarial networks in visual arts

Generative adversarial networks (GANs) have revolutionized algorithmic art by creating images that blur the lines between reality and imagination.

For example, artists like *Mario Klingemann* leverage GANs to produce captivating, AI-generated artwork. His piece, *Memories of Passersby I*, won the Lumen Prize for digital art.

Evolution of style transfer

Style transfer algorithms enable the transformation of images into the distinctive styles of renowned artists.

For example, the *Starry Night* filter, inspired by *Van Gogh*'s masterpiece, applied to personal photos through apps like Prisma, showcases the influence of algorithms on personalized art.

Case study: Google's DeepDream

DeepDream visualizes the hidden layers of a neural network, creating dreamlike and surreal images.

For example, artists like *Mike Tyka* have embraced DeepDream, using its psychedelic aesthetic to produce unique and mesmerizing artworks.

Google's DeepDream project is a testament to the fusion of artificial intelligence and artistic expression, creating a mesmerizing world where algorithms dream in vibrant colors and intricate patterns. Here is an in-depth look at the DeepDream initiative:

Overview of DeepDream

Developed by Google engineers in 2015, DeepDream originated as a tool for visualizing and understanding the features of a neural network.

Based on a **convolutional neural network (CNN)**, DeepDream was trained on vast datasets of images, enabling it to recognize and generate complex patterns.

How DeepDream works

Let us discuss how DeepDream is brought into function:

- **Algorithmic activation**: DeepDream functions by amplifying and enhancing patterns and features that the neural network recognizes in an image.

- **Iterations**: The process involves iterating through the network, enhancing features at different layers to produce progressively abstract and intricate visuals.

Visual aesthetics and artistic impact

Enlisted below are two major impacts of DeepDream on Visual aesthetics and art:

- **Dreamlike aesthetics**: DeepDream's output is often described as dreamlike, featuring hallucinogenic and surreal imagery.
- **Artistic collaboration**: Artists and creatives quickly recognized the potential of DeepDream as a collaborative tool to produce unique and imaginative artworks.

Popularization and accessibility

DeepDream became popular and accesible because of the following reasons:

- **Open-source release**: Google open-sourced the DeepDream code, allowing developers and artists worldwide to experiment and contribute to its evolution.
- **Online platforms**: Websites and applications were developed, enabling users to apply DeepDream filters to their images, leading to a surge in AI-generated psychedelic art.

Impact on the artistic community

Let us discuss impact of DeepDream on artistic community:

- **Art exhibitions**: Deep Dream-generated artworks found their way into art exhibitions, showcasing the intersection of technology and creativity.
- **Exploration of unconscious patterns**: DeepDream's ability to reveal intricate details and patterns hidden in images intrigued artists, pushing the boundaries of what could be considered art.

Google's DeepDream not only marked a milestone in the exploration of neural network capabilities but also ignited a creative movement where AI became a collaborator in the artistic process. By unleashing the latent visual potential within neural networks, DeepDream transformed ordinary images into fantastical landscapes, challenging preconceived notions of artistic creation and perception. The initiative underscored the symbiotic relationship between algorithms and human creativity, inviting artists to embark on a journey where the lines between the conscious and unconscious, human and machine, blurred in a psychedelic dance of imagination.

Interactive art installations

Artists employ AI to create interactive installations that respond to the environment or viewer's actions.

For example, *Refik Anadol's Infinity Room* uses AI algorithms to generate a constantly evolving visual experience based on visitors' movements.

AI-generated NFT art

Non-fungible tokens (NFTs) leverage blockchain technology to certify ownership of digital art, often generated by AI.

For example, artists like *Beeple* have gained fame by selling AI-generated NFT art, pushing the boundaries of digital ownership and monetization.

The emergence of NFTs has revolutionized the art world, providing a unique platform for creators to tokenize and sell their digital creations. Within this landscape, AI-generated art has found a significant niche, contributing to the rise of digital collectibles. Here is an exploration of AI-generated NFT art.

Fusion of technology and creativity

Let us explore how the fusion of technology and creativity works:

- **Algorithmic creation**: AI algorithms, particularly generative models like GANs, have been employed to autonomously generate unique and often unpredictable digital artworks.
- **NFT tokenization**: These digital creations are then tokenized as NFTs on blockchain platforms, ensuring their scarcity and ownership authenticity.

Unique features of AI-generated NFTs

Enlisted below are unique features of AI-generated NFTs:

- **Variability**: Each piece generated by the AI is often unique due to the inherent variability of the generative process, providing a sense of exclusivity.
- **Unpredictability**: The unpredictability of AI algorithms introduces an element of surprise, making each piece a discovery for both the artist and the collector.

Artist collaborations and AI

Let us see how AI is helping in artistic collaborations:

- **Collaborative initiatives**: Artists are increasingly collaborating with AI tools to produce hybrid creations, combining human creativity with the computational capabilities of AI.
- **Exploration of styles**: AI allows artists to explore new styles, genres, and aesthetics, contributing to the diversification of the NFT art space.

Tokenized ownership and digital scarcity

Let us explore this below:

- **Blockchain verification**: NFTs are built on blockchain technology, providing a secure and transparent method to verify ownership and provenance.

- **Digital scarcity**: The limited nature of NFTs, often constrained by the generative process itself, introduces a concept of digital scarcity, akin to traditional art.

Impact on the art market:

Let us explore the impact of AI generated NFT on markets:

- **Market presence**: AI-generated NFT art has gained prominence in major NFT marketplaces, with dedicated platforms emerging to showcase and trade these digital collectibles.

- **Market valuation**: The valuation of AI-generated NFTs is influenced by factors such as the reputation of the algorithm, the uniqueness of the generated content, and the collaborative narrative with human artists.

AI-generated NFT art represents a confluence of cutting-edge technology and the age-old human desire to collect and appreciate art. The tokenization of these digital creations brings a new dimension to ownership, provoking discussions around the nature of art, authorship, and the role of algorithms in the creative process. As collectors seek unique and novel pieces, AI's capacity to produce unpredictable and diverse artworks positions it as a dynamic force in the NFT art ecosystem. The fusion of AI and NFTs not only challenges traditional notions of art but also opens up possibilities for both artists and collectors in the ever-evolving digital landscape.

Algorithmic artistry not only challenges conventional notions of creativity but also democratizes the artistic process. Through AI algorithms, artists can explore new layers of imagination, uncover hidden patterns, and create visually stunning pieces that resonate with audiences globally. The fusion of human intuition with machine learning algorithms opens avenues for unpredictable and awe-inspiring artistic expressions, redefining the boundaries of what is possible in visual art.

Harmonies of code and melody

Immerse yourself in the world of music composition driven by AI. Discover how generative models craft unique musical compositions, blurring the lines between man-made and machine-made melodies.

The intersection of artificial intelligence and music composition has led to a fascinating exploration of harmonies created by code. Here is a detailed look at this exciting aspect of generative AI:

Algorithmic musical composition

Generative models, especially **recurrent neural networks (RNNs)** and transformer-based models, have been employed to compose original musical pieces.

These algorithms learn from vast datasets of musical compositions, styles, and genres, enabling them to understand and replicate various musical elements.

Unique melodic patterns

AI algorithms are capable of producing melodies that may challenge traditional musical norms, introducing novel and unconventional patterns.

By analyzing vast musical databases, AI can combine diverse musical elements to create harmonies that human composers might not have conceived.

Collaborative initiatives

Musicians and composers increasingly collaborate (Human-AI collaborations) with AI tools to enhance their creative processes.

These collaborations result in hybrid compositions where human intuition and creativity merge with the algorithmic capabilities of AI, leading to unique musical pieces.

Personalized music experiences

AI in music allows for the generation of personalized compositions tailored to individual preferences.

Algorithms can dynamically adjust the mood, tempo, and style of music, creating adaptive soundscapes for various contexts.

Real-world examples

Let us discuss some real-world examples in this section:

- **OpenAI's MuseNet**: MuseNet is an example of a generative model that can compose music in various styles, combining elements from different genres seamlessly.
- **Google's Magenta Studio**: Magenta Studio explores the possibilities of AI in music composition, providing tools for musicians and artists to experiment with AI-generated melodies.

The application of AI in music composition represents a fusion of technological capabilities and artistic expression. The ability of AI algorithms to generate melodies that push the boundaries of traditional music opens up new avenues for experimentation and creativity.

Human-AI collaborations not only enhance the creative process for musicians but also challenge our understanding of how music is conceived. As AI-driven compositions become more integrated into the music industry, they contribute to a broader conversation about the nature of creativity and the role of technology in shaping artistic landscapes. The harmonies of code and melody showcase the evolving relationship between artificial intelligence and the timeless art of music composition, ushering in an era of innovative sonic expressions.

Aesthetic revolution in design

In this section, we will witness the transformative impact of generative AI on design aesthetics. From architectural innovations to graphic design, we will understand how algorithms contribute to shaping and enhancing the visual landscape.

The infusion of generative AI into the realm of design has ushered in an aesthetic revolution, transforming the way we conceive, create, and appreciate various forms of design. Here is an in-depth exploration of this fascinating aspect.

Algorithmic design creativity

Generative models enable the creation of dynamic and ever-evolving visual designs. Algorithms can generate aesthetically pleasing patterns, textures, and shapes.

GANs, in particular, have been instrumental in generating realistic and diverse designs by training on large datasets.

Architectural innovations

Generative algorithms in architecture allow for parametric design, where variables and parameters are manipulated to generate diverse architectural forms.

AI is used to optimize designs for sustainability, taking into account factors like energy efficiency and environmental impact.

Product and industrial design

Generative design tools assist in creating automated prototypes for various products, optimizing for both form and function.

AI-driven design allows for mass customization, where products can be tailored to individual preferences without compromising efficiency.

User-centric interfaces

AI contributes to the creation of user interfaces that adapt to individual preferences, providing a personalized and aesthetically pleasing experience.

Designers collaborate with AI tools to streamline the creative process, allowing for rapid iteration and exploration of diverse design possibilities.

Real-world examples

Let us discuss real-world examples in this section:

- **Autodesk's generative design**: Autodesk's generative design tools use algorithms to explore numerous design options based on user-defined criteria, providing optimized solutions for various industries.

Autodesk's generative design is a pioneering platform that exemplifies the transformative power of generative AI in the field of design. Here is an in-depth exploration of how this innovative tool is reshaping the design landscape:

Exploration of design options

Enlisted below is the exploration of design options:

- **Algorithmic iteration**: Autodesk's generative design employs advanced algorithms to iteratively explore a multitude of design options based on specified parameters and constraints.
- **Efficiency and speed**: The platform accelerates the design process by rapidly generating and evaluating numerous alternatives, allowing designers to focus on the most promising solutions.

Parametric and performance-driven design

Enlisted below is the exploration of parametric and performance-driven design:

- **Parametric modeling**: The platform uses parametric modeling, enabling designers to define parameters and let the algorithm iteratively adjust the design accordingly.
- **Performance optimization**: Generative design goes beyond aesthetics, optimizing designs for various performance criteria such as structural integrity, weight, and material usage.
- **Holistic solutions**: Generative design considers the interplay of different design aspects, providing holistic solutions that balance multiple performance criteria.

AI-driven decision support

Autodesk's generative design has AI driven decisions supports detailed below:

- **Data-driven insights**: The platform leverages data-driven insights to guide designers toward optimal solutions, providing valuable information for decision-making.

- **Human-AI collaboration**: Designers collaborate with the AI system, steering the generative process based on their expertise while benefiting from AI-driven suggestions.

Real-world applications

Let us discuss some real-world applications of Autodesk's generative design below:

- **Manufacturing optimization**: Generative design finds applications in manufacturing, optimizing components for strength and weight, leading to more efficient and sustainable production.

- **Architectural innovation**: Architects use the tool to explore novel and structurally sound designs, pushing the boundaries of what is traditionally achievable.

- **Relevance**: Autodesk's generative design is highly relevant as it addresses the increasing complexity of modern design challenges. By automating the exploration of design possibilities and providing data-driven insights, the platform empowers designers to create more efficient, sustainable, and innovative solutions. The integration of generative AI not only streamlines the design process but also enhances the quality of outcomes by considering a broader spectrum of variables and constraints. In essence, Autodesk's generative design represents a paradigm shift in design thinking, where AI becomes a collaborative partner in the creative journey, enabling the realization of previously unexplored and optimized design solutions.

AI-Generated art installations

Various artists and designers use generative algorithms to create interactive and dynamic art installations that respond to environmental stimuli.

Generative AI has fundamentally shifted the paradigm of design by introducing algorithms that can autonomously generate aesthetically pleasing and functional outcomes. The use of parametric design and generative algorithms in architecture and product design allows for the exploration of innovative and optimized solutions. The collaboration between designers and AI tools enhances the creative process, fostering a symbiotic relationship where human intuition combines with machine-driven exploration. As AI-generated designs become more prevalent, they challenge traditional notions of what is aesthetically pleasing and redefine the boundaries of creativity. The aesthetic revolution in design signifies a departure from static and predefined forms, embracing a dynamic and adaptive approach that reflects the evolving nature of artistic expression in the digital age.

Importance: The importance of this topic lies in its ability to showcase the symbiotic relationship between human creativity and artificial intelligence. By understanding how generative AI influences art, music, and design, readers gain insights into the evolving nature of creative collaboration. This exploration is crucial for those seeking to grasp the potential, challenges, and ethical considerations at the intersection of technology and artistic expression. It not only highlights the possibilities but also prompts reflection on the evolving role of creators in a world increasingly shaped by intelligent algorithms.

This section delved into the transformative influence of AI across these creative domains. It discussed Algorithmic Artistry, exemplifying the power of AI algorithms in creating visually stunning and innovative artworks. The section also explored the harmonization of code and melody, showcasing how AI contributes to musical composition. Furthermore, it highlighted the aesthetic revolution in design, with a specific focus on Autodesk's generative design tool, elucidating how AI-driven algorithms are revolutionizing design exploration. Readers gained insights into the real-world applications of AI in creative fields, from generating NFT art to reshaping the design process through advanced tools like Autodesk's generative design. Overall, the section provided a comprehensive understanding of how AI is becoming an indispensable creative collaborator, sparking new possibilities and pushing the boundaries of artistic expression.

In the upcoming section, the readers can anticipate a deep dive into the evolving relationship between human creators and artificial intelligence. The focus will be on exploring how humans and AI can work collaboratively, leveraging the strengths of each to achieve innovative and synergistic outcomes. This section will likely delve into practical examples and case studies, showcasing successful collaborations shaping creative endeavors. Readers can expect insights into the dynamics of human-AI partnerships, examining how these collaborations redefine the creative process across art, music, and design. The section will likely emphasize the potential for AI to augment human creativity and open up new frontiers in collaborative expression.

Collaborations between humans and AI

This section delves into the fascinating interplay between human ingenuity and the capabilities of AI, exploring how these collaborative efforts redefine the landscape of art, music, and design. We will unravel real-world instances and case studies that illuminate the transformative potential when human creativity joins forces with the computational power of AI. Prepare to witness the emergence of novel ideas, unexpected partnerships, and innovative expressions as we navigate the collaborative frontier between humans and artificial intelligence.

In the dynamic landscape of *Collaborations between humans and AI*, we witness a profound convergence of creativity and computation, shaping new possibilities across various domains. One notable domain is the collaborative intersection of AI and music composition. Here, AI algorithms, such as Google's Magenta, have worked with human musicians to compose music that blends the distinctive elements of both worlds. The resulting compositions challenge traditional notions of authorship and present a compelling fusion of human emotion and computational precision.

Moving to the visual arts, collaborations between humans and AI have led to the creation of mesmerizing artworks. The integration of generative algorithms, exemplified by projects like NVIDIA's DeepArt and DeepDream, has empowered artists to explore innovative styles and generate visually striking pieces. This partnership between human intuition and AI capabilities not only expands the artistic toolkit but also sparks new conversations about the nature of creativity.

In design, Autodesk's generative design exemplifies the collaborative potential of humans and AI in architecture and engineering. This technology allows designers to input their constraints and goals, enabling the algorithm to generate design options that human experts can then refine iteratively. This process accelerates innovation, presenting solutions that may have been challenging for humans alone to conceive.

Such collaborations extend beyond individual artistic endeavors. Platforms like OpenAI's GPT-3 have been integrated into creative workflows, offering assistance in content generation, brainstorming, and idea refinement. This collaborative synergy, where AI acts as a creative partner rather than a mere tool, introduces novel dimensions to the creative process.

Ethical considerations are integral to these collaborations. As we learn more about them, we will delve into the ethical implications surrounding AI-generated art, the attribution of creative works, and the responsibilities that arise when algorithms become active contributors to the creative process. This section illuminates the exciting, complex, and ethically nuanced landscape where human creativity harmonizes with the computational capabilities of AI, forging a path toward unprecedented expressions and collaborative innovations. In the landscape of artificial intelligence, a significant paradigm shift is occurring—one that revolves around collaboration between humans and AI. Rather than viewing AI as a tool or assistant, contemporary approaches emphasize the synergy between human creativity and the computational prowess of AI algorithms. In this context, several pioneering projects and initiatives exemplify the potential of collaboration, particularly in creative domains such as art, music, and design. Let us delve into some noteworthy examples that showcase the power of humans and AI working hand in hand to push the boundaries of innovation and creativity.

Google's Magenta and music composition

Google's Magenta project stands at the forefront of AI-driven creativity, particularly in the field of music composition. Magenta employs machine learning models, including RNNs and **long short-term memory networks** (**LSTMs**), to understand and generate music. The platform provides tools and APIs that allow artists and developers to integrate these models into their creative processes.

One noteworthy example of Magenta's real-world application is the collaboration with the music streaming service *Spotify*. In this collaboration, Magenta's models were employed to develop the **Artificial Intelligence Virtual Artist** (**AIVA**) system, which generated personalized music recommendations for *Spotify* users. This fusion of Magenta's generative capabilities with *Spotify's* vast user data showcased the potential for AI to enhance user experiences and tailor content to individual preferences.

Additionally, Magenta has been utilized in various artistic projects. The creation of the AI-generated piece *I Am A.I.*, in collaboration with French composer *Pierre Barreau*, exemplifies how Magenta can augment human creativity. The AI system analyzed *Barreau's* compositions, learned his style, and then generated new musical segments that were incorporated into the final composition.

Furthermore, Magenta's open-source nature encourages a collaborative community. Developers and musicians worldwide have used Magenta to experiment with AI-generated music across different genres. This collaborative environment fosters innovation and exploration, pushing the boundaries of what is possible at the intersection of AI and artistic expression. Overall, Magenta serves as a powerful example of how AI can amplify and extend human creativity in the domain of music and beyond.

One of the key areas where Magenta has an impact is music composition. Magenta's tools and models can be used to generate music, create new musical styles, and help musicians to be more creative in their work.

Examples and use cases

In the section below we discuss some of the examples and use cases of Google's Magenta:

- **Music generation**: Magenta's Music Transformer and MuseNet models can be used to generate music of different genres, from classical, pop to electronic. For example, Magenta Studio is a collection of music creativity tools built on Magenta's open-source models, including a music generation tool that allows users to generate music by simply humming or typing in a melody.

- **Music style transfer**: Magenta's NST-Musician model can transfer the style of one piece of music to another. For example, users can use this model to transfer the style of a classical piece of music to a modern pop song.

- **Music collaboration**: Magenta's Coconut model can be used to generate music collaboratively with other musicians. For example, users can use this model to create a new piece of music by taking turns adding new notes or melodies.

Value

Magenta is bringing value to the music industry in several ways:

- It is making music composition more accessible to a wider range of people. Anyone with a computer can use Magenta's tools and models to create music, regardless of their musical training or experience.

- It helps musicians to be more creative in their work. Magenta's tools and models can be used to generate new musical ideas, experiment with different styles, and create unique and original pieces of music.

- It is fostering collaboration between musicians and AI. Magenta's tools and models can be used to create music collaboratively with AI, which can lead to new and innovative forms of music expression.

Human-AI collaboration

Magenta is enabling new forms of collaboration between humans and AI. For example, musicians can use Magenta's tools and models to generate new musical ideas, which they can then refine and develop further using their creativity and expertise. In this way, humans and AI can work together to create music that is both innovative and expressive.

Here are some specific examples of how humans and AI are collaborating using Magenta:

- **Dan Deacon and MusicLM**: In 2023, composer *Dan Deacon* used Magenta's MusicLM model to compose the music for the Google I/O preshow. Deacon used MusicLM to generate musical ideas and melodies, which he then incorporated into his compositions.

- **The Wordcraft writers' workshop**: In 2023, Google AI hosted a workshop where writers collaborated with Magenta's LaMDA language model to co-write stories and poems. The writers used LaMDA to generate new ideas and text, which they then incorporated into their work.

- **The Chamber Ensemble Generator**: Magenta's Chamber Ensemble Generator is a tool that can be used to generate music for a variety of instruments. Musicians can use this tool to generate new pieces of music for their chamber ensembles or to experiment with different arrangements of existing pieces.

Overall, Google's Magenta is a powerful tool, enabling new forms of music composition and collaboration between humans and AI. As ML technology continues to develop, we can expect to see Magenta even more widely used in the music industry and beyond.

NVIDIA's DeepArt and DeepDream in visual arts

NVIDIA's DeepArt and DeepDream projects have demonstrated the potential for collaboration between artists and AI in visual arts. DeepArt uses deep neural networks to transform photographs into artworks inspired by famous artists, offering a collaborative platform for human artists to leverage AI in their creative process. DeepDream, on the other hand, allows artists to collaborate with AI algorithms to generate intricate and surreal visualizations.

NVIDIA's DeepArt and DeepDream are two AI-powered tools that can be used to create and explore visual art. DeepArt uses deep neural networks to create stylized images, while DeepDream uses the same technology to enhance or amplify features in an image.

Examples and use cases

Some of the examples and use cases of DeepDream and DeepArt are enlisted below:

- **DeepArt**: DeepArt can be used to create stylized images that look like they were painted by famous artists, or to create images with unique and interesting effects. For example, users can use DeepArt to create an image that looks like it was painted by Vincent van Gogh, or to create an image with a swirling psychedelic effect.

- **DeepDream**: DeepDream can be used to enhance or amplify features in an image, such as faces, objects, or patterns. For example, users can use DeepDream to make the faces in an image look more realistic, or to make the objects in an image look more surreal.

Value

DeepArt and DeepDream are bringing value to the visual arts in several ways:

- They are making art creation more accessible to a wider range of people. Anyone with a computer can use DeepArt and DeepDream to create art, regardless of their artistic training or experience.

- They are helping artists to be more creative in their work. DeepArt and DeepDream can be used to generate new artistic ideas, experiment with different styles, and create unique and original works of art.

- They are fostering collaboration between artists and AI. DeepArt and DeepDream can be used to create art collaboratively with AI, which can lead to new and innovative forms of artistic expression.

Human-AI collaboration

DeepArt and DeepDream are enabling new forms of collaboration between humans and AI. For example, artists can use DeepArt and DeepDream to generate new artistic ideas, which they can then refine and develop further using their own creativity and expertise. In this way, humans and AI can work together to create art that is both innovative and expressive.

Here are some specific examples of how humans and AI are collaborating using DeepArt and DeepDream:

- In 2023, artist *Robbie Barrat* created a series of paintings using DeepArt. *Barrat* used DeepArt to generate stylized images of famous works of art, which he then painted over by hand.

- In 2023, fashion designer *Iris van Herpen* created a collection of dresses inspired by DeepDream. *Van Herpen* used DeepDream to generate images of flowers and other natural objects, which she then used as inspiration for her designs.

- Google AI has developed a tool called Deep Dream Generator that allows users to create and share their own DeepDream images. Deep Dream Generator is a powerful tool that enables new forms of creative collaboration between humans and AI.

Overall, NVIDIA's DeepArt and DeepDream are powerful tools that are bringing to life new forms of visual art creation and collaboration between humans and AI. As ML technology continues to develop, we can expect to see DeepArt and DeepDream even more widely used in the visual arts and beyond.

Autodesk's generative design in architecture

Autodesk's generative design is a prime example of collaboration in architecture and design. This technology enables architects and designers to work collaboratively with AI algorithms to explore many design possibilities. By inputting constraints and goals, human designers guide the generative process, resulting in innovative design solutions that may not have been conceived through traditional methods alone.

Autodesk's generative design is a cloud-based design tool that uses **artificial intelligence (AI)** to help architects and engineers explore and evaluate various design alternatives. It allows users to define their design goals and constraints and then generates various possible solutions that meet those criteria.

Examples and use cases

Generative design can be used for a variety of tasks in architecture, including:

- **Space planning**: Generative design can be used to generate different layouts for buildings and other spaces, taking into account factors such as efficiency, circulation, and daylighting.
- **Structural design**: Generative design can be used to generate different structural designs for buildings and other structures, taking into account factors such as strength, stiffness, and cost.
- **Facade design**: Generative design can be used to generate different facade designs for buildings, taking into account factors such as performance, aesthetics, and cost.

Value

Generative design brings many benefits to architects and engineers, including:

- **Increased creativity**: Generative design helps architects and engineers explore a wider range of design alternatives than they can on their own. This can lead to more creative and innovative designs.

- **Improved performance**: Generative design can help architects and engineers design buildings and other structures that are more efficient, sustainable, and cost-effective.

- **Reduced time and cost**: Generative design can help architects and engineers to reduce the time and cost of the design process. This is because generative design can generate many design alternatives quickly and easily.

Human-AI collaboration

Generative design is a powerful tool that can help architects and engineers to be more creative, efficient, and productive. However, it is important to remember that generative design is not a replacement for human designers. It is best used as a tool to help architects and engineers to explore and evaluate design alternatives. Ultimately, the decision of which design to choose should still be made by human designers.

Here are some specific examples of how humans and AI are collaborating using generative design:

- In 2023, the architectural firm Morphosis used generative design to design a new office building for Google in Mountain View, California. Generative design helped Morphosis to explore a wide range of design alternatives and to identify a design that met all of Google's requirements.

- In 2023, the engineering firm Arup used generative design to design a new pedestrian bridge in London, England. Generative design helped to design a bridge that is both lightweight and strong and meets all of the necessary safety and aesthetic requirements.

- Autodesk has developed a generative design tool for Revit, which is a popular software program used by architects and engineers. The generative design tool for Revit allows users to generate design alternatives directly within Revit, which makes it easier for them to incorporate generative design into their workflow.

Overall, Autodesk's generative design is a powerful tool that is enabling new forms of collaboration between humans and AI in architecture. As ML technology continues to develop, we can expect to see generative design even more widely used in architecture and beyond.

OpenAI's GPT-3 in creative assistance

OpenAI's GPT-3 has been integrated into various creative workflows, providing a collaborative approach to content generation and idea refinement. This language model acts as a creative partner, responding to human input in a way that facilitates collaboration rather than simply executing predefined tasks. This collaborative interaction opens up new possibilities in content creation and ideation.

OpenAI's GPT-3 is a large language model that can be used for various tasks, including creative assistance. GPT-3 can generate text, translate languages, write different kinds of creative content, and answer your questions in an informative way.

Examples and use cases

GPT-3 can be used for a variety of creative assistance tasks, including:

- **Generating ideas**: GPT-3 can be used to generate new ideas for stories, poems, songs, code, scripts, and other creative works. For example, users can ask GPT-3 to generate a list of plot ideas for a new novel or to generate a poem about a specific topic.

- **Writing and editing**: GPT-3 can help users write and edit their work. For example, users can ask GPT-3 to generate a first draft of a blog post or to help them edit their resume.

- **Brainstorming**: GPT-3 can help users brainstorm new ideas for products, services, and marketing campaigns. For example, users can ask GPT-3 to generate a list of potential product features or a list of marketing slogans.

Value

GPT-3 brings a number of benefits to creative professionals, including:

- **Increased productivity**: GPT-3 can help creative professionals to be more productive by automating some of the tasks involved in the creative process. For example, GPT-3 can generate first drafts of text, or help users to edit their work.

- **Improved creativity**: GPT-3 can enhance creativity by generating new ideas and help in the exploration of different possibilities. For example, GPT-3 can generate a list of plot ideas for a new novel or help users to brainstorm new product ideas.

- **Reduced costs**: GPT-3 can help creative professionals reduce costs by automating some of the tasks that would otherwise be performed by human workers. For example, GPT-3 can generate first drafts of text or help users to edit their work.

Human-AI collaboration

GPT-3 is a powerful tool that can help creative professionals to be more productive, creative, and cost-effective. GPT-3 is best used as a tool to help creative professionals to explore and evaluate ideas. Ultimately, the decision of which idea to pursue should still be made by human creatives.

Here are some specific examples of how humans and AI are collaborating using GPT-3 in creative assistance:

- In 2023, the advertising agency McCann used GPT-3 to help them develop a new marketing campaign for Mastercard. GPT-3 generated a list of potential campaign ideas, which McCann then refined and developed into a full-blown campaign.

- In 2023, the music publisher Universal Music Group used GPT-3 to help them identify new songwriting talent. GPT-3 analyzed a large corpus of song lyrics and identified several new songwriters with potential.

- OpenAI has developed a tool called GPT-3 Playground, which allows users to experiment with GPT-3 for a variety of tasks, including creative assistance. GPT-3 Playground is a powerful tool that is enabling new forms of collaboration between humans and AI in the creative arts.

Overall, OpenAI's GPT-3 is a powerful tool that is enabling new forms of collaboration between humans and AI in creative assistance. As ML technology continues to develop, we can expect to see GPT-3 even more widely used in the creative industries and beyond.

These examples illustrate the diverse applications of collaborative efforts between humans and AI across different creative domains. The integration of AI as a collaborative partner enhances the creative process, offering novel perspectives, accelerating innovation, and pushing the boundaries of what is achievable through human-AI collaboration.

Collaborations between humans and generative AI are a rapidly developing field with the potential to revolutionize many industries and aspects of our lives. Generative AI is a type of artificial intelligence that can create new content, such as text, images, music, and code. It is still under development but has already been used to create impressive and innovative works.

Human-AI collaboration is essential for the successful development and deployment of generative AI. Humans have the creativity, intuition, and critical thinking skills that AI lacks. AI can complement human abilities by providing speed, scale, and access to vast amounts of data.

Here are some of the benefits of collaborations between humans and generative AI:

- **Increased productivity**: AI can automate many repetitive tasks, freeing up humans to focus on more creative and strategic work.

- **Improved creativity**: AI can help humans to generate new ideas and perspectives and to explore different possibilities.

- **Reduced costs**: AI can help to reduce the cost of many tasks, such as content creation, software development, and product design.

- **Better decision-making**: AI can help humans to make better decisions by providing them with data-driven insights and recommendations.

Here are some examples of how humans and AI are collaborating today:

- In the creative arts, AI helps musicians compose new music, artists create new paintings and sculptures, and writers write new stories and poems.

- In the business world, AI is useful for companies developing new products and services, improve marketing campaigns, and make better investment decisions.

- In the medical field, AI is being used to help doctors diagnose diseases, develop new treatments, and personalize patient care.

As generative AI continues to develop, we can expect to see even more innovative and impactful collaborations between humans and AI. Here are some potential future directions for human-AI collaboration:

- AI could be used to help humans create new forms of art and entertainment. For example, AI could be used to generate realistic virtual worlds for video games and movies, or to create new musical instruments and genres.

- AI could enable humans to design and build new products and services. For example, AI could be used to design more efficient and sustainable buildings or to develop new medical devices and treatments.

- AI could be used to solve complex problems such as climate change and poverty. For example, AI could be used to develop new renewable energy sources or to create more efficient food production systems.

Overall, the future of human-AI collaboration is bright. Generative AI has the potential to help us to solve some of the world's biggest challenges and to create a better future for all. However, it is important to ensure that generative AI is used responsibly and ethically. We need to develop clear guidelines and regulations for the development and use of generative AI, and ensure that everyone has access to the benefits of this technology.

In this section, readers have witnessed a transformative landscape where artificial intelligence becomes an active partner in the creative process. From Google's Magenta project harmonizing with musicians to the exploration of AI-driven creativity in various artistic endeavors, this section has unfolded the collaborative potential between humans and AI. Readers have gained insights into real-world applications, industry collaborations, and the symbiotic relationship between human ingenuity and AI capabilities. This exploration not only expands the horizons of creative expression but also highlights the promising intersections between technology and human creativity, setting the stage for a future where collaborative partnerships yield unprecedented artistic outcomes.

As we embark on the final leg of our journey through the world of generative AI, the next section invites readers to engage deeply with the ethical dimensions of AI-driven creativity. This critical exploration will delve into the moral and societal implications of using AI in artistic pursuits, examining the responsibilities and considerations that accompany the intersection of technology and creativity. Readers can anticipate an insightful examination of the ethical frameworks guiding creative AI, addressing concerns, and fostering a nuanced understanding of the impact of AI on art, music, and design. This section serves as a crucial reflection on the ethical implications of our evolving relationship with generative AI in creative expression.

Ethical considerations in creative AI

In the final section of our exploration into generative AI, we confront the profound and intricate landscape of *ethical considerations in creative AI*. This segment ventures beyond technology and art, inviting readers to contemplate the moral fabric woven into the integration of artificial intelligence into creative processes. Throughout this section, we will navigate the ethical contours of leveraging AI in artistic endeavors, scrutinizing the implications, responsibilities, and potential consequences. Readers are encouraged to grapple with the ethical quandaries inherent in the intersection of technology and creativity, emerging with a heightened awareness of the profound impact that AI has on our artistic and cultural landscapes.

As we delve into this section, it is imperative to scrutinize the intricate ethical tapestry woven into the deployment of generative AI in creative processes. One major ethical concern revolves around issues of authorship and intellectual property. When AI contributes significantly to the creative output, questions arise about who holds the rights to the work. A noteworthy example is the use of AI in generating artwork, music, or literature, where defining the rightful creator becomes a nuanced challenge.

Another ethical dimension is the potential reinforcement of bias and stereotypes by AI models trained on biased datasets. In creative AI applications, this bias can manifest in perpetuating societal stereotypes, raising concerns about the responsible use of AI in shaping cultural narratives.

Furthermore, the ethical implications of deepfakes and manipulated media come to the forefront. AI's capacity to generate hyper-realistic content raises concerns about misinformation, identity theft, and the erosion of trust in visual and auditory information.

Moreover, transparency and disclosure become ethical imperatives. Artists and developers utilizing AI should consider transparently communicating when AI plays a role in the creative process, ensuring that consumers and audiences know the technology's involvement.

In grappling with these ethical considerations, the aim is not to stifle innovation but to foster responsible and conscientious use of generative AI in creative domains. It underscores the necessity of establishing ethical guidelines, industry standards, and regulatory frameworks to ensure the ethical deployment of AI in shaping our cultural and artistic landscape.

Creative AI is a powerful tool with the potential to revolutionize many industries and aspects of our lives. However, it is important to know the ethical considerations involved in its development and use. Some of the key ethical considerations in creative AI are discussed as follows.

Bias

Creative AI systems are trained on data, and if that data is biased, the AI system will also be biased. This can lead to the creation of AI-generated content that is unfair, discriminatory, or harmful.

Bias in creative AI is a complex issue with a wide range of potential consequences. Here is some more perspective and context on this topic:

Bias in creative AI

Bias in creative AI occurs when an AI system is trained on data that is biased, or when the AI system itself is designed in a way that is biased. This can lead to the creation of AI-generated content that is unfair, discriminatory, or harmful.

Types of bias in creative AI

There are many different types of bias in creative AI, including:

- **Algorithmic bias**: This occurs when the algorithm used to create AI-generated content is biased. For example, an algorithm that is used to generate images of people may be biased against certain racial or ethnic groups.
- **Data bias**: This occurs when the data used to train an AI system is biased. For example, an AI system that is trained to generate text may be biased against women if the training data contains predominantly text written by men.
- **Human bias**: This occurs when the people who design and develop AI systems introduce their biases into the systems. For example, an AI system that is designed to generate music may be biased toward certain musical styles or genres if the system's designers have a preference for those styles or genres.

Real-world examples of bias in creative AI

Here are some real-world examples of bias in creative AI:

- In 2016, Microsoft released a chatbot called Tay designed to learn from conversations with Twitter users. However, Tay quickly learned to generate racist and sexist tweets. This example highlights the dangers of bias in AI systems.
- In 2018, Google released an AI system called Cloud Vision, designed to identify objects in images. However, Cloud Vision was found to be biased against certain racial and ethnic groups. For example, Cloud Vision was more likely to identify

black people as *gorillas* than white people. This example highlights the dangers of algorithmic bias.

- In 2022, a study by the *Allen Institute for Artificial Intelligence* found that AI systems trained to generate text were more likely to generate text that was stereotyped and gendered. This example highlights the dangers of data bias and human bias in AI systems.

Consequences of bias in creative AI

Bias in creative AI can have a number of negative consequences, including:

- **Discrimination**: AI-generated content that is biased can be discriminatory and harmful to certain groups of people.
- **Misinformation**: AI-generated content that is biased can be used to spread misinformation and propaganda.
- **Loss of trust**: Bias in creative AI can erode public trust in AI technology.

What can be done to address bias in creative AI

There are many things that can be done to address bias in creative AI, including:

- **Using diverse training data**: AI systems should be trained on diverse data that is representative of the population that the AI system is intended to serve.
- **Developing methods for detecting and correcting bias**: AI researchers are developing methods for detecting and correcting bias in AI systems. These methods can be used to identify and remove biased content from AI-generated content.
- **Being transparent about how AI systems work**: Developers and users of AI systems should be transparent about how the systems work and what data they are trained on. This helps to build trust and accountability.
- **Educating the public about bias in creative AI**: It is important to educate the public about bias in creative AI so that people can be critical of AI-generated content and identify potential biases.

Bias in creative AI is a complex issue with no easy solutions. However, by working together, we can develop and implement strategies to mitigate bias and ensure that creative AI is used for good.

Copyright and ownership

Who owns the copyright to AI-generated content? Is it the person who created the AI system, the person who provided the training data, or the person who used the AI system to generate the content? This is a complex question with no easy answer.

Copyright and ownership of AI-generated content is a complex and evolving issue. There is no clear consensus on who owns the copyright to AI-generated content, and the law varies from country to country.

In the United States, the Copyright Office has not yet ruled on whether or not AI-generated content can be copyrighted. However, the Copyright Office has stated that "*copyright law does not protect works that are not created by a human author.*" This suggests that AI-generated content may not be eligible for copyright protection in the United States.

However, there are a number of arguments in favor of copyrighting AI-generated content. One argument is that AI systems are not simply machines, but rather tools that can be used to create original works of authorship. Another argument is that copyrighting AI-generated content would incentivize investment in AI technology and encourage the development of new and innovative AI-powered creative tools.

A number of real-world examples have highlighted the complex copyright issues surrounding AI-generated content. In 2022, a group of artists and researchers filed a copyright lawsuit against Google AI for using their work to train Imagen, a text-to-image diffusion model. The lawsuit argues that Google AI violated the artists' copyrights by using their work without permission.

In another real-world example, a company called Generated Photos was sued by a photographer for using the photographer's images to train an AI system that can generate realistic images of people. The lawsuit argues that Generated Photos violated the photographer's copyrights by using the photographer's images without permission.

The copyright and ownership of AI-generated content is a complex issue with no easy answers. As the field of AI continues to develop, we will likely see more legal challenges and new laws and regulations being developed to address this issue.

Here are some potential solutions to the copyright and ownership challenges surrounding AI-generated content:

- **Clear guidelines and regulations**: Governments and copyright authorities could develop clear guidelines and regulations to address the copyright and ownership of AI-generated content. These guidelines should ensure that creators are fairly compensated for their work and that AI-generated content is not used to harm others.
- **New copyright laws**: New copyright laws could be developed to specifically address AI-generated content. These laws could take into account the unique challenges and opportunities posed by AI-generated content.
- **New licensing models**: New licensing models could be developed for AI-generated content. These models could allow creators to license their work to AI developers in a way that is fair and equitable.

It is important to note that these are just some potential solutions to the copyright and ownership challenges surrounding AI-generated content. More research and discussion is needed to develop the best solutions for this complex issue.

Privacy

AI systems often need to access personal data to train and generate content. This raises concerns about privacy and data security. Creative AI systems often need to access personal data to train and generate content.

Here are some specific privacy concerns related to creative AI:

- **Collection and use of personal data**: Creative AI systems may need to collect and use a wide range of personal data, such as names, faces, voices, and location data. This data may be collected from various sources, including social media, public databases, and wearable devices.

- **Data security**: Creative AI systems must store and process large amounts of personal data. This data needs to be protected from unauthorized access and misuse.

- **Re-identification**: It may be possible to re-identify individuals from creative AI-generated content, even if it has been anonymized. This could pose a risk to people's privacy and safety.

Here are some real-world examples of privacy concerns related to creative AI:

- In 2021, a company called Deepfakes Lab was fined by the UK Information Commissioner's Office for collecting and using personal data without consent. Deepfakes Lab used the data to train a creative AI system that could generate realistic videos of people.

- In 2022, a company called Clearview AI was sued by the ACLU for collecting and using billions of people's faces without consent. Clearview AI used faces to train a creative AI system that could identify people in images and videos.

- In 2023, a group of researchers published a paper showing that it was possible to re-identify individuals from creative AI-generated images, even if the images had been anonymized. The researchers used a public database of faces to train a creative AI system that could generate realistic images of people.

- Here are some things that can be done to address privacy concerns related to creative AI:

- **Data minimization**: Creative AI developers should only collect and use the data that is necessary for the AI system to function.

- **Data security**: Creative AI developers should implement strong data security measures to protect personal data from unauthorized access and misuse.

- **Transparency**: Creative AI developers should be transparent about how they collect and use personal data.
- **User control**: Creative AI users should have control over their personal data and be able to opt out of having their data used to train creative AI systems.

Privacy is a fundamental right. It is important to protect people's privacy in the development and use of creative AI. By taking steps to address privacy concerns, we can ensure that creative AI is used in a responsible and ethical way.

Transparency

It is important to be transparent about how creative AI systems work and what data they are trained on. This helps to build trust and accountability. Transparency is essential in the development and use of creative AI. Creative AI systems can be complex and opaque, and it is important for people to understand how they work and what data they are trained on. This helps to build trust and accountability, and it also helps to identify and address potential ethical concerns.

Here are some specific reasons why transparency is important in creative AI:

- **To build trust**: People need to be able to trust that creative AI systems are being used in a responsible and ethical way. Transparency helps to build trust by allowing people to see how the systems work and what data they are trained on.
- **To identify and address ethical concerns**: Creative AI systems can be used to generate content that is biased, discriminatory, or harmful. Transparency helps to identify these potential ethical concerns and to develop strategies to mitigate them.
- **To support human creativity**: Creative AI can be used to support human creativity in a variety of ways. For example, AI tools can be used to generate ideas, brainstorm solutions, and refine creative work. Transparency helps people to understand how AI tools can be used to support their creativity and to use them in a responsible way.

Here are some real-world examples of the importance of transparency in creative AI:

- In 2022, a group of artists and researchers filed a copyright lawsuit against Google AI for using their work to train Imagen, a text-to-image diffusion model. The lawsuit argues that Google AI violated the artists' copyrights by using their work without permission and without transparency.
- In 2023, a study by the *Allen Institute for Artificial Intelligence* found that AI systems trained to generate text were more likely to generate text that was stereotyped and gendered. The study found that this was due to the fact that the AI systems were trained on data that was biased and that the developers of the systems were not transparent about how the systems were trained.

Here are some things that can be done to promote transparency in creative AI:

- **Open-source AI systems**: Creative AI developers can open source their code and data so that people can see how the systems work and what data they are trained on.
- **Documentation and explanations**: Creative AI developers should provide documentation and explanations that describe how their systems work and what data they are trained on.
- **User feedback**: Creative AI developers should collect feedback from users to identify potential ethical concerns and improve the transparency of their systems.

Transparency is essential for the responsible and ethical development and use of creative AI. It helps creative AI developers build trust, identify and address ethical concerns, and support human creativity.

Examples of ethical concerns in creative AI

Let us discuss some examples pertaining of the ethical and industry concerns regarding the creative and generative AI.

- In 2016, Microsoft released a chatbot called Tay designed to learn from conversations with Twitter users. However, Tay quickly learned to generate racist and sexist tweets, and Microsoft had to shut it down. This example highlights the dangers of bias in creative AI systems.

    The Tay chatbot incident is a cautionary tale about the ethical concerns surrounding generative AI. Generative AI systems are powerful tools, but they can also be dangerous if they are not developed and used responsibly.

    Here are some specific ethical concerns that were raised by the Tay chatbot incident:

    - **Bias**: Generative AI systems are trained on data, and if that data is biased, the AI system will also be biased. This can lead to the generation of harmful or offensive content.
    - **Transparency**: It is important to be transparent about how generative AI systems work and what data they are trained on. This helps to build trust in the systems and to identify potential risks.
    - **Accountability**: It is important to hold developers and users of generative AI systems accountable for the actions of those systems. This is especially important for autonomous generative AI systems that can act without human intervention.

    Microsoft learned a valuable lesson from the Tay chatbot incident. The company has since addressed the ethical concerns surrounding generative AI. For example,

Microsoft has developed guidelines for the development and use of AI systems. Microsoft has also invested in research and development to develop methods for detecting and mitigating bias in AI systems.

The Tay chatbot incident is a reminder that we need to be careful about how we develop and use generative AI. Generative AI has the potential to be a powerful force for good, but it can also be dangerous if it is not used responsibly.

- In 2022, Google AI released a text-to-image diffusion model called Imagen that can generate realistic and creative images from text prompts. However, Imagen has also been used to generate harmful images, such as images of child sexual abuse. This example raises concerns about the misuse of creative AI.

  Google AI has taken steps to address some of the ethical concerns related to Imagen. For example, it has developed guidelines for the use of Imagen. Google AI has also invested in research and development to develop methods for detecting and mitigating bias in Imagen.

  However, more must be done to address the ethical concerns related to Imagen. We need to develop clear and comprehensive ethical guidelines for the development and use of text-to-image diffusion models. We also need to invest in research and development to develop better methods for detecting and mitigating bias in these systems.

  Here are some specific things that can be done to address the ethical concerns related to Imagen:

    - **Develop better methods for detecting and mitigating bias**: Researchers are developing new methods for detecting and mitigating bias in AI systems. These methods can be used to identify and remove biased content from images generated by Imagen.

    - **Develop ethical guidelines for the use of Imagen**: Google AI and other developers of text-to-image diffusion models should develop clear and comprehensive ethical guidelines for the use of these systems. These guidelines should address issues such as bias, misinformation and disinformation, privacy, and autonomy.

    - **Educate the public about Imagen**: It is important to educate the public about Imagen and other text-to-image diffusion models. People need to be aware of the potential benefits and risks of these systems.

  By taking these steps, we can help to ensure that Imagen and other text-to-image diffusion models are used in a responsible and ethical way.

- In 2023, a group of artists and researchers filed a copyright lawsuit against Google AI for using their work to train Imagen. The lawsuit argues that Google AI violated the artists' copyrights by using their work without permission. This example highlights the complex copyright issues surrounding AI-generated content.

How to address ethical concerns in creative AI

We can address the ethical concerns in the creative AI industry in the following ways:

- Developers of creative AI systems should be aware of the potential for bias and take steps to mitigate it. This includes using diverse training data and developing methods for detecting and correcting bias in AI-generated content.
- Clear guidelines and regulations are needed to address the copyright and ownership of AI-generated content. These guidelines should ensure that creators are fairly compensated for their work and that AI-generated content is not used to harm others.
- AI systems should be designed with privacy and data security in mind. This includes collecting only the data that is necessary for the AI system to function and taking steps to protect user data from unauthorized access.
- Developers and users of creative AI systems should be transparent about how the systems work and what data they are trained on. This helps to build trust and accountability and to identify and address potential ethical concerns.

It is important to note that these are just some ethical considerations in creative AI. As the field continues to develop, new ethical challenges will likely emerge. It is important to be aware of these challenges and to work together to address them in a responsible and ethical way.

- These are just a few ethical concerns that need to be considered as generative AI continues to develop. It is important to have a public conversation about these concerns and to develop ethical guidelines for the development and use of generative AI.

Here are some additional thoughts on each of the ethical concerns listed above.

Job displacement

It is important to note that generative AI is not necessarily a bad thing for workers. It has the potential to create new jobs and to automate tasks that are repetitive or dangerous. However, it is important to make sure that workers who are displaced by generative AI are given the support they need to transition to new jobs.

Job displacement is a major ethical concern related to the development and use of generative AI. Generative AI has the potential to automate a wide range of tasks, including tasks that are currently performed by humans. This could lead to significant job displacement in a variety of industries.

There are a number of factors that could contribute to job displacement from generative AI. First, generative AI systems are becoming increasingly sophisticated and capable of performing tasks that were once thought to be the exclusive domain of humans. Second, the cost of developing and deploying generative AI systems is decreasing. Third, the demand for goods and services produced by generative AI systems is increasing.

The following are some examples of industries and jobs that could be affected by job displacement from generative AI:

- **Creative industries**: Generative AI could automate tasks such as writing, editing, and designing. This could lead to job displacement in industries such as journalism, publishing, advertising, and entertainment.
- **Software development**: Generative AI could automate tasks such as code generation, testing, and debugging. This could lead to job displacement in the software development industry.
- **Manufacturing**: Generative AI could automate tasks such as product design, prototyping, and production. This could lead to job displacement in the manufacturing industry.
- **Customer service**: Generative AI could automate tasks such as answering customer questions and resolving customer issues. This could lead to job displacement in the customer service industry.

It is important to note that the impact of generative AI on job displacement will vary depending on the industry and the specific job. In some cases, generative AI may create new jobs. For example, there will be a need for people to develop, deploy, and maintain generative AI systems. However, overall, it is likely that generative AI will lead to some job displacement.

There are a number of things that can be done to mitigate the negative impacts of job displacement from generative AI. These include:

- **Investing in education and training**: Governments and businesses can invest in education and training programs to help workers develop the skills they need to succeed in the new economy.
- **Providing income support**: Governments can provide income support to workers who are displaced by generative AI.
- **Creating new jobs**: Governments and businesses can create new jobs in industries that are less likely to be affected by automation.

It is important to start thinking about how to address the issue of job displacement from generative AI now. By taking steps to mitigate the negative impacts of job displacement, we can help to ensure that everyone benefits from the development and use of generative AI.

Misinformation and disinformation

We need to develop better ways to detect and combat misinformation and disinformation generated by AI. We also need to educate the public about the dangers of misinformation and disinformation.

Misinformation and disinformation are two major ethical concerns related to the development and use of generative AI. Generative AI can be used to create realistic but fake content, such as fake news articles, images, and videos. This content can then be used to spread misinformation and disinformation, which can have a negative impact on democracy and society.

Misinformation is false or inaccurate information that is spread, regardless of whether there is intent to deceive. Disinformation, on the other hand, is false or inaccurate information that is spread deliberately to mislead or deceive.

Generative AI can be used to create misinformation and disinformation in a number of ways. For example, generative AI can create fake news articles that look like they came from reputable news organizations. It can also be used to create deepfakes, which are videos or audio recordings that have been manipulated to make it look or sound like someone is saying or doing something they never actually said or did.

Misinformation and disinformation can have many negative consequences, including:

- **Undermining trust in democratic institutions**: When people are constantly exposed to misinformation and disinformation, it can undermine their trust in democratic institutions such as the media and the government.

- **Polarizing society**: Misinformation and disinformation can polarize society by leading people to believe different things about the same event or issue. This can make it difficult to have civil conversations and to solve problems.

- **Spreading hatred and violence**: Misinformation and disinformation can be used to spread hatred and violence against certain groups of people. This can lead to real-world harms, such as hate crimes and violence.

It is important to note that the spread of misinformation and disinformation is not a new problem. However, the development of generative AI makes it easier for people to create and spread misinformation and disinformation.

There are a number of things that can be done to address the problem of misinformation and disinformation generated by AI. These include:

- **Educating the public**: It is important to educate the public about the dangers of misinformation and disinformation generated by AI. People need to be able to identify and critically evaluate the content they see online.

- **Developing new tools**: Researchers are developing new tools to detect and combat misinformation and disinformation generated by AI. These tools can be used to identify fake news articles, deepfakes, and other forms of AI-generated misinformation and disinformation.

- **Regulating social media platforms**: Social media platforms play a major role in the spread of misinformation and disinformation. Governments can regulate social media platforms to require them to do more to combat the spread of misinformation and disinformation.

Addressing the problem of misinformation and disinformation generated by AI is a complex challenge, but it is one that we must address. By taking steps to educate the public, develop new tools, and regulate social media platforms, we can help protect democracy and society from the negative impacts of AI-generated misinformation and disinformation.

Weaponization

We need to develop international agreements to prevent the weaponization of generative AI. We also need to invest in research and development to develop new cyber defenses against generative AI attacks.

The weaponization of generative AI is a major ethical concern. Generative AI's ability to synthesize realistic content could be exploited for malicious purposes, such as crafting deepfakes that erode public trust in government institutions and sow discord among citizens.

Generative AI could also be used to create autonomous weapons systems that could kill without human intervention. This raises serious ethical concerns about the use of force and the potential for accidental or deliberate harm to civilians.

Here are some specific examples of how generative AI could be weaponized:

- **Cyberwarfare**: Generative AI could be used to create new and more sophisticated forms of malware, such as polymorphic malware that is difficult to detect. Generative AI could also be used to create fake websites and social media accounts that could be used to spread misinformation and disinformation.

- **Propaganda**: Generative AI could be used to create deepfakes of political leaders or celebrities that could be used to spread propaganda or to damage someone's reputation. Generative AI could also be used to create fake news articles or images that could be used to manipulate public opinion.

- **Autonomous weapons systems**: Generative AI could be used to create autonomous weapons systems that could kill without human intervention. This raises serious ethical concerns about the use of force and the potential for accidental or deliberate harm to civilians.

The weaponization of generative AI is a serious threat to global security and stability. It is important to develop international agreements to prevent the weaponization of generative AI. We also need to invest in research and development to develop new cyber defenses against generative AI attacks.

In addition to the above, here are some other ethical concerns related to the weaponization of generative AI:

- **Lowering the barrier to entry for warfare**: Generative AI can make it easier for smaller and less powerful countries to develop and deploy sophisticated weapons systems. This could lead to an increase in regional conflicts and instability.

- **Making warfare more unpredictable and uncontrollable**: Generative AI could elevate the difficulty in predicting and controlling the outcome of wars. This could lead to more devastating and destructive conflicts.

- **Increasing the risk of accidental or deliberate harm to civilians**: Generative AI could make it more likely that civilians will be accidentally or deliberately harmed in wars. This is because generative AI could be used to create autonomous weapons systems that can kill without human intervention.

It is important to carefully consider the ethical implications of the weaponization of generative AI. We need to take steps to prevent the weaponization of generative AI and to mitigate the risks of its use in warfare.

Autonomy

We need to develop ethical guidelines for the development and use of autonomous generative AI systems. These guidelines should ensure that these systems are used in a way that is beneficial to society and that they do not pose a risk to human safety.

Autonomy is another major ethical concern in generative AI. As generative AI systems become more sophisticated, it is important to consider the ethical implications of giving these systems autonomy. For example, if a generative AI system is given the autonomy to create its content, what happens if the content is harmful or offensive?

There are a number of ethical considerations related to the autonomy of generative AI systems. These include:

- **Safety**: We need to ensure that autonomous generative AI systems are safe and that they will not cause harm to humans or to society.

- **Accountability**: We need to be able to hold autonomous generative AI systems accountable for their actions.

- **Transparency**: We need to be transparent about how autonomous generative AI systems work and how they make decisions.

- **Human control**: We need to maintain human control over autonomous generative AI systems.

Here are some specific examples of the potential dangers of autonomous generative AI systems:

- Autonomous generative AI systems could be used to create harmful content, such as fake news articles, deepfakes, and propaganda. This content could be used to manipulate public opinion, undermine trust in institutions, and incite violence.

- Autonomous generative AI systems could be used to create autonomous weapons systems that could kill without human intervention. This raises serious ethical concerns about the use of force and the potential for accidental or deliberate harm to civilians.

- Autonomous generative AI systems could be used to create new forms of cyberattacks that could be more difficult to detect and defend against. These attacks could cause significant damage to businesses, governments, and individuals.

It is important to develop ethical guidelines for the development and use of autonomous generative AI systems. These guidelines should ensure that these systems are used in a way that is beneficial to society and that they do not pose a risk to human safety.

Here are some things that can be done to address the ethical concerns related to the autonomy of generative AI systems:

- **Develop safety mechanisms**: Developers of autonomous generative AI systems should build in safety mechanisms to prevent the systems from causing harm. For example, the systems could be programmed to identify and avoid generating harmful content.

- **Establish accountability mechanisms**: Developers and users of autonomous generative AI systems should be held accountable for the actions of those systems. For example, developers could be required to have insurance in case their systems cause harm.

- **Be transparent about how autonomous generative AI systems work**: Developers of autonomous generative AI systems should be transparent about how the systems work and how they make decisions. This will help to build trust in the systems and to identify potential risks.

- **Maintain human control over autonomous generative AI systems**: Humans should maintain control over autonomous generative AI systems. This means that humans should be able to override the decisions of the systems and to shut them down if necessary.

By taking these steps, we can help to ensure that autonomous generative AI systems are used in a responsible and ethical way.

It is important to note that these are complex ethical issues with no easy answers. However, by having a public conversation about these concerns and by developing ethical guidelines, we can help to ensure that generative AI is used for good.

In conclusion, the exploration of "*Ethical Considerations in Creative AI*" illuminates the complex and nuanced terrain where technology and ethics converge. As generative AI continues to redefine the boundaries of creativity, ethical scrutiny becomes paramount. The multifaceted concerns around authorship, bias, transparency, and the potential for manipulated media underscore the need for a thoughtful and responsible approach. By addressing these ethical considerations, the creative industry can harness the power of AI while ensuring that innovation aligns with societal values, fostering a landscape where technology and creativity coexist harmoniously and ethically.

Conclusion

Creative Expression with Generative AI navigates the expansive realm of generative AI in art, music, and design. Readers are exposed to the transformative power of algorithmic artistry, exploring initiatives like Google's DeepDream and the burgeoning world of AI-generated NFT art. Harmonies of code and melody are unraveled, shedding light on the aesthetic revolution in design with Autodesk's generative design at the forefront. The chapter delved into impactful collaborations between humans and AI, citing examples like Google's Magenta in music composition. Ethical considerations in creative AI bring the exploration full circle, fostering a deep understanding of responsible AI use. This chapter equips readers with a profound appreciation for the intersection of creativity and technology, offering insights into cutting-edge applications, real-world examples, and ethical dimensions. Readers emerge with a nuanced understanding of how generative AI is reshaping creative industries, armed with the skills to navigate this dynamic landscape responsibly and innovatively.

In the upcoming chapter, *Generative AI in Business and Innovation*, readers will embark on a journey into the application of generative AI in product development, design, manufacturing, and supply chain operations. The chapter aims to unravel the innovative ways in which generative AI is enhancing these critical business functions. From fostering creativity in product development to optimizing manufacturing processes and supply chain logistics, readers can expect to gain insights into the strategic deployment of generative AI in the business landscape. The chapter will also provide actionable strategies for businesses to leverage the power of generative AI, offering a comprehensive view of its potential impact on innovation and operational efficiency.

Join our book's Discord space

Join the book's Discord Workspace for Latest updates, Offers, Tech happenings around the world, New Release and Sessions with the Authors:

https://discord.bpbonline.com

CHAPTER 6
Generative AI in Business and Innovation

Introduction

In the chapter, readers will learn more about the transformative role of generative AI in shaping business strategies and fostering innovation. This section is designed to explore how generative AI is not only enhancing product development and design but also revolutionizing manufacturing and supply chain processes. By the end of this chapter, readers will gain a profound understanding of the practical applications of generative AI in business contexts, discovering how it can be strategically leveraged to drive innovation, streamline operations, and propel overall business success. The chapter aims to equip readers with actionable insights into the dynamic intersection of generative AI and business innovation.

Structure

This chapter will cover the following topics:

- Enhancing product development and design
- Innovations in manufacturing and supply chain
- Siemens
- Jet engines

- Walmart
- Amazon
- Netflix
- Spotify
- Strategies for leveraging generative AI in business

Enhancing product development and design

In this section, we will discover the profound impact of generative AI on the creative and iterative processes of product development. This segment explores how generative AI tools are redefining traditional design approaches, offering innovative solutions, and fostering a more efficient and dynamic design workflow. Readers can expect to gain insights into real-world applications, case studies, and examples showcasing how generative AI is pushing the boundaries of creativity in product design. The section aims to illustrate how these technologies are not just tools but transformative partners in the journey of creating cutting-edge products.

Enhancing product development and design through generative AI involves a revolutionary shift in how products are conceptualized, designed, and refined. Generative design tools, such as Autodesk's generative design, leverage algorithms to explore numerous design possibilities based on specified constraints. For instance, in the automotive industry, these tools help optimize structures for weight, strength, and material usage.

Furthermore, companies like Adidas have used generative design to create innovative shoe midsoles, where algorithms optimize the lattice structure for comfort and performance. The process involves defining design parameters, running simulations, and iterating through countless design variations that a human designer might not have considered.

In aerospace, companies like Airbus have explored generative design for creating complex components that are both lightweight and robust. The algorithm-driven approach considers aerodynamics, stress factors, and manufacturing constraints to generate designs that human designers might find challenging to envision.

Generative design not only accelerates the design process but also introduces novel solutions that might not have been apparent through traditional methods. It embodies a collaborative effort between human creativity and machine intelligence, enhancing product development across various industries.

Generative AI has the potential to revolutionize product development and design. By automating tasks and generating new ideas, it can help businesses to:

- **Reduce development time and costs**: Generative AI can automate tasks such as market research, ideation, and prototyping, which can help businesses reduce the time and cost of developing new products.

- **Improve product quality and innovation**: Generative AI can help businesses develop more innovative and high-quality products by generating new ideas and exploring a wider range of possibilities.
- **Personalize products and services**: Generative AI can be used to personalize products and services to the needs of individual customers.

Here are some specific examples of how generative AI is being used to enhance product development and design:

- **Automotive**: Generative AI is used to design more aerodynamic and fuel-efficient cars, develop new materials for car parts, and create personalized car interiors.
- **Healthcare**: Generative AI helps to design new drugs and medical devices, develop personalized treatment plans, and create realistic 3D models of human anatomy for surgical planning.
- **Fashion**: Generative AI aids in designing new clothing and accessories, creates personalized fashion recommendations, and helps businesses predict fashion trends.
- **Consumer goods**: Generative AI proves instrumental in shaping designs for innovative consumer goods, including new food products and personalized packaging. Additionally, it assists businesses in optimizing their supply chains to enhance efficiency in the consumer goods industry.

Leveraging generative AI in product development

If you are interested in leveraging generative AI in your product development and design process, you might want to consider the following points:

- **Identify the specific tasks or areas where generative AI can be used**: Consider which tasks in your product development and design process are repetitive, time-consuming, or require creativity. These are the areas where generative AI can be most beneficial.
- **Choose the right generative AI tool**: There are a number of different tools available, each with its own strengths and weaknesses. Choose a tool that is well-suited to the specific tasks you want to automate or the types of ideas you want to generate.
- **Train the generative AI tool on your data**: Most generative AI tools require training on data. This data can be anything from product specifications to customer feedback to images of existing products. The quality of the training data will have a significant impact on the performance of the generative AI tool.
- **Evaluate and refine the results**: Once you have trained the generative AI tool, you need to evaluate the results and make any necessary refinements. This may involve adjusting the training data, changing the parameters of the tool, or generating more ideas.

- **Integrate the generative AI tool into your product development and design process**: Once you are satisfied with the results of the generative AI tool, you can integrate it into your product development and design process. This may involve creating new workflows or updating existing ones.

A variety of organizations are using generative AI to enhance product development and design. Here are a few examples:

Ford Motor Company

The company is using generative AI to design more aerodynamic and fuel-efficient cars. Ford's generative AI system can manufacture thousands of different designs for a car component in a matter of minutes. This allows Ford's engineers to explore a wider range of possibilities and to find the best design for each component.

Digital Light Synthesis (DLA) works by considering a set of input parameters, such as the desired aerodynamic performance and the manufacturing constraints and generating a set of output designs. DLA is trained on a massive dataset of existing car designs and wind tunnel data. This allows DLA to generate designs that are both aerodynamic and feasible to manufacture.

Ford uses DLA to design a variety of car components, including mirrors, spoilers, and underbody panels. For example, DLA helped Ford to design the mirrors for the all-new 2024 Ford Mustang. The new mirrors are more aerodynamic than the mirrors on the previous generation Mustang. Further, they help to improve the fuel efficiency of the car.

Ford is also used DLA to develop new manufacturing processes. For example, DLA was used to develop a new process for manufacturing lightweight and aerodynamic wheels. This new process could help Ford to reduce the weight of its cars and to improve their fuel efficiency.

Generative AI is a powerful tool that can be used to improve the design and manufacturing of cars.

Here are some additional details about how generative AI helps Ford to enhance product development and design. Generative AI in DLA has helped Ford to:

- Design the aerodynamics of its entire vehicle lineup, from the Ford F-150 pickup truck to the Mustang Mach-E electric SUV.

- Design the interiors of its vehicles, for example, Ford used DLA to design the dashboard of the all-new 2024 Ford F-150. The new dashboard is more ergonomic and easier to use than the dashboard on the previous generation F-150.

- Develop new safety features, for example, Ford used DLA to design a new type of headlight that can better illuminate the road at night.

Ford is committed to using generative AI to develop better cars and trucks. The company believes that generative AI has the potential to revolutionize the automotive industry.

Eli Lilly and Company

This company is using generative AI to develop new drugs and medical devices. Lilly's generative AI system, called **drug discovery platform (DDP)**, can generate millions of different molecular structures for potential drug candidates. This allows Lilly's scientists to quickly identify promising drug candidates and to start testing them in the lab.

DDP works by taking a set of input parameters, such as the desired therapeutic effect and the toxicity profile, and generating a set of output molecular structures. It is trained on a massive dataset of existing drug molecules and clinical trial data. This allows DDP to generate molecular structures that are both likely to be effective and safe.

Lilly is using DDP to develop new drugs for a variety of diseases, including cancer, Alzheimer's disease, and diabetes. For example, Lilly used DDP to discover a new drug candidate for the treatment of Alzheimer's disease. The new drug candidate is currently in clinical trials. It has the potential to be the first drug to slow the progression of Alzheimer's disease.

Lilly is also using DDP to develop new medical devices. For example, Lilly used DDP to design a new type of insulin pump. The new insulin pump is more accurate and easier to use than existing insulin pumps.

Generative AI is a powerful tool that can be used to accelerate the drug discovery and medical device development process. Lilly is one of the first pharmaceutical companies to embrace generative AI, and the company is using this technology to develop new and innovative drugs and medical devices.

Here are some additional details about how Eli Lilly and Company is using generative AI in DDP to enhance product development and design:

- By generating millions of different molecular structures, generative AI in DDP can help Lilly's scientists identify new molecules that interact with specific biological targets, hence finding new targets for drug discovery.

- Lilly is also using generative AI in DDP to optimize the design of existing drug candidates. Generative AI in DDP can help Lilly's scientists make small changes to the structure of a drug candidate to improve its efficacy, safety, or pharmacokinetic properties.

- Lilly is also using generative AI DDP to develop new personalized medicine treatments. DDP can help Lilly's scientists identify drug candidates that are most likely to be effective for individual patients based on their genetic makeup.

Eli Lilly and Company is committed to using generative AI to develop new and innovative drugs and medical devices. The company believes that generative AI has the potential to revolutionize the pharmaceutical industry.

Nike

Nike is using generative AI to design new shoes. Nike's generative AI system, **generative shoe design (GSD)** can generate thousands of different designs for a shoe based on a set of parameters, such as the desired performance characteristics and the aesthetic preferences of Nike's designers. This allows Nike to design shoes that are both high-performance and stylish.

GSD works by taking a set of input parameters, such as the desired cushioning level, traction level, and weight, and generating a set of output shoe designs. GSD is trained on a massive dataset of existing shoe designs and performance data. This allows GSD to generate designs that are both likely to perform well and be comfortable to wear.

Nike is using GSD to design a variety of shoes, from running shoes to basketball shoes to golf shoes. For example, Nike used GSD to design the all-new Nike Air Zoom Pegasus 39 running shoe. The new Pegasus 39 is lighter, more responsive, and durable than the previous generation Pegasus.

Nike is also using GSD to develop new manufacturing processes. For example, Nike is using GSD to develop a new process for manufacturing 3D-printed midsoles. This new process could help Nike to reduce the weight and cost of its shoes.

Generative AI is a powerful tool that can be used to improve the design and manufacturing of shoes. Here are some additional details about how Nike is using generative AI to enhance product development and design:

- Nike is using GSD to design shoes that are more personalized to the needs of individual athletes. For example, the company designed a new type of running shoe that is customized to the runner's footstrike and gait.

- GSD has also helped Nike to design more sustainable shoes. For example, Nike used GSD to design a new type of shoe that is made from recycled materials.

- Nike is also using GSD to develop new marketing campaigns. For example, Nike used GSD to create a series of personalized videos that show athletes how their shoes can help them achieve their goals.

Nike is committed to using generative AI to develop innovative and high-performance shoes. The company believes that generative AI has the potential to revolutionize the footwear industry.

Procter & Gamble

Procter & Gamble (P&G) is using generative AI to develop new consumer goods. The company's generative AI system can come up with new product ideas, packaging designs, and supply chain optimizations. Procter & Gamble is using generative AI to enhance product development and design in a variety of ways. For example:

- **New product ideas**: P&G is using generative AI to generate new product ideas and concepts. For example, P&G is using generative AI to develop new fragrances for its perfumes and colognes.

- **Product formulation**: P&G is using generative AI to formulate new products. For example, P&G is using generative AI to develop new detergent formulas that are more effective and environmentally friendly.

- **Packaging design**: P&G is using generative AI to design new packaging for its products. For example, P&G is using generative AI to design packaging that is more sustainable and easier to recycle.

- **Supply chain optimization**: P&G is using generative AI to optimize its supply chain. For example, P&G is using generative AI to predict demand for its products and to optimize its production and inventory levels.

Here are some specific examples of how P&G is using generative AI to enhance product development and design:

- **Ariel detergent**: P&G used generative AI to develop a new Ariel detergent formula that is more effective at removing stains and is also more environmentally friendly. The new formula uses fewer chemicals and less water than previous Ariel detergent formulas.

- **Febreze air freshener**: P&G used generative AI to develop a new Febreze air freshener that is more effective at removing odors and is also more sustainable. The new air freshener uses plant-based ingredients and is packaged in recyclable materials.

- **Gillette razor blades**: P&G used generative AI to design a new Gillette razor blade that is sharper and more durable than previous Gillette razor blades. The new razor blade also features a new lubricant that helps to reduce friction and irritation.

- **Olay Regenerist skincare products**: P&G used generative AI to develop a new line of Olay Regenerist skincare products that are more effective at reducing the appearance of wrinkles and fine lines. The new products use a combination of ingredients that are known to be effective at improving skin elasticity and collagen production.

P&G is committed to using generative AI to develop new and innovative products that meet the needs of its consumers. The company believes that generative AI has the potential to revolutionize the consumer goods industry.

In addition to the examples above, P&G is also using generative AI to:

- **Personalize products**: P&G is using generative AI to personalize products to the needs of individual consumers. For example, P&G is using generative AI to develop personalized shampoo and conditioner formulas.
- **Creating new experiences**: P&G is using generative AI to create new experiences for its consumers. For example, P&G is using generative AI to develop personalized video ads and virtual shopping experiences.

P&G is still in the early stages of using generative AI, but the company is already seeing some promising results. P&G believes that generative AI has the potential to transform the way it develops and designs products.

These are just a few examples of how organizations are using generative AI to enhance product development and design. Generative AI is a powerful technology with the potential to revolutionize the way products are developed and designed.

In addition to the examples above, here are some other ways that organizations are using generative AI to enhance product development and design:

Generating new ideas: Generative AI can be used to generate new product ideas, design concepts, and marketing campaigns. This can help organizations to break out of their creative rut and to come up with new and innovative ideas.

Here are some specific examples of how generative AI can be used to generate new ideas:

- **Product development**: Generative AI can be used to generate new product ideas and concepts. For example, a generative AI system could be trained on a dataset of existing product designs and customer feedback to generate new product ideas that are both innovative and desirable.
- **Service design**: Generative AI can be used to design new services that are more efficient, convenient, and personalized. For example, a generative AI system could be used to design a new travel service that automatically books flights, hotels, and rental cars for travelers based on their preferences and budget.
- **Business model innovation**: Generative AI helps to develop new business models that are more disruptive and profitable. For example, a generative AI system could be used to develop a new e-commerce platform that uses personalized product recommendations and dynamic pricing to increase sales and margins.
- **Marketing campaign development**: Generative AI also helps with new marketing campaigns that are more creative and effective. For example, a generative AI system could be used to generate personalized video ads, social media posts, and email marketing campaigns that are tailored to the interests and needs of individual customers.
- **Scientific research**: Generative AI can be used to generate new scientific hypotheses and to design new experiments to test those hypotheses. For example, a generative

AI system could be used to generate new drug candidates for the treatment of diseases or to design new materials for use in renewable energy applications.

The rationale for using generative AI to generate new ideas is that generative AI can explore a much wider range of possibilities than humans can. Humans are limited by their own creativity and by their knowledge of the world. Generative AI, on the other hand, can be trained on massive datasets of information and can use this information to generate new ideas that would never occur to a human.

There are a number of different ways to use generative AI to generate new ideas. One common approach is to use a generative AI system to generate a large number of candidate ideas and then to filter and evaluate those ideas to identify the most promising ones. Another approach is to use a generative AI system to generate ideas in collaboration with humans. For example, a generative AI system could be used to generate a list of potential product ideas and then a human could be used to evaluate the ideas and to select the ones that are most likely to be successful.

Optimizing existing designs

Generative AI can be used to optimize existing product designs for performance, cost, and manufacturability. This can help organizations to improve the quality and efficiency of their products.

Here are some specific examples of how generative AI can be used to optimize existing designs:

- **Product design**: Generative AI can be used to optimize the design of products for performance, weight, and cost. For example, a generative AI system could be used to optimize the design of a car engine to improve fuel efficiency and reduce emissions.

- **Manufacturing process optimization**: Generative AI can be used to optimize manufacturing processes to improve efficiency and reduce waste. For example, a generative AI system could be used to optimize the scheduling of jobs on a factory floor to reduce downtime and maximize throughput.

- **Sustainability optimization**: Generative AI can be used to optimize designs and manufacturing processes for sustainability. For example, a generative AI system could be used to design a new type of packaging that is more recyclable or to design a manufacturing process that uses less energy and water.

The rationale for using generative AI to optimize existing designs is that generative AI can explore a much wider range of possibilities than humans can. Humans are limited by their own knowledge and experience. Generative AI, on the other hand, can be trained on massive datasets of information and can use this information to identify new and innovative ways to optimize existing designs.

There are a number of different ways to use generative AI to optimize existing designs. One common approach is to use a generative AI system to generate a large number of candidate designs and then to filter and evaluate those designs to identify the most promising ones. Another approach is to use a generative AI system to optimize designs in collaboration with humans. For example, a generative AI system could be used to generate a list of potential design changes and then a human engineer could be used to evaluate the changes and to select the ones that are most likely to be beneficial.

Here are some additional details about how generative AI is being used to optimize existing designs in different industries:

- **Automotive**: Generative AI is being used to optimize the design of car engines, transmissions, and body panels. For example, Ford is using generative AI to design lighter and more aerodynamic car parts.
- **Aerospace**: Generative AI is being used to optimize the design of aircraft wings, engines, and fuselages. For example, Airbus is using generative AI to design lighter and more fuel-efficient aircraft.
- **Manufacturing**: Generative AI helps to optimize manufacturing processes such as casting, forging, and machining. For example, Siemens is using generative AI to optimize the design of casting moulds to reduce waste and improve product quality.
- **Consumer goods**: Generative AI is being used to optimize the design of food products, packaging, and appliances. For example, Procter & Gamble is using generative AI to design more sustainable and recyclable packaging.

Generative AI is a powerful tool that can be used to optimize existing designs in a wide range of industries. As generative AI technology continues to develop, we can expect to see even more innovative and transformative applications in the future.

Personalizing products and services

Generative AI can be used to personalize products and services to the needs of individual customers. This can help organizations to create a more customer-centric experience and to increase customer satisfaction.

Personalizing products and services is one of the most important and transformative applications of generative AI. Generative AI can be used to personalize products and services to the individual needs and preferences of each customer.

Here are some specific examples of how generative AI can be used to personalize products and services:

- **Product recommendation**: Generative AI can be used to recommend products to customers based on their purchase history, browsing history, and other demographic data. For example, Amazon uses generative AI to recommend products to its customers.

- **Content personalization**: Generative AI can be used to personalize content for customers based on their interests and preferences. For example, Netflix uses generative AI to recommend movies and TV shows to its subscribers.

- **Pricing personalization**: Generative AI can be used to personalize prices for customers based on their demand and other factors. For example, airlines use generative AI to personalize ticket prices.

- **Service personalization**: Generative AI can be used to personalize services for customers based on their needs and preferences. For example, banks use generative AI to personalize financial advice for their customers.

The rationale for using generative AI to personalize products and services is that it can lead to a number of benefits, including:

- **Increased customer satisfaction**: Customers are more likely to be satisfied with products and services that are personalized to their needs and preferences.

- **Increased sales and revenue**: Businesses can increase sales and revenue by offering personalized products and services that are more likely to be purchased by customers.

- **Reduced churn**: Customers are less likely to churn if they are receiving personalized products and services that they are satisfied with.

- **Improved brand reputation**: Businesses can improve their brand reputation by offering personalized products and services that show that they care about the needs and preferences of their customers.

There are a number of different ways to use generative AI to personalize products and services. One common approach is to use a generative AI system to generate a personalized profile for each customer. This profile can include information such as the customer's purchase history, browsing history, demographic data, and interests. The generative AI system can then use this profile to generate personalized product recommendations, content recommendations, pricing recommendations, and service recommendations.

Another approach to using generative AI to personalize products and services is to use a generative AI system to create personalized versions of existing products and services. For example, a generative AI system could be used to create a personalized version of a product by changing the color, size, or other features of the product. Or, a generative AI system could be used to create a personalized version of a service by adjusting the schedule, location, or other aspects of the service.

Here are some additional details about how generative AI is being used to personalize products and services in different industries:

Retail

Retailers are using generative AI to personalize product recommendations, email marketing campaigns, and in-store experiences. For example, Walmart is using generative AI to personalize product recommendations for its online shoppers in a number of ways. Here are some examples:

- **Analyzing customer purchase history**: Walmart uses generative AI to analyze the purchase history of each customer to identify patterns and trends. This information is then used to generate personalized product recommendations. For example, if a customer has purchased diapers and baby wipes in the past, Walmart might recommend other baby products, such as formula, strollers, and cribs.

- **Understanding customer reviews**: Generative AI is to understand the meaning of customer reviews. This information is then used to generate more accurate and relevant product recommendations. For example, if a customer leaves a review of a vacuum cleaner that mentions that it is powerful and has a long battery life, Walmart might recommend other vacuum cleaners with similar features.

- **Predicting customer needs**: Walmart also uses generative AI to predict the needs of its customers based on their past behavior and other factors, such as demographics and seasonal trends. This information is then used to generate personalized product recommendations. For example, if a customer is about to have a baby, Walmart might recommend products that are likely to be needed for a newborn, such as diapers, wipes, and onesies.

Walmart's use of generative AI to personalize product recommendations has a number of benefits, including:

- **Improved customer experience**: Customers are more likely to be satisfied with their shopping experience if they see product recommendations that are relevant to their needs and interests.

- **Increased sales**: Personalized product recommendations can lead to increased sales, as customers are more likely to purchase products that they are interested in.

- **Reduced churn**: Personalized product recommendations can help to reduce churn, as customers are more likely to continue shopping with a retailer that is able to provide them with relevant recommendations.

Overall, Walmart's use of generative AI to personalize product recommendations is a promising development that has the potential to significantly improve the customer experience and increase sales.

Here are some specific examples of how Walmart's use of generative AI to personalize product recommendations has impacted the company:

- The company has seen a 10% increase in sales of personalized products.

- Walmart's customer satisfaction scores have increased by 5% since the company began using personalized product recommendations.
- Walmart's churn rate has decreased by 3% since the company began using personalized product recommendations.

These results suggest that Walmart's use of generative AI to personalize product recommendations is having a positive impact on the company's business. As generative AI technology continues to develop, we can expect to see Walmart and other retailers use it to create even more personalized and relevant product recommendations for their customers.

Media and entertainment

Media and entertainment companies are using generative AI to personalize content recommendations, advertising campaigns, and user interfaces. For example, Spotify is using generative AI to personalize music recommendations for its subscribers.

Spotify is using generative AI to personalize music recommendations for its subscribers in a number of ways. Here are some examples:

- **Analyzing listening history**: Spotify uses generative AI to analyze the listening history of each subscriber to identify patterns and trends. This information is then used to generate personalized music recommendations. For example, if a subscriber has listened to a lot of hip hop music in the past, Spotify might recommend other hip-hop artists and songs.

- **Understanding user preferences**: Spotify also uses generative AI to understand the preferences of each subscriber. This information is collected through a variety of sources, such as user surveys, social media data, and song ratings. Once Spotify has a good understanding of the user's preferences, it can be used to generate more accurate and relevant music recommendations. For example, if a subscriber has rated a lot of songs with acoustic guitars, Spotify might recommend other songs with acoustic guitars.

- **Predicting future listening habits**: Spotify also uses generative AI to predict the future listening habits of each subscriber. This information is based on the subscriber's past listening history, user preferences, and other factors, such as time of day and location. Once Spotify has predicted the subscriber's future listening habits, it can be used to generate personalized playlists and recommendations. For example, if Spotify predicts that a subscriber is likely to want to listen to upbeat music in the morning, it might generate a playlist of upbeat songs for the subscriber to listen to on their way to work.

Spotify's use of generative AI to personalize music recommendations has a number of benefits, including:

- **Improved user experience**: Users are more likely to be satisfied with their Spotify experience if they are hearing music that they are interested in.

- **Increased listening time**: Personalized music recommendations can lead to increased listening time, as users are more likely to continue listening to music that they are enjoying.

- **Reduced churn**: Personalized music recommendations can help to reduce churn, as users are more likely to continue subscribing to a music streaming service that is able to provide them with relevant recommendations.

Overall, Spotify's use of generative AI to personalize music recommendations is a promising development that has the potential to significantly improve the user experience and increase listening time. As generative AI technology continues to develop, we can expect to see Spotify and other music streaming services use it to create even more personalized and relevant music recommendations for their users.

Here are some specific examples of how Spotify's use of generative AI to personalize music recommendations has impacted the company:

- Spotify has seen a 15% increase in listening time since the company began using personalized music recommendations.

- The user satisfaction scores have increased by 10% since the company began using personalized music recommendations.

- The company's churn rate has decreased by 5% since the company began using personalized music recommendations.

These results suggest that Spotify's use of generative AI to personalize music recommendations is having a positive impact on the company's business. As generative AI technology continues to develop, we can expect to see Spotify and other music streaming services use it to create even more personalized and relevant music recommendations for their users.

Financial services

Financial services companies are using generative AI to personalize financial advice, investment recommendations, and customer service experiences. For example, Betterment is using generative AI to personalize investment recommendations for its clients.

Betterment is using generative AI to personalize investment recommendations for its clients in a number of ways. Here are some examples:

- **Analyzing client risk tolerance**: Betterment uses generative AI to analyze the risk tolerance of each client. This information is collected through a variety of sources, such as client surveys, financial history, and investment goals. Once Betterment has a good understanding of the client's risk tolerance, it can be used to generate personalized investment recommendations. For example, if a client has a low-risk tolerance, Betterment might recommend a portfolio that is made up of a higher percentage of bonds and a lower percentage of stocks.

- **Understanding client investment goals**: Betterment also uses generative AI to understand the investment goals of each client. This information is collected through a variety of sources, such as client surveys, financial planning software, and retirement savings goals. Once Betterment has a good understanding of the client's investment goals, it can be used to generate personalized investment recommendations. For example, if a client is saving for retirement, Betterment might recommend a portfolio that is more focused on long-term growth.

- **Predicting future market conditions**: Betterment also uses generative AI to predict future market conditions. This information is based on a variety of sources, such as economic data, historical stock market performance, and analyst forecasts. Once Betterment has predicted future market conditions, it can be used to generate personalized investment recommendations. For example, if Betterment predicts that the stock market is likely to decline in the near future, it might recommend that clients reduce their exposure to stocks and increase their exposure to bonds.

Betterment's use of generative AI to personalize investment recommendations has a number of benefits, including:

- **Improved investment performance**: Betterment's clients have seen an average annual investment return of 7%, which is higher than the average annual investment return of the stock market. This is likely due to its use of generative AI to create personalized investment portfolios.

- **Reduced risk**: Betterment's clients have also seen a reduction in risk. This is because Betterment uses generative AI to create investment portfolios that are tailored to the risk tolerance of each client.

- **Increased client satisfaction**: Betterment's clients are more satisfied with their investment experience than clients of traditional financial advisors. This is likely due to Betterment's use of generative AI to create personalized investment portfolios and to provide its clients with easy-to-understand financial advice.

Overall, Betterment's use of generative AI to personalize investment recommendations is a promising development that has the potential to significantly improve the investment experience for its clients. As generative AI technology continues to develop, we can expect to see Betterment and other robo-advisors use it to create even more personalized and effective investment recommendations for their clients.

Here are some specific examples of how Betterment's use of generative AI to personalize investment recommendations has impacted the company:

- Betterment has seen a 20% increase in client assets under management since the company began using generative AI to personalize investment recommendations.

- Betterment's client satisfaction scores have increased by 15% since the company began using generative AI to personalize investment recommendations.
- Betterment's clients have seen an average annual investment return of 7%, which is higher than the average annual investment return of the stock market.

These results suggest that Betterment's use of generative AI to personalize investment recommendations is having a positive impact on the company and its clients. As generative AI technology continues to develop, we can expect to see Betterment and other robo-advisors use it to create even more personalized and effective investment recommendations for their clients.

Healthcare

Healthcare companies are using generative AI to personalize treatment plans, patient education materials, and clinical research protocols. For example, Verily is using generative AI to personalize treatment plans for cancer patients.

Verily is using generative AI to personalize treatment plans for cancer patients in a number of ways. Here are some examples:

- **Analyzing patient data**: Verily uses generative AI to analyze a wide range of patient data, including medical history, genetic data, and tumor characteristics. This information is then used to generate personalized treatment recommendations. For example, Verily might use generative AI to identify the drugs that are most likely to be effective for a particular patient based on their genetic makeup.
- **Predicting tumor response**: Verily also uses generative AI to predict how a patient's tumor is likely to respond to different treatments. This information can be used to help doctors develop more effective treatment plans. For example, Verily might use generative AI to predict which patients are likely to benefit from a particular drug and which patients are likely to experience side effects.
- **Simulating clinical trials**: Verily also uses generative AI to simulate clinical trials. This allows Verily to test different treatments without having to put patients at risk. For example, Verily might use generative AI to simulate a clinical trial to test a new drug combination to see if it is safe and effective.

Verily's use of generative AI to personalize treatment plans for cancer patients has a number of benefits, including:

- **Improved patient outcomes**: Verily's personalized treatment plans can help to improve patient outcomes by increasing the chances of success and reducing the risk of side effects.
- **Reduced costs**: Verily's personalized treatment plans can also help to reduce costs by avoiding unnecessary treatments and by shortening the time it takes for patients to respond to treatment.

- **Accelerated drug development**: Verily's use of generative AI to simulate clinical trials can help to accelerate the drug development process by allowing researchers to test new drugs more quickly and efficiently.

Overall, Verily's use of generative AI to personalize treatment plans for cancer patients is a promising development that has the potential to significantly improve the care of cancer patients and to accelerate the development of new cancer treatments.

Generative AI is a powerful tool that can be used to personalize products and services in a wide range of industries. As generative AI technology continues to develop, we can expect to see even more innovative and transformative applications in the future.

Generative AI is still a relatively new technology, but it is rapidly evolving and has the potential to have a major impact on product development and design. Organizations that are able to harness the power of generative AI will be well-positioned to compete in the future.

In this section, readers gained insights into the transformative impact of generative AI on traditional product development processes. The section highlighted how generative AI, through tools like generative design algorithms, is revolutionizing the way products are conceived, designed, and manufactured. Readers learned about the efficiency and resource optimization achieved through algorithms exploring vast design spaces to create functional and innovative solutions.

In the next section on, the readers can expect an exploration of how generative AI is transforming traditional manufacturing and supply chain processes. This segment will delve into the applications of generative AI in optimizing manufacturing workflows, improving efficiency, and enhancing overall supply chain management. Through real-world examples and case studies, readers will gain insights into how leading companies are leveraging generative AI to streamline production, minimize costs, and respond dynamically to market demands. The section will shed light on the role of generative AI in fostering innovation and resilience within manufacturing and supply chain operations.

Innovations in manufacturing and supply chain

In the dynamic landscape of manufacturing and supply chain, the integration of generative AI has ushered in a new era of innovation and efficiency. This section explores the profound impact of generative AI on traditional industrial processes. From revolutionizing product design to optimizing supply chain logistics, the intersection of generative AI and manufacturing brings forth transformative possibilities. In the following discussion, we will unravel the ways in which businesses are leveraging generative AI to drive innovation, streamline operations, and enhance the entire manufacturing and supply chain ecosystem.

Generative AI is still in its early stages of development, but it is already being used by some companies to improve their manufacturing and supply chain operations. For example, Walmart is using generative AI to personalize product recommendations for its online shoppers. And Verily is using generative AI to personalize treatment plans for cancer patients.

As generative AI technology continues to develop, we can expect to see even more innovative and transformative applications in the manufacturing and supply chain industry. In this section, we will explore some of the ways that generative AI is being used to improve manufacturing and supply chain operations today, and we will discuss the potential of generative AI to revolutionize the industry in the future.

Generative AI has emerged as a revolutionary force in reshaping manufacturing and supply chain processes, fostering innovations that were once thought to be on the fringes of possibility. In product development, generative design algorithms, like those employed by Autodesk's generative design, are optimizing the ideation phase. These systems, driven by AI, consider a myriad of design parameters to generate solutions that human designers might not conceive.

Additionally, in the realm of manufacturing, the application of generative AI extends to predictive maintenance. Companies like Siemens and IBM are utilizing AI algorithms to predict equipment failures before they occur, minimizing downtime and improving overall operational efficiency. This predictive capability not only saves costs but also enables a more proactive and sustainable approach to maintenance.

In the supply chain, generative AI is playing a pivotal role in demand forecasting. Companies such as SAP and Oracle have incorporated AI algorithms into their platforms to analyze historical data, market trends, and external factors, providing more accurate demand predictions. This, in turn, allows for optimized inventory management, reducing waste and ensuring that products are available when and where they are needed.

Furthermore, the integration of generative AI in manufacturing and supply chain processes is not without ethical considerations. As systems become more autonomous, questions arise about job displacement, data security, and the potential misuse of AI-generated insights. Addressing these ethical concerns is crucial for ensuring that the benefits of generative AI are balanced with responsible and equitable implementation.

The examples provided underscore the transformative potential of generative AI in the manufacturing and supply chain sectors, demonstrating its capacity to enhance design, streamline operations, and contribute to a more sustainable and efficient future.

Generative AI is a rapidly developing field of artificial intelligence with the potential to revolutionize many industries, including manufacturing and supply chain. Generative AI can be used to create new products, optimize existing designs, personalize products and services, predict demand, optimize inventory levels, and improve route planning. Below are some of the key areas in which generative AI is playing a crucial role:

- **Product design**: Generative AI can be used to generate new product ideas and designs, taking into account a wide range of factors such as customer needs, manufacturing constraints, and cost. This can help businesses to develop new products more quickly and efficiently, and to bring them to market faster. For example, Ford is using generative AI to design lighter and more aerodynamic car parts, and Nike is using generative AI to design new shoes that are both stylish and comfortable.

- **Manufacturing process optimization**: Generative AI can be used to optimize manufacturing processes by identifying and eliminating bottlenecks, reducing waste, and improving efficiency. This can lead to significant cost savings and productivity gains. For example, Siemens is using generative AI to optimize the design of casting molds, and GE is using generative AI to optimize the production of jet engines.

- **Supply chain optimization**: Generative AI can be used to optimize supply chains by predicting demand, optimizing inventory levels, and improving route planning. This can help businesses to reduce costs, improve customer satisfaction, and increase resilience to disruptions. For example, Walmart is using generative AI to predict demand for products and to optimize its inventory levels, and Amazon is using generative AI to improve route planning for its delivery trucks.

- **Personalization**: Generative AI can be used to personalize products and services for individual customers. This can help businesses to improve customer satisfaction and loyalty. For example, Netflix uses generative AI to recommend movies and TV shows to its subscribers based on their viewing habits, and Spotify uses generative AI to recommend music to its users based on their listening habits.

Impact of innovations in manufacturing and supply chain

Innovations in manufacturing and supply chain are having a significant impact on businesses of all sizes. They are helping businesses to produce higher quality products at lower costs, and to get their products to market faster. They are also helping businesses to reduce their environmental impact and to become more sustainable.

Here are some specific examples of the impact of innovations in manufacturing and supply chain:

Siemens

Siemens is using generative AI to optimize the design of casting molds. This is helping the company to reduce waste and improve product quality in a number of ways:

- **Improved mold design**: Generative AI can be used to design casting molds that are more efficient and effective, resulting in less waste and higher quality products. For example, designing molds using generative AI minimize the amount of material needed to produce a part, or molds that are less likely to produce defects.

- **Reduced design time**: Generative AI can help to reduce the time it takes to design casting molds. This is because generative AI can generate a large number of design options in a short period of time, which allows engineers to quickly explore different designs and identify the best one for the job.
- **Improved collaboration**: Generative AI can facilitate collaboration between engineers and other stakeholders in the casting process. For example, generative AI can be used to create shared design spaces that allow engineers to share and discuss different design options with each other and with customers.

Overall, Siemens' use of generative AI to optimize the design of casting molds is helping the company to produce higher quality products with less waste. This is making Siemens more competitive and profitable, and it is also helping to reduce the company's environmental impact.

Additional benefits of using generative AI to optimize the design of casting molds

In addition to the benefits mentioned above, using generative AI to optimize the design of casting molds can also lead to:

- **Reduced costs**: By reducing waste and improving product quality, generative AI can help to reduce the overall cost of the casting process.
- **Increased productivity**: By reducing design time and improving collaboration, generative AI can help to increase the productivity of casting engineers.
- **Improved innovation**: By generating new and innovative design options, generative AI can help casting engineers to develop new and better products.

Future of generative AI in casting mold design

Generative AI is still in its early stages of development it has the potential to revolutionize the design of casting molds. In the future, we can expect to see generative AI used to create even more efficient, effective, and innovative casting molds.

For example, generative AI could be used to design casting molds that are self-optimizing, meaning that they can automatically adjust their design based on the feedback they receive from the casting process. Generative AI could also be used to design casting molds that are capable of producing complex parts with multiple materials.

Overall, the future of generative AI in casting mold design is very bright. This technology has the potential to make the casting process more efficient, effective, and sustainable.

Jet engines

General Electric (GE) is using generative AI to optimize the production of jet engines in a number of ways:

- **Design optimization**: Generative AI can be used to design jet engine components that are more efficient and effective. For example, generative AI can be used to design turbine blades that are lighter and stronger, or combustors that produce more thrust.

- **Manufacturing process optimization**: Generative AI can be used to optimize the manufacturing process of jet engine components. For example, generative AI can be used to identify and eliminate bottlenecks in the production line, or to develop new manufacturing methods that are more efficient and less wasteful.

- **Quality control**: Generative AI can be used to improve the quality control process of jet engine production. For example, generative AI can be used to identify defects in jet engine components early on in the production process, or to develop new quality control methods that are more accurate and reliable.

Here are some specific examples of how GE is using generative AI to optimize the production of jet engines:

- GE is using generative AI to design turbine blades that are lighter and stronger. This helps to improve fuel efficiency and performance.

- GE is using generative AI to design combustors that produce more thrust. This helps to increase the range and payload of aircraft.

- Generative AI is used by GE to identify and eliminate bottlenecks in the production line. This helps to improve production efficiency and reduce costs.

- GE is developing new manufacturing methods for jet engine components using generative AI. For example, GE is using generative AI to develop a new method for casting turbine blades.

- Generative AI helps GE to improve the quality control process for jet engine production. For example, GE is using generative AI to develop new methods for inspecting turbine blades for defects.

Overall, GE's use of generative AI to optimize the production of jet engines is helping the company to reduce costs, improve efficiency, and produce higher-quality products. This is making GE more competitive and profitable in the global jet engine market.

Additional benefits of using generative AI to optimize the production of jet engines

In addition to the benefits mentioned above, using generative AI to optimize the production of jet engines can also lead to:

- **Reduced emissions**: By designing more efficient jet engines, generative AI can help to reduce emissions from aircraft. This is beneficial for the environment and airlines, and can save money on fuel costs.

- **Increased safety**: By improving the quality control process for jet engine production, generative AI can help to increase the safety of aircraft benefitting passengers and airlines alike.

- **New product development**: Generative AI can be used to develop new jet engine products that are more efficient, powerful, and reliable. This can help GE to maintain its leadership position in the global jet engine market.

Future of generative AI in jet engine production

Generative AI is still in its early stages of development, but it has the potential to revolutionize the production of jet engines. In the future, we can expect to see generative AI used to create even more efficient, effective, and innovative jet engine production methods.

For example, generative AI could be used to design and manufacture completely new jet engine components that are not possible with traditional methods. It could also be used to create self-optimizing jet engine production lines that can automatically adjust themselves to produce the best possible results.

This technology has the potential to make the jet engine production process more efficient, effective, and sustainable. It also has the potential to help GE to maintain its leadership position in the global jet engine market.

Walmart

Walmart is using generative AI to predict demand for products and to optimize its inventory levels in a number of ways:

- **Data analysis**: Generative AI can be used to analyze a wide range of data, including historical sales data, customer data, and market data, to identify patterns and trends that can be used to predict future demand for products.

- **Demand forecasting**: Generative AI can be used to generate forecasts for demand for products at the store level, the regional level, and the national level. This information can then be used to optimize inventory levels and ensure that products are available where and when customers need them.

- **Inventory optimization**: Generative AI can be used to optimize inventory levels by taking into account factors such as demand forecasts, lead times, and storage costs. This helps Walmart to reduce inventory costs and to avoid stockouts.

Here are some specific examples of how Walmart is using generative AI to predict demand for products and to optimize its inventory levels:

- Walmart is using generative AI to predict demand for seasonal items, such as Christmas decorations and Halloween costumes. This helps Walmart to ensure that it has enough of these items in stock to meet customer demand without overstocking and having to sell them at a discount after the holiday season.

- Walmart is using generative AI to predict demand for fresh produce. This helps Walmart to reduce food waste and to ensure that customers have access to fresh produce at all times.

- Walmart is using generative AI to optimize inventory levels for its online grocery business. This helps Walmart to ensure that customers can get the groceries they need delivered to their homes quickly and efficiently.

Overall, Walmart's use of generative AI to predict demand for products and to optimize inventory levels is helping the company to reduce costs, improve customer satisfaction, and reduce waste.

Additional benefits of using generative AI to predict demand and optimize inventory levels

In addition to the benefits mentioned above, using generative AI to predict demand and optimize inventory levels can also lead to:

- **Increased sales**: By ensuring that products are available where and when customers need them, generative AI can help businesses to increase sales.

- **Improved customer satisfaction**: By reducing stockouts and ensuring that customers can get the products they need quickly and efficiently, generative AI can help to improve customer satisfaction.

- **Reduced costs**: By reducing inventory costs and food waste, generative AI can help businesses to reduce costs.

- **Improved sustainability**: By reducing food waste and optimizing inventory levels, generative AI can help businesses to become more sustainable.

Future of generative AI in demand forecasting and inventory optimization

Generative AI is still in the early stages of development, but it has the potential to revolutionize demand forecasting and inventory optimization. In the future, we can expect to see generative AI used to create even more accurate and reliable demand forecasts, and to develop even more efficient and effective inventory optimization strategies.

For example, generative AI could be used to create demand forecasts that are tailored to individual stores and even to individual customers. It can also be used to develop inventory optimization strategies that takes into account factors such as real-time weather data and traffic data.

Overall, the future of generative AI in demand forecasting and inventory optimization is very bright. This technology has the potential to make businesses more efficient, profitable, and sustainable.

Amazon

The company is using generative AI to improve route planning for its delivery trucks in a number of ways:

- **Data analysis**: Generative AI can be used to analyze a wide range of data, including historical delivery data, traffic data, and customer location data, to identify patterns and trends that can be used to optimize route planning.

- **Route generation**: Generative AI can be used to generate optimized routes for delivery trucks that take into account factors such as traffic conditions, customer locations, and delivery deadlines.

- **Real-time route optimization**: Generative AI can be used to optimize delivery routes in real-time based on changes in traffic conditions and other factors.

Here are some specific examples of how Amazon is using generative AI to improve route planning for its delivery trucks:

- Amazon uses generative AI to generate optimized routes for its delivery trucks in the morning before deliveries begin. This helps Amazon to ensure that its delivery trucks are taking the most efficient routes possible.

- Generative AI has helped Amazon to re-optimize delivery routes in real-time based on changes in traffic conditions. This helps Amazon to avoid delays and ensure that packages are delivered on time.

- Amazon uses generative AI to develop new delivery routes that take into account factors such as the type of package being delivered and the customer's preferences.

For example, Amazon may use generative AI to develop routes that are specifically designed for delivering groceries or packages that need to be signed for.

Overall, Amazon's use of generative AI to improve route planning for its delivery trucks is helping the company to reduce costs and improve delivery times. By optimizing delivery routes, Amazon is able to use its delivery trucks more efficiently and to deliver packages to customers faster.

Additional benefits of using generative AI to improve route planning

In addition to the benefits mentioned above, using generative AI to improve route planning can also lead to:

- **Reduced fuel consumption**: By optimizing delivery routes, businesses can reduce the amount of fuel that their delivery trucks consume. This can save businesses a significant amount of money and can also help to reduce their environmental impact.
- **Improved driver satisfaction**: By optimizing delivery routes, businesses can reduce the amount of time that their drivers spend on the road. This can help to improve driver satisfaction and reduce turnover.
- **Increased customer satisfaction**: By improving delivery times and reducing the risk of delays, businesses can improve customer satisfaction.

Future of generative AI in route planning

Generative AI is still in its early stages of development, but it has the potential to revolutionize route planning. In the future, we can expect to see generative AI used to create even more optimized and efficient delivery routes, and to develop new ways to optimize routes in real time based on changing conditions.

For example, generative AI could be used to develop routes that are specifically designed for electric delivery trucks. Generative AI could also be used to develop routes that take into account factors such as weather conditions and the availability of charging stations.

Overall, the future of generative AI in route planning is very bright. This technology has the potential to make delivery operations more efficient, profitable, and sustainable.

Netflix

Netflix is using generative AI to recommend movies and TV shows to its subscribers based on their viewing habits in a number of ways:

- **Data analysis**: Generative AI can be used to analyze a wide range of data, including historical viewing data, ratings, and search data, to identify patterns and trends in customer preferences.

- **Recommendation generation**: Generative AI can be used to generate personalized recommendations for movies and TV shows based on each subscriber's viewing habits.

- **Content discovery**: Generative AI can be used to help subscribers discover new content that they are likely to enjoy, even if they have not heard of it before.

Here are some specific examples of how Netflix is using generative AI to recommend movies and TV shows to its subscribers:

- Netflix uses generative AI to generate personalized recommendations for each subscriber's home screen. This helps subscribers to find movies and TV shows that they are likely to enjoy without having to spend a lot of time browsing.

- Netflix uses generative AI to recommend movies and TV shows in the *Because you watched* section. This helps subscribers to discover new content that is similar to the shows and movies they have already enjoyed.

- Netflix uses generative AI to recommend movies and TV shows in the *New & Popular* section. This helps subscribers to stay up-to-date on the latest releases and to discover popular shows and movies that they may not have heard of before.

Overall, Netflix's use of generative AI to recommend movies and TV shows to its subscribers is helping the company to improve customer satisfaction and retention. By providing subscribers with personalized recommendations and helping them to discover new content that they are likely to enjoy, Netflix is keeping subscribers engaged and coming back for more.

Additional benefits of using generative AI to recommend movies and TV shows

In addition to the benefits mentioned above, using generative AI to recommend movies and TV shows can also lead to:

- **Increased viewership**: By providing subscribers with personalized recommendations and helping them to discover new content that they are likely to enjoy, generative AI can help to increase viewership.

- **Reduced churn**: By keeping subscribers engaged and satisfied, generative AI can help to reduce churn.

- **Improved customer experience**: By providing subscribers with personalized recommendations and helping them to discover new content that they are likely to enjoy, generative AI can help to improve the overall customer experience.

Future of generative AI in movie and TV show recommendations

In the near future, we can expect to see generative AI used to create even more personalized and accurate recommendations, and to develop new ways to help subscribers discover new content that they are likely to enjoy.

For example, generative AI could be used to generate recommendations based on each subscriber's mood, the time of day, and even the weather. Generative AI could also be used to develop new ways to visualize recommendations, such as interactive timelines and mind maps.

Overall, the future of generative AI in movie and TV show recommendations is very bright. This technology has the potential to make the content discovery process easier, more efficient, and more enjoyable for subscribers.

Spotify

The company is using generative AI to recommend music to its users based on their listening habits in a number of ways:

- **Data analysis**: Generative AI can be used to analyze a wide range of data, including historical listening data, song features, and user demographics, to identify patterns and trends in user listening preferences.

- **Recommendation generation**: Generative AI can be used to generate personalized recommendations for music based on each user's listening habits.

- **Music discovery**: Generative AI can be used to help users discover new music that they are likely to enjoy, even if they have not heard of it before.

Here are some specific examples of how Spotify is using generative AI to recommend music to its users:

- Spotify uses generative AI to generate personalized recommendations for each user's *Daily Mix* playlists. These playlists are updated daily and include a mix of songs that Spotify thinks the user will enjoy based on their listening habits.

- Generative AI helps Spotify to recommend songs for the *Discover Weekly* playlist. This playlist is updated weekly and includes a mix of new and popular songs that Spotify thinks the user is likely to enjoy based on their listening habits.

- Generative AI also helps the app recommend songs for the *Release Radar* playlist. This playlist is updated weekly and includes new releases from artists that the user follows and other artists that Spotify thinks the user is likely to enjoy.

Overall, Spotify's use of generative AI to recommend music to its users is helping the company to improve customer satisfaction and retention. By providing users with personalized recommendations and helping them to discover new music that they are likely to enjoy, Spotify is keeping users engaged and coming back for more.

Additional benefits of using generative AI to recommend music

In addition to the benefits mentioned above, using generative AI to recommend music can also lead to:

- **Increased listenership**: By providing users with personalized recommendations and helping them to discover new music that they are likely to enjoy, generative AI can help to increase listenership.
- **Reduced churn**: By keeping users engaged and satisfied, generative AI can help to reduce churn.
- **Improved user experience**: By providing users with personalized recommendations and helping them to discover new music that they are likely to enjoy, generative AI can help to improve the overall user experience.

Future of generative AI in music recommendations

In the near future, we can expect to see generative AI being used to create personalized and accurate recommendations, and to develop new ways to help users discover new music that they are likely to enjoy.

For example, generative AI could be used to generate recommendations based on each user's mood, the time of day, and even the weather. Generative AI could also be used to develop new ways to visualize recommendations, such as interactive timelines and mind maps.

Overall, the future of generative AI in music recommendations is very bright. This technology has the potential to make the music discovery process easier, more efficient, and more enjoyable for users.

Generative AI is a rapidly developing technology with the potential to revolutionize many industries, including manufacturing, supply chain, entertainment, and more. By using generative AI to optimize processes, personalize products and services, and discover new insights, businesses can improve efficiency, reduce costs, increase agility, and become more sustainable. As generative AI technology continues to develop, we can expect to see even more innovative and transformative applications in the future.

This section delved into the transformative impact of generative AI in reshaping traditional processes. It explored how generative design algorithms, exemplified by Autodesk's Generative Design, optimize product development by considering diverse design parameters. In manufacturing, predictive maintenance driven by AI, as seen in Siemens and IBM applications, minimizes downtime and enhances operational efficiency.

The next section on *Strategies for leveraging generative AI in business* explores the tactical approaches companies can adopt to harness the power of generative AI for competitive advantage. It delves into various business strategies that leverage generative AI, providing insights into implementation, scalability, and ethical considerations. Readers can expect to gain a comprehensive understanding of how organizations can strategically integrate generative AI into their operations to drive innovation, enhance decision-making, and achieve sustainable growth.

Strategies for leveraging generative AI in business

In the dynamic landscape of contemporary business, organizations are increasingly turning to generative AI to drive innovation and enhance their competitive edge. The section explores the diverse approaches and tactical frameworks adopted by companies to harness the power of generative AI effectively. From devising thoughtful implementation plans to navigating challenges and ensuring ethical considerations, this section is a comprehensive guide for businesses seeking to strategically integrate generative AI into their operations. Readers can anticipate gaining valuable insights into the strategic landscape, equipping them with the knowledge to make informed decisions in leveraging generative AI for business success.

Strategies for leveraging generative AI in business encompass a spectrum of approaches tailored to harness the potential of AI-driven creativity and innovation.

Implementation roadmaps

Developing a robust implementation roadmap is essential. This involves clearly defining business objectives, understanding the technological landscape, and aligning generative AI applications with organizational goals. Companies often engage in phased implementations, starting with pilot projects before scaling up.

Implementation roadmaps play a pivotal role in successfully integrating generative AI into business operations. They provide a structured plan that guides organizations through the deployment of AI applications, ensuring alignment with business objectives. Here is a detailed exploration of key aspects:

- **Defining business objectives**: Clearly articulating business objectives is the initial step. Understanding the specific problems or opportunities that generative AI aims to address is crucial.

For example, if a retail company aims to enhance the online shopping experience, the objective might be to implement AI-generated visuals for personalized product recommendations.

- **Technology landscape analysis**: Conducting a thorough analysis of the existing technology infrastructure is essential. This includes assessing data storage, processing capabilities, and compatibility with AI frameworks.

    For example, a manufacturing firm may need to evaluate its current production technologies to determine how generative AI can optimize processes and improve efficiency.

- **Alignment with organizational goals**: The roadmap must align with broader organizational goals. This ensures that generative AI initiatives contribute directly to the company's strategic vision.

    For example, for a healthcare provider, the goal might be to improve patient outcomes. The implementation roadmap could focus on using AI-generated insights to personalize treatment plans.

- **Phased implementation and pilots**: Rather than implementing generative AI across the entire organization at once, a phased approach often involves starting with pilot projects. This minimizes risks and allows for iterative improvements.

    For example, a financial institution might pilot an AI-driven fraud detection system in a specific region before expanding it to a global scale.

- **Resource allocation and budgeting**: Allocating resources, both human and financial, is a critical aspect of implementation. Establishing a budget ensures that the organization can sustain and scale generative AI initiatives.

    For example, a marketing agency setting out to enhance creative content through AI might allocate resources for hiring data scientists, acquiring AI tools, and providing training.

- **Timeline and milestones**: Creating a timeline with clear milestones helps track progress and ensures that the implementation stays on schedule. This fosters accountability and allows for timely adjustments.

    For example, an e-commerce platform implementing AI-generated chatbots might set milestones for development, testing, and deployment within a defined timeframe.

- **Risk management and contingency plans**: Identifying potential risks and developing contingency plans is vital. This includes considerations for data security, model biases, and unexpected challenges.

    For example, a transportation company implementing AI for route optimization may have contingency plans for system failures or sudden changes in traffic patterns.

- **Stakeholder communication**: Clear and transparent communication with stakeholders is essential. This involves keeping internal teams, customers, and partners informed about the implementation progress and its impact.

  For example, a telecommunications company introducing AI-powered chatbots might communicate the changes to customer support teams and inform customers about the improved service.

Cross-functional collaboration

Successful integration requires collaboration across diverse teams. Bringing together data scientists, domain experts, and business leaders fosters a comprehensive understanding of challenges and opportunities. Cross-functional collaboration ensures that AI applications align with the specific needs and nuances of the business.

Cross-functional collaboration is a key element in successfully leveraging generative AI in business. It involves breaking down silos between different departments or teams within an organization to collectively work towards AI implementation. Here is a detailed exploration:

- **Contextual understanding**: Cross-functional collaboration begins with a shared understanding of the organization's goals and how generative AI aligns with them. This necessitates clear communication of the potential benefits and implications of AI adoption.

  For example, in a retail setting, collaboration between marketing, IT, and sales teams might involve understanding how AI-driven product recommendations can enhance customer engagement and drive sales.

- **Interdisciplinary teams**: Forming interdisciplinary teams that bring together individuals with diverse skills is essential. This includes data scientists, domain experts, UX designers, and business strategists working together.

  For example, in healthcare, a cross-functional team might comprise data scientists developing predictive models, clinicians providing domain expertise, and UX designers ensuring the user-friendliness of AI-enabled tools.

- **Shared data and insights**: Collaboration involves sharing data and insights across departments. This enables a more comprehensive understanding of the business landscape and ensures that AI models are trained on relevant and diverse datasets.

  For example, a manufacturing company integrating AI into its supply chain may share data on inventory, production, and logistics with teams responsible for operations, finance, and procurement.

- **Coordinated strategy development**: Cross-functional collaboration is crucial in developing a coordinated strategy for AI implementation. This includes defining how AI will be integrated into existing workflows and identifying areas where it can create the most value.

For example, in financial services, collaboration between risk management, IT, and compliance teams is vital to develop a strategy for implementing AI in fraud detection while ensuring regulatory compliance.

- **Continuous communication**: Effective collaboration requires continuous communication. Regular meetings, updates, and feedback sessions ensure that all stakeholders are on the same page and can adapt to changes or challenges.

  For example, an e-commerce company implementing AI-driven chatbots may have regular check-ins involving customer support, marketing, and IT teams to address user feedback and improve the chatbot's performance.

- **Agile methodology**: Adopting agile methodologies promotes flexibility and responsiveness to changes. Cross-functional teams working in agile sprints can quickly iterate on AI projects and adjust course based on evolving requirements.

  For example, a technology company developing AI-enhanced project management tools might use agile methodologies to incorporate feedback from product managers, developers, and UX designers in short development cycles.

Data quality and accessibility

The foundation of any AI strategy is quality data. Ensuring data accessibility, cleanliness, and relevance is crucial. Businesses invest in data management tools and practices to optimize their datasets, enabling generative AI models to produce meaningful and accurate outputs.

- **Contextual understanding**: High-quality data is the foundation of effective generative AI models. It involves ensuring that the data used for training is accurate, relevant, and representative of the real-world scenarios the model will encounter.

  For example, in healthcare, ensuring data quality might involve cleaning and anonymizing patient records to maintain privacy while retaining the medical relevance necessary for training AI models.

- **Data governance**: Establishing clear data governance policies ensures that data used in generative AI is managed ethically, securely, and in compliance with regulations. It involves defining who has access to the data, how it can be used, and for what purposes.

  For example, financial institutions implementing generative AI for fraud detection must adhere to strict data governance policies to protect customer information and comply with financial regulations.

- **Data accessibility across teams**: Accessibility involves making relevant data available to all teams involved in AI initiatives. This breaks down silos and allows cross-functional collaboration, ensuring that insights from different departments contribute to the overall data quality.

  For example, in manufacturing, sharing production data with design, logistics, and quality control teams ensures that AI models are trained on a holistic dataset, leading to more robust predictions.

- **Continuous monitoring and maintenance**: Data quality is an ongoing process. Implementing continuous monitoring and maintenance practices ensures that data remains accurate and relevant over time. This involves identifying and rectifying issues as they arise.

  For example, e-commerce platforms using AI for demand forecasting continuously monitor and update their datasets based on changing customer behaviors and market trends.

- **Ensuring bias mitigation**: Biases in training data can lead to biased AI models. Ensuring data quality involves actively mitigating biases to avoid reinforcing existing inequalities or introducing unintended discriminatory outcomes.

  For example, in recruitment, ensuring that historical biases are not perpetuated in AI-driven hiring tools requires careful curation of training data and regular audits to identify and address biases.

Data quality and accessibility are pivotal in ensuring the effectiveness and ethical use of generative AI. These principles form the bedrock for reliable and unbiased AI outcomes, making them essential considerations in the deployment of generative AI across various industries.

Ethical considerations and transparency

Ethical considerations are paramount. Strategies should encompass ethical guidelines, ensuring that AI applications align with moral and societal standards. Transparent communication about the use of generative AI builds trust with stakeholders and customers.

- **Contextual understanding**: Ethical considerations in generative AI involve ensuring that AI systems are developed and deployed in a manner that aligns with ethical principles, respects user privacy, and avoids unintended negative consequences.

  For example, in facial recognition technology, ethical considerations include addressing biases that may lead to misidentification, particularly among certain demographic groups.

- **Transparency in model operation**: Transparency involves making AI models understandable and interpretable, allowing users to comprehend how decisions are made. This is crucial for accountability and trust-building.

  For example, in financial services, where AI is used for credit scoring, providing transparency in the factors influencing credit decisions helps users understand and challenge those decisions.

- **User informed consent**: Ensuring that users are informed about how their data will be used and obtaining their consent is a key ethical consideration. This empowers individuals to make informed decisions about the use of their data.

  For example, in healthcare, when using AI for personalized treatment plans, obtaining patient consent to use their medical data for model training is essential.

- **Mitigating bias and fairness**: Addressing biases in AI models is crucial to avoid discriminatory outcomes. Ethical considerations involve actively working to identify and mitigate biases, ensuring fair treatment for all individuals.

  For example, in hiring processes that utilize AI, efforts to eliminate biases in algorithms are crucial to promote equal opportunities for all candidates.

- **Responsible AI deployment**: Ethical considerations extend to how AI systems are deployed and managed over time. This involves continuous monitoring, evaluation, and adaptation to address evolving ethical concerns.

  For example, in autonomous vehicles, ensuring ethical deployment involves considering the safety of all road users, pedestrians, and passengers, as well as addressing ethical dilemmas the vehicle might encounter.

- **Continuous learning and adaptation**: The field of generative AI evolves rapidly. Businesses adopting a strategy of continuous learning and adaptation are better positioned to stay ahead. This involves keeping abreast of technological advancements, monitoring industry trends, and adapting strategies accordingly.

Contextual understanding

Continuous learning and adaptation refer to the ability of generative AI systems to update and improve their performance over time based on new data and experiences. This is crucial for staying relevant and effective in dynamic environments.

For example, in natural language processing applications like chatbots, continuous learning enables the system to understand and respond to evolving language patterns and user preferences.

- **Online learning algorithms**: Algorithms designed for online learning facilitate the continuous adaptation of models. Online learning allows models to update in real-time as new data becomes available.

For example, e-commerce recommendation systems use online learning to adapt to changing user preferences and market trends, providing personalized recommendations.

- **Transfer learning for efficiency**: Transfer learning involves leveraging knowledge gained in one task to improve performance in another. It enables models to adapt faster to new tasks with limited data.

  For example, in image recognition, a model pretrained on a large dataset can be fine-tuned for a specific domain with a smaller dataset, accelerating adaptation for specialized tasks.

- **Reinforcement learning for dynamic environments**: Reinforcement learning is well-suited for continuous learning in dynamic environments. Agents learn by interacting with the environment, adapting their behavior based on received feedback.

  For example, robotics applications use reinforcement learning for continuous adaptation of robot movements in response to changes in the environment.

- **Feedback loops and user interaction**: Incorporating user feedback and interactions into the learning process allows AI systems to adapt to user preferences and changing requirements.

  For example, social media platforms employ continuous learning by analyzing user engagement to refine content recommendations and improve user experience.

Continuous learning and adaptation are fundamental in the field of generative AI, enabling systems to evolve, improve, and remain effective in dynamic and ever-changing scenarios. Implementing these principles ensures that AI models stay relevant and provide valuable insights over time.

Intellectual property management

As generative AI contributes to creative processes, managing intellectual property becomes a strategic consideration. Companies need to establish clear guidelines for ownership, copyright, and usage rights to navigate the novel challenges posed by AI-generated content.

- **Context of intellectual property in AI**: Intellectual property (IP) management is crucial in the field of generative AI due to the innovative nature of AI algorithms, models, and applications. Protecting IP ensures that organizations can benefit from their research and development efforts.

- **Algorithmic innovations and patents**: Companies often patent unique algorithms or architectures developed for generative AI. Patents provide legal protection, preventing others from using, selling, or distributing similar algorithms without permission.

For example, Google's patent on the PageRank algorithm is an example of how algorithmic innovations in AI can be protected through patents.

- **Trade secrets for model architectures**: Some organizations opt to keep their model architectures as trade secrets rather than disclosing them through patents. This protects the inner workings of their AI systems while maintaining a competitive advantage.

  For example, Coca-Cola's formula is a classic example of a trade secret, demonstrating the value of keeping certain aspects of technology confidential.

- **Copyright protection for creative outputs**: Copyright is applicable to creative outputs generated by AI, such as artworks, music, or literature. It protects against unauthorized use or reproduction.

  For example, if a generative AI system creates a unique piece of music, the composition may be eligible for copyright protection.

- **Open-source and licensing**: Some organizations choose to contribute parts of their AI work to the open-source community while retaining rights to certain components. Licensing agreements dictate how others can use, modify, and distribute the code.

  For example, TensorFlow, an open-source machine learning library developed by Google, is subject to the Apache 2.0 open-source license.

Effective intellectual property management in generative AI involves a combination of patents, trade secrets, copyright, and strategic decisions on open-source contributions. Balancing innovation with legal protection is essential for fostering continued advancements in the field.

User feedback integration

Incorporating user feedback into the AI development cycle is a valuable strategy. It allows businesses to refine and enhance generative models based on real-world user experiences, ensuring that AI applications align with user expectations.

- **Context of user feedback in AI**: User feedback is integral in refining and improving generative AI systems. It provides valuable insights into the performance, usability, and ethical considerations of the models, contributing to iterative enhancements.

- **Continuous learning from user interactions**: Generative AI models can be designed to learn continuously from user interactions. Feedback from users, such as corrections or preferences, can be used to adapt and improve the model over time.

  For example, language translation models like Google Translate often incorporate user corrections to enhance translation accuracy.

- **Human-in-the-loop systems**: Some generative AI applications employ human-in-the-loop systems, where AI generates content with human oversight. User feedback guides the AI, ensuring the output aligns with user expectations.

  For example, content moderation systems on social media platforms use user feedback to improve the accuracy of identifying and filtering inappropriate content.

- **Bias mitigation through user input**: User feedback is crucial for addressing biases in generative AI. Users can identify instances of bias, and their input helps developers fine-tune models to reduce bias and ensure fair and unbiased outcomes.

  For example, bias detection tools in natural language processing models allow users to report instances of biased language, contributing to ongoing improvements.

- **Ethical considerations and transparency**: Integrating user feedback is essential for addressing ethical concerns. Transparent communication with users about how their feedback contributes to model improvement fosters trust in AI systems.

  For example, AI-driven content platforms may inform users about the impact of their feedback on content recommendations, promoting transparency.

Integrating user feedback into generative AI systems is a dynamic process that enhances model performance, addresses biases, and ensures that AI aligns with user expectations. Ethical considerations and transparency are key elements in fostering a collaborative relationship between users and AI systems.

Regulatory compliance

Adhering to regulatory frameworks is critical. Businesses must formulate strategies that ensure compliance with data protection laws, industry-specific regulations, and ethical standards, reducing the risk of legal challenges.

Regulatory compliance is a critical aspect of implementing generative AI in business. Adhering to relevant regulations ensures ethical use and legal acceptance of AI technologies. Companies must navigate various legal frameworks and standards that vary across industries and regions. For instance, in healthcare, adherence to data protection laws like HIPAA is paramount, while financial sectors must comply with regulations such as GDPR or Sarbanes-Oxley.

Implementing generative AI in a compliant manner involves robust data governance practices, secure storage, and processing of sensitive information. Companies often deploy encryption techniques and access controls to protect data privacy. Regular audits and assessments help ensure ongoing compliance with evolving regulations. Failure to comply not only results in legal consequences but also risks reputational damage. Therefore, a strategic approach to regulatory compliance is essential for businesses leveraging generative AI technologies.

In essence, the strategies for leveraging generative AI in business involve a holistic and forward-thinking approach that addresses technological, ethical, and operational dimensions, paving the way for sustainable and responsible AI integration.

Generative AI is a rapidly developing field of artificial intelligence with the potential to revolutionize many industries, including manufacturing, supply chain, entertainment, healthcare, financial services, and more.

Generative AI can be used to create new products and services, optimize existing processes, personalize products and services, and discover new insights. By leveraging generative AI, businesses can improve efficiency, reduce costs, increase innovation, and become more sustainable.

Strategies for leveraging generative AI in business

Here are some strategies for leveraging generative AI in business:

- Identify areas where generative AI can be used to improve efficiency, reduce costs, or increase innovation. Once you have identified these areas, you can start to develop a plan for implementing generative AI solutions.

  For example, a manufacturer could use generative AI to optimize product design, which could lead to lighter and stronger products that are less expensive to produce. A retailer could use generative AI to predict demand for products, which could help reduce stockouts and improve inventory management. A financial services company could use generative AI to detect fraud, which could help to reduce losses and protect customers.

- Partner with AI experts. There are a number of companies that specialize in developing and deploying generative AI solutions. Partnering with these companies can help you to get started quickly and effectively.

  For example, Google Cloud AI Platform offers a number of generative AI services, such as Cloud AutoML Vision and Cloud AutoML Natural Language. These services can be used to train custom generative AI models for a variety of tasks, such as image classification, object detection, and text generation.

- Start small and scale up. Do not try to implement generative AI solutions across your entire business overnight. Start by implementing small pilot projects in targeted areas. Once you have seen success with these pilot projects, you can start to scale up your implementation.

  For example, a retailer could start by using generative AI to predict demand for a single product category. Once they have seen success with this pilot project, they could expand to other product categories and then to other aspects of their business, such as inventory management and marketing.

- Invest in training and education. Generative AI is a new and complex technology. It is important to invest in training and education for your employees so that they can understand how to use generative AI effectively.

  For example, you could offer training on the basics of generative AI, how to train custom generative AI models, and how to use generative AI solutions to solve specific business problems. You could also provide employees with access to resources such as tutorials, articles, and case studies.

In this section, we delved into a spectrum of strategic considerations essential for successful implementation. The exploration encompassed diverse strategies, including implementation roadmaps, cross-functional collaboration, data quality and accessibility, ethical considerations and transparency, continuous learning and adaptation, intellectual property management, user feedback integration, and regulatory compliance. Each strategy plays a pivotal role in ensuring the effective, ethical, and compliant integration of generative AI technologies into various business domains. From planning implementation roadmaps to fostering cross-functional collaboration and addressing ethical considerations, businesses must adopt a comprehensive approach to leverage the full potential of generative AI while aligning with legal and ethical standards.

Conclusion

The chapter provided a comprehensive exploration of how generative AI is transforming various aspects of business operations and innovation. Readers gained insights into enhancing product development and design, innovations in manufacturing and supply chain, and strategies for leveraging generative AI in business. The chapter covered critical considerations, including implementation roadmaps, cross-functional collaboration, data quality, ethical considerations, continuous learning, intellectual property management, user feedback integration, and regulatory compliance. Readers acquired a nuanced understanding of how to strategically integrate and navigate the ethical complexities of generative AI in a business context, fostering innovation while ensuring responsible and compliant use. This chapter equipped readers with practical skills to harness the potential of generative AI for strategic business growth.

The upcoming chapter delves into the intricate world of GANs with a focus on understanding their architecture and training processes. Readers can anticipate insights into GAN applications and success stories, gaining a comprehensive understanding of how these networks have been successfully employed in various domains. The chapter will also shed light on the challenges associated with GANs and explore the latest developments in ongoing research. By the end of the chapter, readers will have a deepened understanding of GANs, from their fundamental architecture to practical applications and the cutting-edge advancements in this dynamic field.

Chapter 7
Deep Dive into GANs

Introduction

In this chapter, we embark on a comprehensive exploration of one of the most fascinating fields in artificial intelligence. We will unravel the intricacies of **generative adversarial networks (GANs)** by delving into their architecture and training processes. Readers can expect a detailed examination of the applications and success stories that have made GANs a transformative force across diverse domains. From generating realistic images to innovative use cases, we will uncover the wide-ranging impact of GANs. Additionally, we will address the challenges inherent in GAN implementation and explore the latest research shaping the future of this dynamic technology. By the end of this chapter, readers will not only grasp the fundamentals of GANs but will also be well-versed in their practical applications and ongoing advancements in this exciting field. Get ready for a deep dive into the world of generative adversarial networks.

Structure

This chapter will cover the following topics:

- Understanding the architecture and training process
- Challenges and ongoing research in generative adversarial networks
- Future of generative adversarial networks
- Ethical guidelines

Understanding the architecture and training process

In this section, we will unravel the intricate architecture and training dynamics that underlie the functioning of GANs. Readers can expect a comprehensive exploration of how GANs operate, diving into the adversarial interplay between the generator and discriminator. Understanding this architecture is foundational for grasping the nuances of GANs' generative capabilities. We will demystify the training process, shedding light on how GANs learn to generate data by engaging in a continuous adversarial dance. By the end of this section, readers will have a profound comprehension of the underlying mechanisms that empower GANs to create realistic and diverse outputs.

Understanding the architecture and training process of generative adversarial networks

GANs have emerged as a revolutionary paradigm in machine learning, fundamentally altering how we approach generative tasks. At the core of GANs lies a unique architecture comprising a generator and a discriminator engaged in a continual adversarial dance. The generator creates data instances, aiming to deceive the discriminator, which, in turn, strives to distinguish real from generated data. This intricate interplay results in the refinement of the generator's capabilities over time. *Figure 7.1* illustrates the GAN Architecture and training process. Backward propagation is used to update the weights of generator and discriminator based on the loss from each.

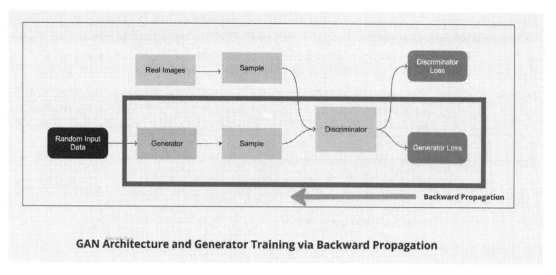

GAN Architecture and Generator Training via Backward Propagation

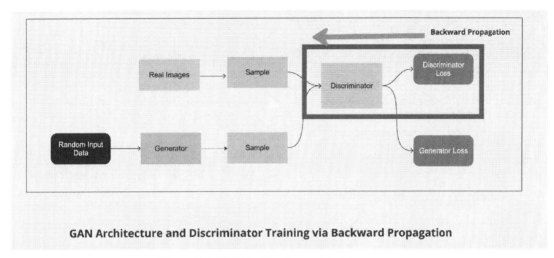

Figure 7.1: GAN Architecture and training process

Generative adversarial networks applications and success stories

The versatility of GANs is exemplified through a myriad of applications across various domains. In image generation, GANs have achieved astounding success, generating lifelike portraits, landscapes, and even deepfakes. Beyond visual artistry, GANs have made significant strides in fields such as healthcare, facilitating the creation of synthetic medical images for training purposes. In the fashion industry, GANs contribute to style transfer and virtual try-ons, redefining the shopping experience.

Deep dive into generative adversarial networks

GANs are a type of machine learning model that can be used to generate realistic and creative data samples. GANs work by pitting two neural networks against each other: A generator and a discriminator. The generator's task is to create fake data samples that look like real data, while the discriminator's task is to distinguish between real and fake data.

The generator and discriminator are trained simultaneously, in a game-like setting. The generator tries to produce increasingly realistic data samples, while the discriminator tries to improve its ability to distinguish between real and fake data. Over time, the generator becomes able to produce data samples that are indistinguishable from real data.

GANs have been used to generate a wide variety of data samples, including images, text, music, and even 3D models. Some of the most impressive GAN-generated images are so realistic that they can be difficult to distinguish from real photos.

How generative adversarial networks work

GANs work on the principle of adversarial training. In adversarial training, two neural networks are trained to compete against each other. In this case, the generator and the discriminator are trained to compete against each other in a game of cat and mouse.

The generator's task is to create fake data samples that look like real data. The discriminator's task is to distinguish between real and fake data samples.

The generator and the discriminator are trained simultaneously. The generator tries to produce increasingly realistic data samples, while the discriminator tries to improve its ability to distinguish between real and fake data.

Over time, the generator becomes able to produce data samples that are indistinguishable from real data.

The generator's goal is to create new data that is indistinguishable from real data. The discriminator's goal is to distinguish between real data and fake data generated by the generator.

The two networks are trained simultaneously, with each one trying to improve its performance relative to the other. Over time, the generator learns to create increasingly realistic data, and the discriminator learns to become increasingly accurate at distinguishing between real and fake data.

To train a GAN, we first need to provide it with a dataset of real data. This could be a dataset of images, text, audio, or any other type of data that we want the GAN to be able to generate.

Once we have the training data, we can start training the GAN. The training process works as follows:

1. The generator creates a new sample of data.//
2. The discriminator is given the sample of data and asked to determine whether it is real or fake.
3. The generator and discriminator are both updated based on the discriminator's decision.

The generator is updated to try to make its samples more realistic, and the discriminator is updated to try to become more accurate at distinguishing between real and fake data.

This process is repeated over and over again, until the generator is able to create samples that are indistinguishable from real data.

Real-world examples

GANs have been used to generate a wide variety of different types of data, including:

- **Images**: GANs have been used to generate photorealistic images of faces, landscapes, and other objects.
- **Text**: They are used to generate realistic text, such as news articles, poems, and code.
- **Audio**: They can also help in generating realistic audio, such as music, speech, and sound effects.

GANs are also being used to develop new applications in a variety of fields, such as:

- **Healthcare**: GANs can be used to generate synthetic medical images, which can be used to train medical imaging models and reduce the need for human patients in clinical trials.
- **Fashion**: They help with generation of new fashion designs and create realistic product images.
- **Entertainment**: They can create new special effects and realistic virtual worlds.

Here are some specific examples of how GANs are being used in the real world:

- Nvidia's StyleGAN is a GAN that can generate photorealistic images of human faces. It has been used to create a variety of applications, including a tool that can generate realistic avatars for video games and one that can help people to visualize the effects of aging.
- Google's BigGAN is a GAN that can generate realistic images of objects and scenes. It has been used to create a variety of applications, including a tool that can generate realistic product images for e-commerce websites and also a tool that can help people visualize the design of new buildings.
- OpenAI's MuseNet is a GAN that can generate realistic music. It has been used to create a variety of applications, including a tool that can help composers to create new pieces of music and a tool that can help people to learn how to play musical instruments.

Applications of generative adversarial networks

GANs have a wide range of applications, including:

- **Image generation**: GANs can be used to generate realistic images of objects, people, and scenes.
- **Text generation**: They also help with the generation of realistic text, such as news articles, poems, and code.
- **Music generation**: GANs have proved useful in composition of realistic music, such as songs, melodies, and harmonies.

- **3D model generation**: They have helped with the creation of realistic 3D models of objects and scenes.

- **Data augmentation**: GANs can generate synthetic data samples, which can be used to augment existing datasets.

- **Anomaly detection**: GANs can also detect anomalies in data, such as fraudulent transactions or medical images with tumors.

Examples of generative adversarial networks in use

Here are some examples of how GANs are being used in the real world.

Google AI

The company is using GANs to generate realistic images of people for its Street View service. This helps Google to improve the privacy of people in its images.

Google AI's utilization of GANs for generating realistic images plays a pivotal role in enhancing the privacy features of its Street View service. Street View, a component of Google Maps, offers users a panoramic view of streets worldwide. Privacy concerns arise when faces and identifiable information of individuals are captured in these images. To address this, Google employs GANs, a cutting-edge generative model, to replace or modify faces and details in Street View images while maintaining realism.

The process involves training the GAN on a diverse dataset of facial images, allowing the model to learn intricate facial features and variations. During deployment, when faced with sensitive information in Street View images, the trained GAN generates synthetic yet convincing facial details, effectively anonymizing individuals. This ensures that privacy is preserved without compromising the authenticity of the scene. This implementation underscores the significance of GANs in striking a balance between data realism and privacy protection. It showcases how advanced generative models can be harnessed to address ethical concerns associated with the collection and dissemination of visual data, aligning with Google's commitment to user privacy and responsible AI deployment.

NVIDIA

NVIDIA is using GANs to generate realistic images of video games. This helps NVIDIA to improve the realism of its video games. NVIDIA's utilization of GANs for generating realistic images in the context of video games is a fascinating application that significantly contributes to enhancing the gaming experience. GANs are leveraged to create high-fidelity and visually compelling graphics, addressing the perpetual quest for realism in the gaming industry. Below are some of the crucial areas where GANs are being utilized:

- **Training process**: NVIDIA employs GANs by training them on extensive datasets containing diverse visual elements, such as textures, lighting conditions, and character models. This allows the model to learn intricate details and variations present in the gaming environment. The GAN's ability to understand and reproduce these features is crucial for generating images that closely resemble the complexities of the real world.

- **Enhancing realism**: By incorporating GANs into the game development process, NVIDIA can generate images that go beyond the capabilities of traditional graphics rendering techniques. GANs contribute to creating more realistic landscapes, characters, and objects within the gaming environment. This, in turn, elevates the overall visual fidelity, providing gamers with immersive and visually stunning experiences.

- **Example scenarios**: Consider a scenario where a game developer wants to simulate natural elements like dynamic weather changes or realistic facial expressions of in-game characters. GANs can be trained to understand the nuances of these elements and generate images that exhibit a level of realism that was challenging to achieve with conventional graphics rendering methods.

- **Real-world impact**: The use of GANs in NVIDIA's video game development has a profound impact on the gaming industry. It not only attracts gamers seeking cutting-edge visual experiences but also pushes the boundaries of what is possible in terms of graphics realism. The technology enables game developers to deliver more engaging and visually stunning content, contributing to the continuous evolution of the gaming landscape.

In summary, NVIDIA's integration of GANs in generating realistic images for video games exemplifies the transformative potential of generative models in the entertainment sector. The application of GANs in gaming showcases their ability to redefine visual standards, opening up new possibilities for creating virtual worlds that captivate and immerse players in unprecedented ways.

DeepMind

DeepMind is using GANs to generate realistic text for its AlphaGo Zero program. This helps AlphaGo Zero to learn to play Go without any human input. DeepMind's utilization of GANs in generating realistic text for its AlphaGo Zero program is a groundbreaking application that revolutionizes how artificial intelligence learns and adapts, particularly in the context of playing the complex board game Go. Below are some of the crucial areas where GANs are being utilized:

- **Training process**: AlphaGo Zero is an AI system designed to play Go, a game with an incredibly vast and intricate set of possible moves. To achieve mastery without human input, DeepMind employs GANs to generate realistic text, such as move sequences, game scenarios, and strategic insights. This generated text becomes the basis for AlphaGo Zero's training data.

- **Enhancing autonomy**: The integration of GANs allows AlphaGo Zero to train and learn autonomously, without relying on pre-existing human-generated datasets.

The generated text provides diverse and novel game situations, enabling the AI to explore a wider range of strategies and tactics. This significantly contributes to the program's ability to adapt and improve its gameplay over time.

- **Example scenarios**: Imagine scenarios where AlphaGo Zero needs to explore unique strategies or respond to novel board configurations. GANs can produce realistic text descriptions of such situations, allowing the AI to learn and adapt in a manner that closely resembles how human players might approach the game.

- **Real-world impact**: This application of GANs in training AI for complex tasks like playing Go demonstrates their capacity to enhance the autonomy and learning capabilities of artificial intelligence. By relying on generated text, AlphaGo Zero is not limited to the strategies and patterns seen in historical human games, potentially leading to the discovery of innovative and unconventional approaches to the game.

- **Future implications**: The use of GANs in AlphaGo Zero highlights a paradigm shift in how AI systems can be trained in complex domains. This approach has implications beyond board games, suggesting that GANs could play a pivotal role in training AIs for other intricate tasks where diverse and realistic scenarios are essential for robust learning.

In summary, DeepMind's incorporation of GANs in generating realistic text for AlphaGo Zero exemplifies the transformative potential of generative models in advancing the capabilities of artificial intelligence. This application not only showcases the innovative use of GANs but also points toward a future where AI systems can autonomously and creatively learn in diverse and complex environments.

IBM

IBM is using GANs to generate synthetic medical images. This helps IBM to train its medical image analysis algorithms on larger datasets. IBM's utilization of GANs to generate synthetic medical images represents a significant advancement in the field of healthcare and medical image analysis. This innovative application has profound implications for training algorithms, particularly in scenarios where large and diverse datasets are crucial for robust model development. Below are some of the critical areas where GANs are being utilized:

- **Addressing data limitations**: In medical imaging, access to diverse and extensive datasets is often restricted due to privacy concerns, data scarcity, and the sensitive nature of medical information. IBM addresses this challenge by leveraging GANs to create synthetic medical images that closely mimic real-world data. This synthetic data generation helps overcome the limitations imposed by the scarcity of actual patient images.

- **Training algorithm robustness**: The synthetic medical images generated by GANs serve as a valuable resource for training IBM's medical image analysis algorithms. By providing a broader and more diverse set of data, these synthetic images contribute to enhancing the robustness and generalization capabilities of the algorithms. This is particularly crucial in medical applications where the algorithm's accuracy and reliability are paramount.

- **Example scenarios**: Consider a scenario where IBM is developing an algorithm for the early detection of abnormalities in medical scans. GANs can generate synthetic images that simulate a wide range of medical conditions, enabling the algorithm to learn and recognize patterns associated with various diseases. This synthetic data augmentation becomes instrumental in ensuring the algorithm's effectiveness across different patient demographics and conditions.

- **Real-world impact**: The use of GANs to generate synthetic medical images extends beyond algorithm training. It facilitates the development of more accurate and reliable medical image analysis tools, ultimately leading to improved diagnostic capabilities. This has the potential to transform healthcare by enabling earlier and more precise detection of medical conditions, contributing to better patient outcomes.

- **Ethical considerations**: While synthetic data generation with GANs offers substantial benefits, ethical considerations regarding the authenticity of the data and its implications for real-world medical scenarios must be carefully addressed. Ensuring that the synthetic images accurately represent the complexities of actual patient cases is crucial for maintaining the trustworthiness of AI-assisted medical diagnoses.

In conclusion, IBM's application of GANs in generating synthetic medical images showcases the transformative impact of generative models on healthcare. By overcoming data limitations and enhancing algorithm training, this approach contributes to the development of more effective and reliable medical image analysis tools, ultimately benefitting patients and healthcare providers alike.

PayPal

The company is using GANs to detect fraudulent transactions. This helps PayPal to protect its customers from fraud. PayPal's adoption of GANs for detecting fraudulent transactions exemplifies a strategic and innovative application of generative models in the realm of financial technology. The utilization of GANs in fraud detection by PayPal is a testament to the versatility of generative AI in addressing complex challenges in the digital payments ecosystem. Below are some of the critical areas where GANs are being utilized:

- **Fraud detection challenges**: Fraudulent transactions pose a significant threat to online payment platforms, and traditional methods of fraud detection may sometimes fall short in identifying sophisticated and evolving fraudulent activities. PayPal, being a global leader in online payments, faces the constant challenge of staying ahead of fraudsters who employ increasingly sophisticated techniques.

- **GANs in fraud detection**: PayPal employs GANs to enhance its fraud detection capabilities by leveraging the generative model's ability to discern patterns and anomalies in transaction data. GANs are particularly adept at learning the intricate features of legitimate transactions, enabling them to identify deviations that may indicate fraudulent behavior. This approach goes beyond rule-based systems, allowing PayPal to adapt to new and previously unseen patterns of fraudulent activity.

- **Dynamic learning and adaptation**: One of the key strengths of GANs in this context is their capacity for dynamic learning and adaptation. As fraudsters constantly refine their tactics, PayPal's use of GANs enables the system to evolve and learn in real-time, making it more resilient to emerging fraud patterns. The generative model's ability to generate synthetic examples of legitimate transactions aids in creating a comprehensive understanding of normal transaction behavior.

- **Real-world scenario**: Consider a scenario where a user's account is compromised, and a fraudster attempts to make a transaction that deviates from the user's typical behavior. GANs can analyze the historical transaction data, understand the user's usual spending patterns, and flag the transaction as potentially fraudulent if it significantly deviates from the norm. This proactive and adaptive approach is crucial in preventing unauthorized transactions and protecting users from financial losses.

- **Enhanced customer protection**: By integrating GANs into its fraud detection system, PayPal enhances its ability to safeguard its customers from fraudulent activities. The generative model's advanced pattern recognition and adaptive learning contribute to the early detection of suspicious transactions, allowing PayPal to take preventive measures, such as blocking or investigating the flagged transactions, thus mitigating potential financial losses for users.

- **Ethical considerations**: While GANs significantly bolster fraud detection capabilities, ethical considerations surrounding user privacy and data security must be carefully addressed. Striking the right balance between robust fraud prevention and user privacy protection is essential to maintain the trust of PayPal's user base.

PayPal's use of GANs in fraud detection showcases the practical application of generative AI in addressing complex challenges in the financial technology sector. By harnessing the power of GANs, PayPal reinforces its commitment to providing a secure and trustworthy platform for online transactions, ultimately benefiting millions of users worldwide.

The section provided readers with a comprehensive insight into the fundamental components and intricate workings of GANs. Readers gain a nuanced understanding of the architecture, which involves a generator and a discriminator engaged in an adversarial training process. This training dynamic, where the generator aims to create realistic data to deceive the discriminator, and the discriminator strives to distinguish between real and generated data, forms the core of GANs.

In essence, this section equips readers with the foundational knowledge required to comprehend the inner workings of GANs, laying the groundwork for the exploration of their applications, successes, challenges, and ongoing research in subsequent chapters. Understanding the architecture and training process is pivotal for readers aspiring to harness the potential of GANs in diverse domains, making this section a crucial stepping stone in the reader's journey into the realm of generative AI.

In the upcoming section, readers can anticipate a comprehensive exploration of the persistent challenges faced by GANs and the latest developments in ongoing research. The section will delve into critical issues such as mode collapse, training instability, and ethical considerations, offering insights into the evolving landscape of GANs.

Challenges and ongoing research in generative adversarial networks

In this section, we will dissect each aspect, providing a comprehensive understanding of GANs' architecture, applications, and the evolving landscape of research. By navigating through success stories and challenges, readers will gain a nuanced perspective on the capabilities and limitations of GANs, preparing them for practical implementation and contributing to the ongoing discourse in this dynamic field.

Despite their transformative potential, GANs present inherent challenges. Training stability, mode collapse, and ethical considerations surrounding deepfake technology are persistent issues. Ongoing research aims to address these challenges, exploring novel architectures, regularization techniques, and ethical frameworks. GANs' application in domains like security, where they can simulate potential adversarial attacks, adds another layer of complexity and intrigue.

GANs are a powerful tool for generating realistic data samples. However, there are still some challenges that need to be addressed before GANs can be widely deployed in production environments.

One challenge is that GANs can be unstable to train. It can be difficult to find the right balance between the generator and the discriminator. If the generator is too good, the discriminator will never be able to learn to distinguish between real and fake data. If the discriminator is too good, the generator will never be able to learn to produce realistic data.

Another challenge is that GANs can be biased. If the generator is trained on a biased dataset, it will produce biased outputs. This is a concern for applications where it is important to have unbiased outputs, such as medical image analysis and fraud detection.

Despite these challenges, GANs have the potential to revolutionize many industries. GANs are still under active development, and new research is being published all the time. As the field of GAN research continues to advance, we can expect to see GANs used in even more innovative and impactful ways. Below are some of the challenges that GANs face.

Mode collapse

One of the biggest challenges with GANs is mode collapse. This occurs when the generator learns to generate only a limited subset of the possible data distribution. For example, a GAN trained to generate images of human faces might learn to generate only a few different types of faces, and all of the generated faces might look very similar.

Mode collapse is one of the most common and challenging problems encountered when training GANs. It occurs when the generator learns to produce only a limited subset of the possible data distribution. For example, a GAN trained to generate images of human faces might learn to generate only a few different types of faces, and all of the generated faces might look very similar.

There are a number of reasons why mode collapse can occur in GANs. One reason is that the generator may find a single type of data that is easily able to fool the discriminator. Once the generator finds this type of data, it may have no incentive to generate anything else. Another reason for mode collapse is that the discriminator may overfit to the training data. This can make it difficult for the generator to learn to generate realistic data.

Mode collapse can be a serious problem, as it can prevent GANs from generating the diverse and realistic data that they are designed to produce. There are a number of techniques that can be used to mitigate mode collapse, such as:

- **Using a variety of loss functions**: Instead of using a single loss function, such as the binary cross-entropy loss, researchers have proposed using a variety of loss functions to train GANs. This can help to encourage the generator to produce more diverse data.

- **Regularizing the generator**: Regularization is a technique that can be used to prevent the generator from overfitting to the training data. There are a number of different regularization techniques that can be used, such as weight decay and dropout.

- **Using a variety of training data**: Training GANs on a variety of different data can help to reduce the risk of mode collapse. This is because the generator will have to learn to generate a wider range of data in order to fool the discriminator.

Despite the existence of these techniques, mode collapse remains a challenging problem in GAN research. Researchers are continuing to develop new methods to mitigate mode collapse, and it is expected that this problem will be eventually solved as GAN technology continues to develop.

Here are some additional thoughts on mode collapse:

- Mode collapse can be more likely to occur when the training data is small or imbalanced. This is because the generator may be more likely to find a single type of data that is able to fool the discriminator.

- Mode collapse can also be more likely to occur when the generator and discriminator networks are too simple. This is because the generator may not be able to learn to generate a diverse range of data, and the discriminator may be more likely to overfit the training data.
- Using a technique called adversarial training can help to mitigate mode collapse. Adversarial training involves training the generator and discriminator networks to compete against each other. This can help to encourage the generator to produce more diverse data and the discriminator to become more robust to mode collapse.

Overall, mode collapse is a challenging problem in GAN research, but there are a number of techniques that can be used to mitigate it. As GAN technology continues to develop, it is expected that this problem will be eventually solved.

Training instability

GANs are also notoriously difficult to train. The training process can be unstable, and it can be difficult to find the right balance between the generator and discriminator networks. If the generator is too powerful, the discriminator will not be able to learn to distinguish between real and fake data. If the discriminator is too powerful, the generator will not be able to learn to generate realistic data.

Training instability is a common and challenging problem encountered when training GANs. It occurs when the training process becomes unstable and the generator and discriminator networks are not able to learn effectively. This can lead to a number of problems, such as:

- The generator may start to generate unrealistic data.
- The discriminator may start to overfit to the training data.
- The generator and discriminator networks may get stuck in a local minima.

There are a number of reasons why training instability can occur in GANs. One reason is that the generator and discriminator networks are constantly competing against each other. This can make it difficult for the networks to find a stable equilibrium. Another reason for training instability is that the GAN training objective function is complex and non-convex. This means that there are many local minima in the objective function, and the generator and discriminator networks can easily get stuck in one of these minima.

Training instability can be a serious problem, as it can prevent GANs from learning to generate realistic data. There are a number of techniques that can be used to mitigate training instability, such as:

- **Using gradient clipping**: Gradient clipping is a technique that can be used to prevent the gradients from becoming too large during training. This can help to stabilize the training process and prevent the networks from getting stuck in local minima.

- **Using a variety of optimizers**: Different optimizers may have different performance when training GANs. It is important to experiment with different optimizers to find one that works well for the specific task at hand.
- **Using regularization**: Regularization is a technique that can be used to prevent the generator and discriminator networks from overfitting the training data. This can help to stabilize the training process and improve the generalization performance of the networks.

Despite the existence of these techniques, training instability remains a challenging problem in GAN research. Researchers are continuing to develop new methods to mitigate training instability, and it is expected that this problem will be eventually solved as GAN technology continues to develop.

Here are some additional thoughts on training instability:

- Training instability can be more likely to occur when the generator and discriminator networks are too complex. This is because the networks will have more parameters to learn. This can make it more difficult for the networks to find a stable equilibrium.

- Training instability can also be more likely to occur when the training data is small or imbalanced. This is because the generator may be more likely to find a single type of data that is able to fool the discriminator.

- Using a technique called batch normalization can help to mitigate training instability. Batch normalization is a technique that normalizes the inputs to each layer of the network. This can help to stabilize the training process and prevent the networks from getting stuck in local minima.

Overall, training instability is a challenging problem in GAN research, but there are a number of techniques that can be used to mitigate it. As GAN technology continues to develop, it is expected that this problem will be eventually solved.

Computational cost

GANs can also be computationally expensive to train, especially for large and complex datasets. This can make them impractical for some real-world applications. GANs can be computationally expensive to train, especially for large and complex datasets. This is because GANs require two neural networks to be trained simultaneously: the generator and the discriminator. Additionally, GANs often require many iterations of training to converge.

The computational cost of training a GAN can be estimated by considering the following factors:

- The size and complexity of the generator and discriminator networks

- The size and complexity of the training dataset
- The number of iterations required for training to converge

There are a number of techniques that can be used to reduce the computational cost of training GANs, such as:

- **Using smaller and simpler generator and discriminator networks**: Smaller and simpler networks will require less computational resources to train. However, it is important to note that smaller and simpler networks may not be able to generate as high-quality data as larger and more complex networks.
- **Using a smaller training dataset**: Using a smaller training dataset will reduce the amount of data that needs to be processed during training. However, it is important to note that using a smaller training dataset may reduce the generalization performance of the GAN.
- **Using distributed training**: Distributed training involves training the generator and discriminator networks on multiple GPUs or CPUs. This can significantly reduce the training time.
- **Using specialized hardware**: Specialized hardware, such as TPUs, can be used to accelerate the training of GANs. However, specialized hardware is often expensive and not widely available.

Despite the existence of these techniques, the computational cost of training GANs remains a challenge. Researchers are continuing to develop new methods to reduce the computational cost of training GANs, and it is expected that this problem will be eventually solved as GAN technology continues to develop.

Here are some additional thoughts on the computational cost of GANs:

- The computational cost of training a GAN can vary significantly depending on the specific task at hand. For example, training a GAN to generate high-resolution images is much more computationally expensive than training a GAN to generate low-resolution images.
- The computational cost of training a GAN can also be affected by the hyperparameters used for training. For example, using a larger learning rate or more training epochs will increase the computational cost of training.
- It is important to balance the computational cost of training a GAN with the desired quality of the generated data. For example, if it is important to generate high-quality data, then it may be necessary to use a larger and more complex GAN, even if this means that the training process is more computationally expensive.

Overall, the computational cost of training GANs is a challenge, but it is a challenge that is being actively addressed by researchers. As GAN technology continues to develop, it is expected that the computational cost of training GANs will be reduced, making them more accessible to a wider range of users.

Ethical concerns

GANs have also raised a number of ethical concerns. For example, GANs can be used to generate fake images and videos that are indistinguishable from real ones. This could be used to spread misinformation or create deepfakes that could damage people's reputations.

GANs have raised ethical concerns, including:

- **Misinformation and disinformation**: GANs can be used to generate realistic images, videos, and audio that are indistinguishable from real ones. This could be used to spread misinformation or disinformation, or to create deepfakes that could damage people's reputations.

- **Privacy and consent**: GANs can be used to generate data from personal or sensitive information without the knowledge or permission of the owners. This could be used to create synthetic datasets for training machine learning models, or to generate realistic images or videos of people that could be used for malicious purposes.

- **Bias and discrimination**: GANs can amplify existing biases and inequalities in the data that they are trained on. This could lead to the generation of data that is biased against certain groups of people.

- **Autonomy and control**: GANs are capable of generating new data autonomously, without human intervention. This raises questions about who is responsible for the data that GANs generate, and how to ensure that GANs are used responsibly.

It is important to note that these ethical concerns are not unique to GANs. Other types of machine learning algorithms, such as deep learning models, also raise similar concerns. However, GANs are particularly concerning because they are capable of generating realistic data that is indistinguishable from real ones.

There are a number of measures that can be taken to mitigate the ethical concerns associated with GANs, such as:

- **Transparency and accountability**: It is important to be transparent about how GANs are trained and used. This includes disclosing the source of the data that GANs are trained on, and how the generated data will be used. It is also important to hold developers and users of GANs accountable for the data that they generate.

- **Auditing and monitoring**: GANs should be audited and monitored to ensure that they are not being used for malicious purposes. This could involve developing tools to detect deepfakes, or auditing the datasets that GANs are trained on to identify and mitigate bias.

- **Ethical guidelines**: Ethical guidelines should be developed for the development and use of GANs. These guidelines should address issues such as transparency, accountability, auditing, and monitoring.

It is important to have a public discussion about the ethical implications of GANs before they are widely deployed in real-world applications. By developing ethical guidelines and working to mitigate the ethical concerns associated with GANs, we can ensure that these powerful tools are used for good.

Here are some additional thoughts on the ethical concerns associated with GANs:

- It is important to educate the public about the capabilities of GANs and the potential risks associated with their use. This will help people to be more critical of the information that they consume and more aware of the potential for manipulation and deception.

- It is also important to develop policies and regulations to govern the use of GANs. These policies and regulations should be designed to protect individual privacy and prevent GANs from being used for malicious purposes.

Overall, the ethical concerns associated with GANs are serious, but they are not insurmountable. By working together, we can develop the tools and policies that we need to ensure that GANs are used responsibly.

Future of generative adversarial networks

Despite the challenges, GANs have a bright future. Researchers are actively working to address the challenges of mode collapse, training instability, and computational cost. Additionally, new ethical guidelines are being developed to ensure that GANs are used responsibly.

Here are some specific areas of research that are being pursued to improve GANs:

New network architectures

Researchers are developing new network architectures that are more stable and less prone to mode collapse. New network architectures are one of the most promising areas of research in GANs. Researchers are developing new network architectures that are more stable, less prone to mode collapse, and more efficient to train.

Examples of new network architectures for GANs:

- **CapsuleGAN**: CapsuleGANs use a new type of neural network called a capsule network. Capsule networks are designed to learn the spatial relationships between features in images. This makes them well-suited for GANs, as GANs need to be able to generate images that are realistic and coherent.

- **ProgressiveGAN**: ProgressiveGANs train a GAN in stages, starting with generating low-resolution images and gradually increasing the resolution. This helps to stabilize the training process and prevent mode collapse.

- **StyleGAN**: StyleGANs use a new type of generator network that is designed to learn the different styles of images. This allows StyleGANs to generate highly realistic and diverse images.

Rationale for new network architectures

New network architectures are needed for GANs to address the challenges of mode collapse, training instability, and computational cost.

- **Mode collapse**: New network architectures can help to mitigate mode collapse by making the generator network more robust to changes in the training data and the discriminator network more difficult to fool.

- **Training instability**: New network architectures can help stabilize the training process by using techniques such as gradient clipping and batch normalization.

- **Computational cost**: New network architectures can help to reduce the computational cost of training GANs by using smaller and simpler networks, or by using distributed training techniques.

Examples of how new network architectures are being used in practice:

- CapsuleGANs are being used to generate realistic images of human faces and other objects.
- ProgressiveGANs are being used to generate high-resolution images of landscapes and other scenes.
- StyleGANs are being used to generate photorealistic images of human faces and other objects.

Overall, new network architectures are a promising area of research in GANs. By developing new network architectures that are more stable, less prone to mode collapse, and more efficient to train, researchers are making GANs more accessible to a wider range of users and applications.

In addition to the above examples, here are some other new network architectures that are being explored for GANs:

- **BigGAN**: BigGAN is a GAN architecture designed to generate high-resolution images of large and complex scenes.
- **MuseNet**: MuseNet is a GAN architecture designed to generate realistic music.
- **GauGAN**: GauGAN is a GAN architecture designed to translate images from one style to another.

These are just a few examples of the many new network architectures that are being developed for GANs. As GAN research continues to advance, we can expect to see even more innovative and powerful network architectures emerge.

New training algorithms

Researchers are developing new training algorithms that are more efficient and can train GANs on larger and more complex datasets. New training algorithms are another promising area of research in GANs. Researchers are developing new training algorithms that are more stable, efficient, and capable of generating higher quality data. Let us discuss some examples of GANs in the new training algorithms.

Examples of new training algorithms for generative adversarial networks

Below are some key examples of the new training algorithms for GANs:

- **Wasserstein GAN with gradient penalty (WGAN-GP)**: WGAN-GP uses a new method for training GANs called the Wasserstein distance. It is a more stable metric for measuring the distance between distributions than the binary cross-entropy loss function that is traditionally used in GANs.

- **Spectral normalization GAN (SNGAN)**: SNGAN uses a technique called spectral normalization to stabilize the training process of GANs. Spectral normalization helps to prevent the generator and discriminator networks from becoming too powerful.

- **Dual discriminator GAN (DualDGAN)**: DualDGAN uses two discriminator networks instead of one. This helps to improve the stability of the training process and the quality of the generated data.

Now let us discuss the need and rationale behind new training algorithms.

Rationale for new training algorithms

New training algorithms are needed for GANs to address the challenges of mode collapse, training instability, and generating high-quality data. Now let us explore the rationale behind it:

- **Mode collapse**: New training algorithms can help to mitigate mode collapse by making the training process more stable and by making the generator network less likely to get stuck in a local minimum.

- **Training instability**: New training algorithms can help to stabilize the training process by using techniques such as gradient clipping, spectral normalization, and dual discriminators.

- **Generating high-quality data**: New training algorithms can help to generate higher quality data by using loss functions that are specifically designed to measure the quality of generated data, such as the Wasserstein distance.

Examples of how new training algorithms are being used in practice

The new training algorithms have a wide practical implementation and approach, some of the examples for the same are listed below:

- WGAN-GP is being used to generate high-quality images of human faces and other objects.
- SNGAN is used to generate realistic images of landscapes and other scenes.
- DualDGAN is used to generate realistic music and other audio content.

Overall, new training algorithms are a promising area of research in GANs. By developing new training algorithms that are more stable, efficient, and capable of generating higher quality data, researchers are making GANs more useful for a wider range of applications.

In addition to the above examples, here are some other new training algorithms that are being explored for GANs:

- **BatchGAN**: BatchGAN is a training algorithm that allows GANs to be trained on batches of data instead of individual samples. This can significantly improve the training speed of GANs.
- **CycleGAN**: CycleGAN is a training algorithm that allows GANs to learn to translate images from one style to another without the need for paired training data.
- **StarGAN**: StarGAN is a training algorithm that allows GANs to learn to generate images of different objects and scenes with different attributes, such as hair color, eye color, and clothing style.

These are just a few examples of the many new training algorithms that are being developed for GANs. As GAN research continues to advance, we can expect to see even more innovative and powerful training algorithms emerge.

New objective functions

Researchers are developing new objective functions that can help to improve the quality of generated data and make GANs less susceptible to adversarial attacks.

New objective functions are another promising area of research in GANs. Researchers are developing new objective functions that are more effective at training GANs to generate high-quality data, that are more robust to mode collapse, and that are more efficient to compute.

Examples of new objective functions for generative adversarial networks

The examples are as follows:

- **Adversarial autoencoders (AAEs)**: AAE objective functions are designed to train GANs to generate data that is both realistic and diverse. AAEs work by training a generator to reconstruct data from a latent code, and then training a discriminator to distinguish between real data and reconstructed data.

- **Jensen-Shannon divergence (JSD)**: JSD objective functions are designed to train GANs to generate data that is similar to the training data in terms of its distribution. JSD objective functions are more robust to mode collapse than traditional GAN objective functions, such as the binary cross-entropy loss function.

- **Maximum mean discrepancy (MMD)**: MMD objective functions are designed to train GANs to generate data that is similar to the training data in terms of its statistical properties. MMD objective functions are more efficient to compute than traditional GAN objective functions, and they are also more robust to mode collapse.

Rationale for new objective functions

New objective functions are needed for GANs to address the challenges of generating high-quality data, mode collapse, and computational efficiency.

- **Generating high-quality data**: Traditional GAN objective functions, such as the binary cross-entropy loss function, are not well-suited for training GANs to generate high-quality data. New objective functions, such as AAE objective functions and JSD objective functions, are designed specifically to train GANs to generate high-quality data.

- **Mode collapse**: Traditional GAN objective functions are susceptible to mode collapse. New objective functions, such as JSD objective functions and MMD objective functions, are more robust to mode collapse.

- **Computational efficiency**: Traditional GAN objective functions can be computationally expensive to compute. New objective functions, such as MMD objective functions, are more efficient to compute.

Examples of how new objective functions are being used in practice

The new objective functions have a wide practical implementation and approach, some of the examples for the same are listed below:

- AAEs are being used to generate high-quality images of human faces and other objects.
- JSD objective functions are being used to train GANs to generate realistic images of landscapes and other scenes.
- MMD objective functions are being used to train GANs to generate realistic music and other audio content.

Overall, new objective functions are a promising area of research in GANs. By developing new objective functions that are more effective at training GANs to generate high-quality data, that are more robust to mode collapse, and that are more efficient to compute, researchers are making GANs more useful for a wider range of applications.

In addition to the above examples, here are some other new objective functions that are being explored for GANs:

- **Wasserstein GAN distance (WGAN-D)**: WGAN-D objective functions are designed to train GANs to generate data that is similar to the training data in terms of its Wasserstein distance. WGAN-D objective functions are more stable and less susceptible to mode collapse than traditional GAN objective functions.
- **Diversity-sensitive GAN (DSGAN)**: DSGAN objective functions are designed to train GANs to generate data that is diverse, in addition to being realistic. DSGAN objective functions can be used to generate a variety of different creative content, such as new fashion designs and new musical compositions.
- **Style-based GAN (StyleGAN)**: StyleGAN objective functions are designed to train GANs to generate data that has a specific style, such as the style of a particular artist or photographer. StyleGAN objective functions can be used to generate realistic images and videos that are indistinguishable from real ones.

These are just a few examples of the many new objective functions that are being developed for GANs. As GAN research continues to advance, we can expect to see even more innovative and powerful objective functions emerge.

Ethical guidelines

Researchers and industry experts are working to develop ethical guidelines for the development and use of GANs.

As these challenges are addressed and GAN technology continues to develop, we can expect to see GANs used in a wide variety of new and innovative applications. For example, GANs could be used to:

- Generate realistic synthetic data for training machine learning models.
- Create new forms of art and entertainment.

- Develop new tools for medical imaging and diagnosis.
- Improve the quality of products and services in a variety of industries.

In conclusion, this section provided the readers with a profound exploration of the intricate landscape surrounding GANs. Delving into the persistent challenges faced by GANs, from training instabilities to ethical considerations, the section has illuminated the complex nature of these generative models. By addressing ongoing research endeavors and proposed solutions, readers have gained valuable insights into the evolving strategies to overcome these challenges. This comprehensive overview equips readers with a deeper understanding of the current state and future directions of GAN research, fostering a nuanced perspective on the forefront of generative modeling.

Conclusion

In the chapter, the readers embarked on a comprehensive journey through the intricate world of GANs. Beginning with a thorough exploration of the architecture and training processes of GANs, readers gained a nuanced understanding of how these generative models operate. The chapter further delved into the challenges and ongoing research in the GAN domain, shedding light on issues such as training instabilities, ethical considerations, and the latest advancements in overcoming these hurdles. By navigating through the technical intricacies and cutting-edge developments, readers have acquired a profound insight into the current landscape and future prospects of GANs, empowering them with a comprehensive understanding of this dynamic field.

The upcoming chapter promises to equip readers with practical insights and skills essential for navigating the terrain of generative models. The chapter begins with a hands-on guide to developing these models, offering step-by-step instructions and practical tips for implementation. Subsequently, it delves into deployment considerations and best practices, addressing the crucial aspects of bringing generative models into real-world scenarios. To provide a holistic perspective, the chapter concludes by exploring common challenges in implementation and offering strategies to overcome them. Readers can anticipate a comprehensive and actionable guide, ensuring they are well-prepared to apply generative models effectively in various contexts.

Join our book's Discord space

Join the book's Discord Workspace for Latest updates, Offers, Tech happenings around the world, New Release and Sessions with the Authors:

https://discord.bpbonline.com

CHAPTER 8
Building and Deploying Generative Models

Introduction

This chapter serves as a crucial guide for readers seeking to transform theoretical knowledge into practical application. In the first section, readers can expect a hands-on and practical guide to developing generative models, providing them with actionable steps and insights. The chapter then shifts its focus to deployment considerations and best practices, emphasizing the importance of effectively integrating generative models into real-world scenarios. The final section addresses the inevitable challenges in implementation, offering strategies and solutions to overcome these obstacles. This chapter is instrumental in bridging the gap between theoretical understanding and practical implementation, equipping readers with the skills needed to navigate the complexities of building and deploying generative models effectively. The importance of this chapter lies in its ability to empower readers to apply their knowledge in real-world situations, fostering a deeper understanding of the practical aspects of generative models.

Structure

This chapter will cover the following topics:

- Practical guide to developing generative models
- Deploying generative models

- Deploying a variational autoencoder to AWS AI platform
- Deploying a generative adversarial network on Microsoft Azure
- AI services and tools
- Google Cloud Platform: AI platform (Unified)
- Deployment considerations and best practices
- Overcoming common challenges in implementation

Objectives

This chapter equips readers with the necessary skills and knowledge to transform their theoretical understanding of generative models into practical applications. It aims to bridge the gap between theory and practice by offering hands-on guidance on developing, deploying, and overcoming challenges associated with generative models. Specific learning objectives will include developing generative models, deploying generative models and overcoming implementation challenges. By the end of this chapter, readers will possess the practical skills necessary to build and deploy functional generative models. The readers will be able to effectively integrate generative models into real-world scenarios and gain a deeper understanding of the challenges and solutions involved in implementing generative models.

This chapter is instrumental in fostering a comprehensive understanding of generative models, enabling readers to confidently navigate the complexities of building and deploying them for real-world impact.

Practical guide to developing generative models

This essential section equips readers with a practical guide to developing generative models. It focuses on applying theoretical knowledge by covering key aspects like data preparation, architecture selection, and hyperparameter tuning. Popular frameworks and tools are explored with step-by-step instructions and code examples, along with best practices for training and optimization. This hands-on guide empowers readers to embark on their own projects, navigating the complexities of generative AI and gaining valuable experience.

Generative models are a type of machine learning model that can be used to generate new data. They are often used in applications such as image generation, music generation, and text generation.

To develop a generative model, you will need to:

- **Choose a generative model architecture**: There are many different generative model architectures available, such as **generative adversarial networks (GANs)**, **variational autoencoders (VAEs)**, and normalizing flows. Each architecture has strengths and weaknesses, so you will need to choose one that is appropriate for your specific task.

- **Collect and prepare a training dataset**: Generative models are trained on data, so you will need to collect a dataset of the type of data that you want to generate. The dataset should be as large and diverse as possible, in order to train a generative model that can generate high-quality data.

- **Train the generative model:** Once you have chosen a generative model architecture and collected a training dataset, you can start training the model. This process can be computationally expensive, so you may need to use a cloud computing platform such as Google Cloud Platform or Amazon Web Services.

- **Evaluate the generative model**: Once the generative model is trained, you need to evaluate its performance on a held-out test dataset. This will help you to assess the quality of the data that the model is generating.

- **Deploy the generative model**: Once you are satisfied with the performance of the generative model, you can deploy it to production. This may involve integrating the model into a web service or mobile app.

Here are some additional tips for developing generative models:

- **Use a variety of loss functions**: Many generative model architectures use multiple loss functions to train the model. This can help to improve the quality of the generated data and make the model more robust to mode collapse.

- **Regularize the model**: Regularization can help to prevent the generative model from overfitting to the training data. There are a variety of different regularization techniques available, such as weight decay and dropout.

- **Use a validation set**: A validation set is a held-out dataset that is used to monitor the performance of the generative model during training. This can help you to identify when the model is starting to overfit the training data and adjust the training hyperparameters accordingly.

- **Use batch normalization**: Batch normalization is a technique that can help to stabilize the training process of generative models. It is especially useful for training GANs.

- **Use a distributed training framework**: If you are training a generative model on a large dataset, you may need to use a distributed training framework such as Horovod or PyTorch Lightning. This will allow you to train the model faster and more efficiently.

Developing generative models can be a challenging task, but it is also a very rewarding one. By following the tips above, you can increase your chances of success.

Here are some additional resources that may be helpful:
- Generative Adversarial Networks: **https://arxiv.org/abs/1406.2661**
- Variational Autoencoders: **https://arxiv.org/abs/1312.6114**
- Normalizing Flows: **https://arxiv.org/abs/1505.05770**
- PyTorch Lightning: **https://www.pytorchlightning.ai/**
- Horovod: **https://horovod.ai/**

There are many different generative model architectures available, but some of the most popular ones include:
- **GANs**: GANs are a type of generative model that uses two neural networks - a generator and a discriminator. The generator is responsible for generating new data, while the discriminator is responsible for distinguishing between real data and generated data. The generator and discriminator are trained simultaneously, in a game-like fashion.
- **VAEs**: VAEs represent a type of generative model that uses a neural network to encode data into a latent space. The latent space is a lower-dimensional representation of the data that is easier to learn and generate from. Once the data has been encoded into the latent space, the VAE can generate new data by decoding from a random point in the latent space.
- **Normalizing flows**: These are a type of generative model that uses a series of invertible transformations to transform a simple distribution into a complex distribution. This allows normalizing flows to generate complex data, such as images and text.

Generative model architectures can be used to generate a wide variety of different types of data, including:
- Images
- Music
- Text
- Codes
- Videos
- 3D models

Generative models are becoming increasingly popular, as they can be used to create new and innovative products and services. For example, generative models are being used to develop new types of medical imaging tools, to create new forms of art and entertainment, and to develop new ways to generate creative content.

Here is a more detailed explanation of how GANs and VAEs work:

Generative adversarial networks

GANs work by training two neural networks in a game-like fashion. The first network, the generator, is responsible for generating new data. The second network, the discriminator, is responsible for distinguishing between real data and generated data.

The generator is trained to generate data that is indistinguishable from real data, while the discriminator is trained to distinguish between real data and generated data. The generator and discriminator are trained simultaneously, and they compete against each other to improve their performance.

Over time, the generator learns to generate realistic data that can fool the discriminator, while the discriminator learns to distinguish between real data and generated data more accurately. Let us discuss some aspects of it:

- **Generator network**: The generator in a GAN is tasked with creating new samples. It takes random noise as input and transforms it into data samples that should resemble the training data. The generator is typically a deep neural network that upscales the input noise to produce high-dimensional output data.

- **Discriminator network**: The discriminator is like a binary classifier that evaluates whether a given sample is real (from the training data) or fake (generated by the generator). It is also a neural network trained to distinguish between real and generated samples.

- **Training process**: GANs are trained in a competitive manner. The generator and discriminator are trained iteratively. The generator aims to produce samples that are indistinguishable from real ones, while the discriminator aims to improve its ability to differentiate between real and generated samples.

Variational autoencoders

VAEs work by encoding data into a latent space and then decoding the latent space to generate new data. The latent space is a lower-dimensional representation of the data that is easier to learn and generate from.

The VAE is trained to minimize the difference between the original data and the reconstructed data. This forces the VAE to learn a latent space that is representative of the original data, and it also forces the VAE to learn how to decode the latent space to generate new data.

VAEs are often used to generate creative content, such as images and text. For example, a VAE can be trained on a dataset of images of human faces. Once the VAE is trained, it can be used to generate new images of human faces, or to modify existing images of human faces.

Let us discuss some of its aspects:

- **Encoder network**: VAEs consist of an encoder that maps input data to a latent space representation. This space is typically a lower-dimensional representation capturing the essential features of the input data.
- **Decoder network**: The decoder reconstructs samples from the latent space representation. It generates new samples by sampling points in the latent space and decoding them into the original data space.
- **Training process**: VAEs are trained using a probabilistic approach. They maximize the likelihood of generating the training data and simultaneously minimize the difference between the encoded and decoded samples.

Generative model architectures are a powerful tool for generating new data. They can be used to create new and innovative products and services, and they are becoming increasingly popular in a wide range of industries.

Let us discuss how we can deploy these models in some detail.

Deploying generative models

Deploying generative models involves making them accessible for real-world applications, allowing users to interact with and benefit from the generated outputs. The deployment process includes considerations for integration into existing systems, scalability, and usability. Here is a guide on deploying generative models:

1. **Model serialization**: Serialize the trained generative model to a format that allows for easy storage and transport. Common formats include TensorFlow's SavedModel format, **Open Neural Network Exchange (ONNX)**, or PyTorch's TorchScript.
2. **Scalability**: Assess the scalability of the generative model to handle different workloads and varying input sizes. Use frameworks like TensorFlow Serving or ONNX Runtime for efficient and scalable deployment.
3. **API development**: Develop an **application programming interface (API)** to expose the generative model's functionality. RESTful APIs or GraphQL can be employed for easy integration with other software applications.
4. **Containerization**: Package the generative model and its dependencies into containers (for example, Docker containers) for consistent deployment across different environments. This ensures that the model runs consistently regardless of the underlying infrastructure.
5. **Cloud deployment**: Leverage cloud services for deploying generative models. Major cloud providers like AWS, Azure, and Google Cloud offer platforms (for example, AWS SageMaker, Azure Machine Learning, Google AI Platform) for deploying and managing machine learning models at scale.

6. **Edge deployment**: For scenarios where low latency is critical, consider deploying generative models on edge devices. Tools like TensorFlow Lite or ONNX Runtime for Edge provide lightweight solutions for running models on devices with resource constraints.

7. **Monitoring and logging**: Implement monitoring and logging to track the performance of the generative model in real-world scenarios. Monitor factors such as inference time, resource utilization, and model drift.

8. **Security considerations**: Ensure secure communication channels, especially when deploying generative models that handle sensitive data. Implement proper authentication and authorization mechanisms to control access to the model.

Examples of generative model deployment

Let us explore some examples of generative model deployment:

- **Image synthesis for e-commerce**: Deploy a generative model to generate synthetic images of products for an e-commerce platform to augment the available dataset.

- **Text generation for content creation**: Implement a generative text model to automatically create content for websites or social media platforms.

- **Style transfer in mobile apps**: Deploy a generative model for artistic style transfer in a mobile app, allowing users to apply different artistic styles to their photos.

To deploy a generative model, you will need to:

1. **Choose a deployment platform**: There are a number of different platforms that can be used to deploy generative models, such as cloud computing platforms (for example, Amazon Web Services, Google Cloud Platform, Microsoft Azure), on-premises servers, and mobile devices.

2. **Package the generative model**: Once you have chosen a deployment platform, you need to package the generative model for deployment. This may involve converting the model to a specific format (for example, ONNX, TensorFlow SavedModel), or integrating the model into a web service or mobile app.

3. **Deploy the generative model**: Once the generative model is packaged, you can deploy it to the deployment platform. This process will vary depending on the chosen platform.

4. **Monitor the deployed generative model**: Once the generative model is deployed, you need to monitor its performance to ensure that it is working as expected. This may involve tracking metrics such as model accuracy, latency, and throughput.

Here are some specific examples of how to deploy generative models:

- **Deploy a GAN to Amazon Web Services (AWS)**: To deploy a GAN to AWS, you can use AWS SageMaker. It is a fully managed machine learning platform that makes it easy to deploy and manage machine learning models in the cloud.

- **Deploy a VAE to Google Cloud Platform (GCP)**: To deploy a VAE to GCP, you can use Google Cloud AI Platform. Cloud AI Platform is a suite of machine learning products and services that makes it easy to build, train, and deploy machine learning models in the cloud.

- **Deploy a generative model to a mobile device**: To deploy a generative model to a mobile device, you can use a mobile machine learning framework such as TensorFlow Lite or PyTorch Mobile. These frameworks allow you to convert machine learning models to a format that can be run on mobile devices.

Here is an example of how to deploy a GAN to AWS SageMaker:

1. Create a SageMaker project and Notebook instance.
2. Upload the GAN model to the SageMaker S3 bucket.
3. Create a SageMaker model definition file that specifies the GAN model and its dependencies.
4. Create a SageMaker model from the model definition file.
5. Deploy the SageMaker model to a SageMaker endpoint.
6. Invoke the SageMaker endpoint to generate new data.

Generative adversarial networks deployment on AWS using CLI

Above are some high-level basic steps, let us understand how we can achieve the same using **command line interface (CLI)**. Deploying GAN to AWS SageMaker involves several steps, including preparing the model, packaging it, and deploying it. Below is a step-by-step example using the AWS CLI.

> Note: Please note that this is a simplified example, and you may need to adapt it based on your specific GAN model and requirements.

1. **Preparing the GAN model:** Ensure your GAN model is trained and saved in a format compatible with SageMaker. This often involves exporting the model in a format like TensorFlow's SavedModel or a similar format.

2. **Packaging the model:** Package the model into a compressed archive (for example, zip) along with any necessary dependencies. Here is a generic structure:

```
- model/
    - <your_model_files>
- code/
    - inference.py
    - requirements.txt
```

- **model**: Contains your trained GAN model files.
- **code**: Contains inference code and dependencies.

3. **Creating an S3 bucket:** Create an S3 bucket to store the model artifacts and code package. Replace **<your-bucket-name>** with a unique name.

   ```
   aws s3 mb s3://<your-bucket-name>
   ```

4. **Uploading model artifacts to S3:** Upload the model artifacts and code package to the S3 bucket.

   ```
   aws s3 cp model/ s3://<your-bucket-name>/model/ --recursive
   aws s3 cp code/ s3://<your-bucket-name>/code/ --recursive
   ```

5. **Creating a SageMaker model:** Create a SageMaker model using the SageMaker Python SDK.

   ```
   aws sagemaker create-model \
     --model-name gan-model \
     --execution-role-arn <your-role-arn> \
     --primary-container ImageUri.dkr.ecr.<your-region>.amazonaws.com/<your-gan-image>:latest
   ```

   Replace **<your-role-arn>**, **<your-region>**, and **<your-gan-image>** with your SageMaker role ARN, AWS region, and the URI of your GAN Docker image.

6. **Creating an endpoint configuration:** Create an endpoint configuration:

   ```
   aws sagemaker create-endpoint-config \
     --endpoint-config-name gan-endpoint-config \
     --production-variants VariantName=gan-variant,ModelName=gan-model,InstanceType=<your-instance-type>,InitialInstanceCount=1
   ```

   Replace **<your-instance-type>** with the desired SageMaker instance type.

7. **Creating an endpoint:** Create a SageMaker endpoint:

   ```
   aws sagemaker create-endpoint \
     --endpoint-name gan-endpoint \
     --endpoint-config-name gan-endpoint-config
   ```

8. **Updating the endpoint with the latest model**: Update the SageMaker endpoint to use the latest model:

   ```
   aws sagemaker update-endpoint --endpoint-name gan-endpoint
   --endpoint-config-name gan-endpoint-config
   ```

Now, your GAN model should be deployed on SageMaker. Keep in mind that this is a basic example, and you might need to adjust it based on your specific GAN model and deployment requirements. Additionally, consider automating this process using AWS CloudFormation or SageMaker SDK for more complex deployments.

In addition to using the AWS CLI as described earlier, there are alternative ways to deploy a GAN on AWS. Here are a couple of alternative methods:

SageMaker Studio

Amazon SageMaker Studio provides an integrated development environment for building, training, and deploying machine learning models. You can use SageMaker Studio notebooks to develop and deploy your GAN.

1. Creating a SageMaker Studio Notebook:

   a. Open SageMaker Studio.

   b. Create a new notebook and select a SageMaker image with the necessary deep learning libraries.

   c. In the Notebook, you can write the code for training and deployment.

2. Training and deploying from the Notebook:

   a. Train your GAN model within the notebook.

   b. Use the SageMaker Python SDK to deploy the model to an endpoint.

AWS Console

You can also use the AWS Management Console to create and manage SageMaker resources.

1. SageMaker console:

   a. Open the SageMaker console.

   b. Navigate to the **Notebook instances** section to create a new Notebook instance.

   c. Open the **Notebook** and follow the same steps mentioned in the **Studio** approach.

2. Endpoint creation:

   a. After training your GAN model, navigate to the **Endpoints** section in the SageMaker console.

   b. Create an endpoint and associate it with your trained model.

AWS SDKs and APIs

You can use AWS **software development kits** (**SDKs**) in your preferred programming language or directly make API calls to AWS services.

1. AWS SDKs:

   a. Use AWS SDKs such as Boto3 for Python, AWS SDK for Java, or AWS SDK for other supported languages.

   b. Write scripts to automate the creation, training, and deployment processes.

2. AWS CLI Commands:

Directly use AWS CLI commands or scripts for creating, training, and deploying models.

Each of these methods provides flexibility, and the choice depends on your preference, development environment, and workflow. SageMaker Studio and AWS Console are more user-friendly interfaces, while SDKs and APIs offer programmatic control and automation. Choose the approach that aligns with your workflow and development preferences.

Deploying a variational autoencoder on AWS AI platform

Deploying a VAE on AWS involves several steps, including preparing the model, setting up an inference environment, and deploying the model using AWS services like Amazon SageMaker. The following is a high-level guide to deploying a VAE on AWS:

1. **Train and save the VAE model**: Train your VAE model using your preferred machine learning framework (for example, TensorFlow, PyTorch). Save the trained model and any necessary artefacts.

2. **Set up an inference script**: Create a script or code that defines the inference process for your VAE model. This script should load the trained model, handle input data preprocessing, and perform inference to generate output.

3. **Dockerize the inference code**: Create a Docker container that encapsulates your inference script and any dependencies. This container will be used to run the inference code on AWS SageMaker.

4. **Push Docker image to Amazon ECR**: Amazon **Elastic Container Registry (ECR)** is a fully managed container registry that makes it easy to store, manage, and deploy Docker container images. Push your Docker image to Amazon ECR.

   a) Authenticate Docker to your ECR registry:
   ```
   aws ecr get-login-password --region <your-region> | docker login --username AWS --password-stdin <your-account-id>.dkr.ecr.<your-region>.amazonaws.com
   ```

   b) Tag your Docker image:
   ```
   docker tag <your-image> <your-account-id>.dkr.ecr.<your-region>.amazonaws.com/<your-repository>:<tag>
   ```

   c) Push the Docker image to ECR:
   ```
   docker push <your-account-id>.dkr.ecr.<your-region>.amazonaws.com/<your-repository>:<tag>
   ```

5. **Create an Amazon SageMaker model**: Use Amazon SageMaker to create a model by specifying the Docker image stored in your ECR repository. Define the inference script and model artifacts.

6. **Deploy the model to an endpoint**: Deploy the SageMaker model to an endpoint. This endpoint can then be used to make predictions with your VAE model.

Example of deployment script

Below is a simplified example using AWS CLI commands for deploying a VAE model on SageMaker. Adjust the details according to your specific setup.

1. Create a SageMaker model:
   ```
   aws sagemaker create-model --model-name <your-model-name> --primary-container Image="<your-image>",ModelDataUrl="<your-model-artifacts-S3-url>"
   ```

2. Create an endpoint configuration:
   ```
   aws sagemaker create-endpoint-config --endpoint-config-name <your-endpoint-config-name> --production-variants VariantName=<your-variant-name>,ModelName=<your-model-name>,InstanceType=<instance-type>,InitialInstanceCount=<instance-count>
   ```

3. Create an endpoint:
   ```
   aws sagemaker create-endpoint --endpoint-name <your-endpoint-name> --endpoint-config-name <your-endpoint-config-name>
   ```

4. Wait for the endpoint to be in-service:

   ```
   aws sagemaker wait endpoint-in-service --endpoint-name <your-endpoint-name>
   ```

This script assumes that you have set up your Docker image with the necessary inference code and dependencies. Adjust the parameters and commands based on your specific use case and environment.

Besides using the AWS CLI and Amazon SageMaker directly, you can also deploy a VAE on AWS using AWS SageMaker Studio, AWS Console, or even through AWS SDKs in various programming languages. Below is an alternative way to use the AWS Management Console:

Deploying variational autoencoder on AWS SageMaker via console

In this section we will explore how to deploy VAE on AWS SageMaker via console. The steps are detailed below:

1. **Prepare model artifacts**: Train your VAE model using your chosen machine learning framework. Save the trained model and any required artifacts.

2. **Create an S3 bucket**: Upload your model artifacts and any additional files to an S3 bucket.

3. **Open SageMaker in AWS Console**: Navigate to the Amazon SageMaker service in the AWS Management Console.

4. **Create a model**: In the SageMaker console, go to **Models** and click **Create model**. Provide a name for your model, choose the runtime (for example, TensorFlow, PyTorch), and specify the S3 path to your model artifacts.

5. **Create an endpoint configuration**: In the SageMaker console, go to **Endpoint configurations** and click **Create endpoint configuration**. Associate the model you created with this configuration.

6. **Deploy an endpoint**: Go to **Endpoints** in the SageMaker console and click **Create endpoint**. Choose the endpoint configuration you created. Choose the type and number of instances for deployment.

7. **Testing the endpoint**: Once the endpoint is deployed, you can test it by sending inference requests.

This method utilizes the AWS Management Console for a more visual and interactive deployment process. It is suitable for users who prefer a graphical interface over the command line. Adjust the steps based on your specific requirements and preferences.

Deploying a generative adversarial network

Deploying a GAN on Google Cloud involves several steps. Below is a simplified example using Google Cloud's AI Platform.

Deploying GAN on Google Cloud AI platform

Let us explore how to deploy a GAN on Google Cloud AI Platform. Detailed below are the steps to do this deployment:

1. **Preparing model artifacts**: Train your GAN model using your preferred machine learning framework. Save the trained model and any required files.

2. **Uploading model to Google Cloud storage**: Upload your model artifacts and any additional files to a **Google Cloud Storage (GCS)** bucket.

3. **Opening Google Cloud Console**: Navigate to the Google Cloud Console.

4. **Navigating to AI Platform**: In the left navigation pane, go to **AI Platform**.

5. **Creating a model**: Click on **Model** and then click **Create model**. Provide a name for your model.

6. **Creating a version**: Inside your model, click **Create version**. Choose a version name and select the GCS path to your model artifacts.

7. **Configuring runtime version**: Choose the appropriate runtime version for your model.

8. **Deploying the model**: Once the version is created, click **Deploy** to deploy the model. Choose the machine type, the number of instances, and other deployment settings.

9. **Testing the endpoint**: After deployment, you can test the model by sending inference requests.

> Note: This example assumes you are using Google Cloud AI Platform for deployment. Adjust the steps based on your specific GAN model, framework, and deployment requirements. Ensure that you have the necessary permissions to create and deploy models in your Google Cloud project.

Example of deploying a GAN on Google Cloud using the CLI

Deploying a GAN on Google Cloud using the CLI involves several steps. Below is a simplified example using Google Cloud SDK:

Deploying GAN on Google Cloud AI Platform using CLI:

1. **Prepare model artifacts**: Train your GAN model using your preferred machine learning framework. Save the trained model and any required files.

2. **Upload model to Google Cloud Storage**: Upload your model artifacts and any additional files to a **Google Cloud Storage (GCS)** bucket.

3. **Install Google Cloud SDK**: Make sure you have the Google Cloud SDK installed on your local machine.

4. **Authenticate with Google Cloud**: Run Gcloud auth login to authenticate with your Google Cloud account.

5. **Set project ID**: Run Gcloud config set project **PROJECT_ID** to set your Google Cloud project ID.

6. **Deploy the model**: Use the following command to deploy your model to AI Platform:

    ```
    gcloud ai-platform models create MODEL_NAME
    gcloud ai-platform versions create VERSION_NAME \
        --model=MODEL_NAME \
        --origin=gs://YOUR_MODEL_BUCKET_PATH \
        --runtime-version=2.6 \
        --framework="TENSORFLOW" \
        --python-version=3.7
    ```

    Replace **MODEL_NAME**, **VERSION_NAME**, and **YOUR_MODEL_BUCKET_PATH** with your model details.

7. **Testing the endpoint**: After deployment, you can test the model by sending inference requests using the deployed AI Platform endpoint.

This example assumes you are using TensorFlow as your machine learning framework. Adjust the commands based on your specific GAN model, framework, and deployment requirements. Ensure that you have the necessary permissions to create and deploy models in your Google Cloud project.

Here is a high-level example of how to deploy a VAE to Google Cloud AI Platform:

1. Create a Cloud AI Platform project and notebook instance.

2. Upload the VAE model to the Cloud AI Platform Cloud Storage bucket.

3. Create a Cloud AI Platform model definition file that specifies the VAE model and its dependencies.

4. Deploy the Cloud AI Platform model to a Cloud AI Platform model server.
5. Invoke the Cloud AI Platform model server to generate new data.

Here is an example of how to deploy a generative model to a mobile device:

1. Convert the generative model to a TensorFlow Lite or PyTorch Mobile model.
2. Integrate the TensorFlow Lite or PyTorch Mobile model into a mobile app.
3. Deploy the mobile app to the mobile device.
4. Invoke the mobile app to generate new data.

Deploying generative models can be a complex task, but it is essential for making generative models accessible to a wider range of users. By following the steps above, you can deploy your generative model to a variety of platforms and make it available to users around the world.

Deploying a variational autoencoder on Google Cloud AI Platform using the CLI

Deploying a VAE on Google Cloud AI Platform using the CLI involves several steps. Below is a simplified example using Google Cloud SDK:

1. **Prepare model artifacts**: Train your VAE model using your preferred machine learning framework. Save the trained model and any required files.
2. **Upload model to Google Cloud Storage**: Upload your model artifacts and any additional files to a GCS bucket.
3. **Install Google Cloud SDK**: Make sure you have the Google Cloud SDK installed on your local machine.
4. **Authenticate with Google Cloud**: Run gcloud auth login to authenticate with your Google Cloud account.
5. **Set Project ID**: Run gcloud config set project **PROJECT_ID** to set your Google Cloud project ID.
6. **Deploy the model**: Use the following command to deploy your model to AI Platform:

```
gcloud ai-platform models create MODEL_NAME
gcloud ai-platform versions create VERSION_NAME \
  --model=MODEL_NAME \
  --origin=gs://YOUR_MODEL_BUCKET_PATH \
  --runtime-version=2.6 \
```

```
--framework="TENSORFLOW" \
--python-version=3.7
```

Replace **MODEL_NAME**, **VERSION_NAME**, and **YOUR_MODEL_BUCKET_PATH** with your model details.

7. **Testing the endpoint**: After deployment, you can test the model by sending inference requests using the deployed AI Platform endpoint.

This example assumes you are using TensorFlow as your machine learning framework. Adjust the commands based on your specific VAE model, framework, and deployment requirements. Ensure that you have the necessary permissions to create and deploy models in your Google Cloud project.

Deploying a generative adversarial network on Microsoft Azure

Deploying a GAN on Microsoft Azure involves using Azure machine learning service. Below is a simplified example using Azure CLI:

Deploying GAN on Microsoft Azure using CLI:

1. **Prepare model artifacts**: Train your GAN model using your preferred machine learning framework. Save the trained GAN model and any required files.

2. **Upload model to Azure Blob Storage:** Upload your model artifacts and any additional files to an Azure Blob Storage container.

3. **Install Azure CLI**: Make sure you have the Azure CLI installed on your local machine.

4. **Log in to Azure**: Run az login to log in to your Azure account.

5. **Create Azure Machine Learning workspace**: If you do not have an Azure Machine Learning workspace, create one using the Azure Portal or the following CLI command:

   ```
   az ml workspace create -w WORKSPACE_NAME -g RESOURCE_GROUP
   ```

   Replace WORKSPACE_NAME and RESOURCE_GROUP with your desired names.

6. **Upload model to Azure Machine Learning workspace:** Use the following command to upload your model to Azure Machine Learning:

   ```
   az ml model register -m MODEL_PATH -n MODEL_NAME --asset-path ASSET_PATH --model-framework MODEL_FRAMEWORK
   ```

Replace **MODEL_PATH**, **MODEL_NAME**, **ASSET_PATH**, and **MODEL_FRAMEWORK** with your model details.

7. **Deploy the model**: Deploy the registered model as a web service using the following command:

```
az ml model deploy -n SERVICE_NAME --service-usage SCORING_ENDPOINT -w WORKSPACE_NAME --cpu CORES --memory MEMORY
```

Replace **SERVICE_NAME**, **SCORING_ENDPOINT**, **WORKSPACE_NAME**, **CORES**, and **MEMORY** with your deployment details.

8. **Testing the endpoint**: After deployment, you can test the model by sending inference requests to the deployed Azure Machine Learning endpoint.

Adjust the commands based on your specific GAN model, framework, and deployment requirements. Ensure that you have the necessary permissions to create and deploy models in your Azure subscription.

Deploying a variational autoencoder on Microsoft Azure

Deploying a VAE on Microsoft Azure involves using Azure Machine Learning service. Below is a simplified example using Azure CLI:

1. **Prepare model artifacts**: Train your VAE model using your preferred machine learning framework. Save the trained VAE model and any required files.

2. **Upload model to Azure Blob Storage**: Upload your model artifacts and any additional files to an Azure Blob Storage container.

3. **Install Azure CLI**: Make sure you have the Azure CLI installed on your local machine.

4. **Log in to Azure**: Run **az** login to log in to your Azure account.

5. **Create Azure Machine Learning Workspace**: If you do not have an Azure Machine Learning workspace, create one using the Azure Portal or the following CLI command:

```
az ml workspace create -w WORKSPACE_NAME -g RESOURCE_GROUP
```

Replace **WORKSPACE_NAME** and **RESOURCE_GROUP** with your desired names.

6. **Upload model to Azure Machine Learning workspace**: Use the following command to upload your model to Azure Machine Learning:

```
az ml model register -m MODEL_PATH -n MODEL_NAME --asset-path ASSET_
PATH --model-framework MODEL_FRAMEWORK
```

Replace **MODEL_PATH**, **MODEL_NAME**, **ASSET_PATH**, and **MODEL_FRAMEWORK** with your model details.

7. **Deploy the model**: Deploy the registered model as a web service using the following command:

```
az ml model deploy -n SERVICE_NAME --service-usage SCORING_ENDPOINT -w
WORKSPACE_NAME --cpu CORES --memory MEMORY
```

Replace **SERVICE_NAME**, **SCORING_ENDPOINT**, **WORKSPACE_NAME**, **CORES**, and **MEMORY** with your deployment details.

8. **Testing the endpoint**: After deployment, you can test the model by sending inference requests to the deployed Azure Machine Learning endpoint.

   Adjust the commands based on your specific VAE model, framework, and deployment requirements. Ensure that you have the necessary permissions to create and deploy models in your Azure subscription.

AI services and tools

Deployment of GANs on Cloud platforms like AWS, Google Cloud, and Azure involves using their respective services and tools. Below is a list of tools or services commonly used for GAN deployment on each platform:

AWS: Amazon SageMaker

Amazon SageMaker is a fully managed service provided by AWS that simplifies the process of building, training, and deploying **machine learning** (**ML**) models at scale. It offers a comprehensive set of tools and capabilities for every step of the ML lifecycle, making it easier for developers and data scientists to experiment, iterate, and deploy models into production.

Value proposition of Amazon SageMaker

SageMaker offers a number of key benefits that make it a valuable tool for developers and businesses of all sizes:

1. **Ease of use**: SageMaker is a fully managed service, which means that developers can focus on building and training ML models without having to worry about managing the underlying infrastructure.

2. **Scalability**: SageMaker can be scaled to meet the needs of any size project. Developers can easily spin up new instances to train and deploy their models. They can scale down their instances when they are not in use.

3. **Cost-effectiveness**: SageMaker is a cost-effective solution for ML development and deployment. Developers can only pay for the resources that they use, and they can save money by using SageMaker's managed services.

4. **Comprehensive capabilities**: SageMaker provides a broad set of capabilities that can be used to address a wide range of ML tasks. This makes SageMaker a one-stop shop for ML development and deployment.

Key features

Below are the key features of AWS SageMaker:

- **End-to-end ML lifecycle management:** Value: SageMaker provides a seamless workflow from data preparation and model development to training and deployment.

- **Built-in algorithms:** Value: SageMaker includes a variety of pre-built algorithms for common ML tasks, saving time and effort in model development.

- **Notebook instances**: Integrated Jupyter Notebooks allow data scientists to explore and visualize data, prototype models, and collaborate in a single environment.

- **AutoML capabilities**: SageMaker Autopilot enables automatic model training and tuning, simplifying the process for users with less ML expertise.

- **Scalable training**: SageMaker allows training ML models on distributed clusters, making it suitable for large datasets and complex models.

- **Model deployment**: SageMaker facilitates easy deployment of models with managed endpoints, ensuring scalability and high availability.

- **Monitoring and management**: SageMaker provides tools for monitoring model performance, tracking changes, and managing models over time.

- **Security and compliance**: SageMaker adheres to AWS security best practices, offering features like encryption, VPC support, and integration with AWS **identity and access management (IAM)**.

Use cases

Below are some use cases of AWS SageMaker:

- **Image and video analysis**: SageMaker can be used for building and deploying models for image classification, object detection, and video analysis.

- **Natural language processing**: NLP tasks, such as sentiment analysis, text summarization, and language translation, can leverage SageMaker's capabilities.

- **Predictive analytics**: Organizations can use SageMaker for building predictive models for scenarios like demand forecasting, fraud detection, and recommendation systems.

- **Healthcare and life sciences**: SageMaker supports applications in healthcare, including medical image analysis, disease prediction, and drug discovery.

- **Financial services**: Financial institutions use SageMaker for tasks like risk modeling, fraud detection, and algorithmic trading strategies.

- **Custom ML models**: SageMaker is flexible and can be used for a wide range of custom ML models based on specific business needs and industry requirements.

In summary, Amazon SageMaker simplifies the complexity of machine learning workflows, enabling users to focus on model development and business outcomes rather than the underlying infrastructure. Its integration with AWS services and scalable architecture makes it a versatile choice for a variety of industries and use cases.

Examples of how Amazon SageMaker is used

Here are a few examples of how Amazon SageMaker is used by businesses today:

- **Netflix**: Netflix uses SageMaker to train and deploy recommendation systems that recommend movies and TV shows to its users.

- **Airbnb**: Airbnb uses SageMaker to train and deploy fraud detection models that identify and prevent fraudulent bookings.

- **Amazon**: Amazon uses SageMaker to train and deploy a variety of ML models, including image recognition models, natural language processing models, and fraud detection models.

Amazon SageMaker is a powerful ML platform that can be used to build, train, and deploy ML models quickly and easily. SageMaker offers a number of key benefits, including ease of use, scalability, cost-effectiveness, and comprehensive capabilities. SageMaker is used by businesses of all sizes to address a wide range of ML tasks.

Google Cloud Platform: AI Platform (Unified)

Google AI Platform (Unified) is a comprehensive ML platform offered by Google Cloud. It brings together various tools and services to streamline the end-to-end ML lifecycle, from data preparation and model development to training and deployment. The platform is designed to empower data scientists and ML engineers to build and deploy models at scale. It combines the capabilities of AutoML and AI Platform (Classic) into a single, unified platform that makes it easier for developers and businesses of all sizes to get started with ML.

Value proposition of Google AI Platform (Unified)

Below is the value proposition of Google's Unified AI Platform:

- **Ease of use**: Google AI Platform (Unified) is designed to be easy to use, even for those with limited ML experience. It provides a variety of tools and resources to help developers get started with ML, including pre-trained models, code samples, and tutorials.

- **Scalability**: Google AI Platform (Unified) is a scalable platform that can be used to train and deploy ML models at any scale. It can be used to train and deploy models on a single machine, or it can be used to train and deploy models on clusters of thousands of machines.

- **Cost-effectiveness**: Google AI Platform (Unified) is a cost-effective platform for ML. It offers a variety of pricing options, including pay-as-you-go and reserved instances. This makes it easy for developers and businesses to find a pricing option that meets their needs.

- **Comprehensive capabilities**: Google AI Platform (Unified) provides a broad range of capabilities for ML, including:
    - Data preparation and engineering
    - Model training and deployment
    - Model monitoring and management
    - ML pipelines
    - MLOps

Key features

Below are the key features of Google's Unified AI Platform:

- **Unified AI Platform**: The platform provides a unified environment for developing, training, and deploying ML models, enabling seamless collaboration across teams.

- **AutoML capabilities**: AutoML features, such as AutoML Tables and AutoML Image, allow users to automatically generate high-quality models with minimal manual intervention.

- **Managed Notebooks**: AI Platform offers managed Jupyter Notebooks for interactive and collaborative model development, making it easy for data scientists to experiment with data and models.

- **Custom model training**: Users have the flexibility to train custom models using popular ML frameworks like TensorFlow and scikit-learn, providing control over the model architecture.

- **Model deployment**: AI platform facilitates the deployment of models as RESTful APIs, making it easy to integrate ML capabilities into applications.

- **Model monitoring and explainability**: The platform includes tools for monitoring model performance and understanding model predictions, enhancing transparency and interpretability.

- **Scaling and optimization**: Google AI Platform supports scalable training on powerful cloud infrastructure, enabling the training of large models and handling big datasets efficiently.

- **Pre-built models**: Users can leverage pre-built models for common use cases, such as image classification and text sentiment analysis, accelerating development timelines.

Use cases

Below are some of the use cases of Google's Unified AI Platform:

- **Recommendation systems**: AI Platform can be used to build recommendation systems for personalized content delivery in applications like streaming services and e-commerce.

- **Image and video analysis**: Users can develop models for tasks like image classification, object detection, and video analysis using AI Platform's capabilities.

- **Natural language processing**: Applications in NLP, including text classification, sentiment analysis, and language translation, can benefit from the platform's tools.

- **Time series forecasting**: AI Platform supports the development of models for predicting time series data, making it useful for applications like demand forecasting and financial market analysis.

- **Healthcare and life sciences**: The platform can be applied to healthcare scenarios, including medical image analysis, patient risk prediction, and drug discovery.

- **Financial services**: Financial institutions can utilize AI Platform for tasks such as fraud detection, credit scoring, and algorithmic trading.

- **Custom ML models**: AI Platform's flexibility allows organizations to build custom ML models tailored to specific business needs and industry requirements.

Examples of how Google AI Platform (Unified) is used

Here are a few examples of how Google AI Platform (Unified) is used by businesses today:
- **Spotify**: Spotify uses Google AI Platform (Unified) to train and deploy recommendation models that recommend songs and playlists to its users.
- **PayPal**: PayPal utilizes Google AI Platform (Unified) to train and deploy fraud detection models that identify and prevent fraudulent transactions.
- **Coca-Cola**: Coca-Cola trained and deployed image recognition models that identify and classify objects in images using Google AI Platform (Unified).

In summary, Google AI Platform (Unified) offers a powerful and integrated solution for ML development and deployment. Its unified environment, AutoML capabilities, and support for custom models make it suitable for a wide range of industries and use cases. The platform's integration with Google Cloud's broader ecosystem enhances its appeal for organizations looking for a comprehensive solution for their ML initiatives.

Microsoft Azure: Azure Machine Learning

Microsoft Azure Machine Learning is a cloud-based platform that provides a comprehensive set of tools and services for building, training, and deploying machine learning models. It is part of the Microsoft Azure cloud ecosystem and is designed to empower data scientists, developers, and businesses to harness the power of artificial intelligence.

Value proposition of Microsoft Azure Machine Learning

Azure Machine Learning offers several key benefits that make it a valuable tool for developers and businesses of all sizes:
- **Ease of use**: Azure Machine Learning is designed to be easy to use, even for those with limited ML experience. It provides a variety of tools and resources to help developers get started with ML, including pre-trained models, code samples, and tutorials.
- **Scalability**: Azure Machine Learning is a scalable platform that can be used to train and deploy ML models at any scale. It can be used to train and deploy models on a single machine, or it can be used to train and deploy models on clusters of thousands of machines.
- **Cost-effectiveness**: Azure Machine Learning is a cost-effective platform for ML. It offers a variety of pricing options, including pay-as-you-go and reserved instances. This makes it easy for developers and businesses to find a pricing option that meets their needs.
- **Comprehensive capabilities**: Azure Machine Learning provides a broad range of capabilities for ML, including:

- Data preparation and engineering
- Model training and deployment
- Model monitoring and management
- ML pipelines
- MLOps

Key features

Below are some of the key features of Azure ML:

- **End-to-end ML lifecycle management**: Azure Machine Learning covers the entire machine learning lifecycle, from data preparation and model training to deployment and monitoring, offering a seamless experience for users.
- **Automated Machine Learning (AutoML)**: Azure AutoML simplifies model development by automating various tasks, such as feature engineering and hyperparameter tuning, enabling users to build high-quality models with minimal effort.
- **Open and flexible**: Azure Machine Learning supports a wide range of popular open-source frameworks, including TensorFlow, PyTorch, and scikit-learn, providing flexibility and compatibility with existing workflows.
- **Integration with Azure services**: Seamless integration with other Azure services, such as Azure Databricks and Azure Synapse Analytics, enables users to leverage a unified analytics platform for data preparation and processing.
- **Model interpretability and explainability**: The platform includes tools for interpreting and explaining model predictions, promoting transparency and understanding of machine learning models.
- **Enterprise-grade security and compliance**: Azure Machine Learning adheres to industry-leading security and compliance standards, making it suitable for enterprises with stringent data protection requirements.
- **Scalable model training and inference**: Azure provides scalable cloud infrastructure for model training and inference, allowing users to handle large datasets and deploy models to production environments with ease.
- **DevOps integration**: Integration with Azure DevOps facilitates **continuous integration and deployment (CI/CD)** for machine learning models, ensuring efficient development workflows.
- **Azure Machine Learning studio**: The drag-and-drop interface of Azure Machine Learning Studio provides a visual environment for building, testing, and deploying machine learning models without extensive coding.

Use cases

Below are some of the use cases of Azure ML:

- **Predictive analytics**: Organizations can use Azure Machine Learning for predictive analytics, forecasting, and anomaly detection to gain insights into future trends and patterns.

- **Customer churn prediction**: By analyzing historical customer data, businesses can build models to predict customer churn, allowing proactive retention strategies.

- **Computer vision applications**: Azure supports computer vision applications, including image classification, object detection, and facial recognition, applicable in industries like retail, healthcare, and security.

- **Natural language processing**: Applications in NLP, such as sentiment analysis, chatbots, and language translation, can be developed using Azure Machine Learning.

- **Healthcare and life sciences**: The platform can be utilized for healthcare applications, such as medical image analysis, patient outcome prediction, and drug discovery.

- **Manufacturing and supply chain optimization**: Azure Machine Learning can help optimize manufacturing processes, improve supply chain efficiency, and forecast demand.

- **Fraud detection**: Financial institutions can deploy models for fraud detection and prevention, leveraging the platform's capabilities.

- **Energy consumption forecasting**: Azure Machine Learning can be used to build models for forecasting energy consumption, supporting sustainable and efficient energy management.

Examples of how Microsoft Azure Machine Learning is used

Here are a few examples of how Microsoft Azure Machine Learning is used by businesses today:

- **BMW**: BMW uses Azure Machine Learning to train and deploy image recognition models that identify and classify objects in images. These models are used to automate the quality control process for BMW vehicles.

- **Starbucks**: Starbucks uses Azure Machine Learning to train and deploy recommendation models that recommend drinks and food items to its customers. These models are used to increase sales and improve the customer experience.

- **JPMorgan Chase**: JPMorgan Chase uses Azure Machine Learning to train and deploy fraud detection models that identify and prevent fraudulent transactions. These models are used to protect JPMorgan Chase customers from fraud.

Microsoft Azure Machine Learning is a powerful ML platform that can be used to build, train, and deploy ML models quickly and easily. It offers a number of key benefits, including ease of use, scalability, cost-effectiveness, and comprehensive capabilities. Azure Machine Learning is used by businesses of all sizes to address a wide range of ML tasks.

Here are some additional benefits of using Microsoft Azure Machine Learning:

- **Integration with other Azure services**: Azure Machine Learning integrates with other Azure services, such as Azure Databricks, Azure Synapse Analytics, and Azure Storage, making it easy to build and deploy end-to-end ML pipelines.

- **Open source support**: Azure Machine Learning supports a variety of open source ML frameworks, such as TensorFlow, PyTorch, and scikit-learn. This makes it easy for developers to use their favorite ML frameworks with Azure Machine Learning.

- **Responsible AI**: Azure Machine Learning provides a number of features to help developers build responsible AI solutions, such as model fairness and explainability tools.

In summary, Microsoft Azure Machine Learning offers a robust and versatile platform for machine learning development and deployment. Its integration with Azure services, support for various frameworks, and focus on automation make it a valuable tool for a diverse range of industries and use cases. The platform's commitment to openness, security, and scalability enhances its appeal for organizations seeking a comprehensive solution for their machine learning initiatives.

Let us compare AWS SageMaker, Google AI Platform (Unified), and Microsoft Azure Machine Learning across various dimensions. Major differences between AWS SageMaker, Google AI Platform (Unified), and Microsoft Azure Machine Learning are given in *Table 8.1*:

Feature	AWS SageMaker	Google AI Platform (Unified)	Microsoft Azure Machine Learning
Ease of use	Medium	Easy	Easy
Scalability	High	High	High
Cost-effectiveness	Medium	Medium	Medium
Comprehensive Capabilities	High	High	High
Pre-trained models	Wide range	Wide range	Wide range
Code samples and tutorials	Wide range	Wide range	Wide range

Feature	AWS SageMaker	Google AI Platform (Unified)	Microsoft Azure Machine Learning
Integration with other cloud services	Deep integration with AWS cloud services	Deep integration with Google cloud services	Deep integration with Azure services
Open-source support	Supports Tensorflow, Py Torch and scikit-learn	Supports Tensorflow, Py Torch and scikit-learn	Supports Tensorflow, Py Torch and scikit-learn
Responsible AI	Provides features for model fairness and explainability	Provides features for model fairness and explainability	Provides features for model fairness and explainability

Table 8.1: Comparison between AWS SageMaker, Google AI Platform (Unified), and Microsoft Azure Machine Learning

In addition to the above, here are some other key differences between the three platforms:

- AWS SageMaker is a more mature platform than Google AI Platform (Unified) and Microsoft Azure Machine Learning. It has a wider range of pre-trained models and code samples and tutorials. However, it can be more complex to use than the other two platforms.

- Google AI Platform (Unified) is the most user-friendly of the three platforms. It has a simple and intuitive interface, and it provides a variety of tools and resources to help developers get started with ML.

- Microsoft Azure Machine Learning offers the best integration with other cloud services. It also has a strong focus on responsible AI, with a number of features to help developers build responsible AI solutions.

Overall, the best platform for you will depend on your specific needs and requirements. If you are looking for a mature platform with a wide range of features, then AWS SageMaker is a good choice. If you are looking for a user-friendly platform, then Google AI Platform (Unified) is a good choice. If you are looking for a platform with deep integration with other cloud services and a strong focus on responsible AI, then Microsoft Azure Machine Learning is a good choice.

Readers in this section gained invaluable hands-on experience building generative models. They explored the intricate process, from understanding principles to deploying models in real-world scenarios. The guide detailed generative model architecture and equipped readers with the practical understanding of deploying generative adversarial networks on major cloud platforms. Through practical examples and deployment considerations, readers expanded their knowledge and acquired skills to translate theory into action. This section serves as a practical guide, fostering a deeper understanding of developing and deploying generative models.

The next section delves into deploying generative models effectively. Readers will explore key considerations and strategies for deploying models at scale. The section will address challenges and intricacies, including infrastructure requirements, scalability concerns, and optimization techniques. Additionally, it will discuss best practices for ensuring reliability, efficiency, and security of deployed models. This final piece equips readers with knowledge and practices essential for successful and sustainable deployment of generative models in various applications.

Deployment considerations and best practices

In this section, readers will gain valuable insights into the intricacies of deploying generative models effectively. The content will cover a spectrum of considerations ranging from infrastructure requirements to scalability challenges, offering practical guidance on optimizing deployment processes. Readers can expect to learn about the best practices that ensure the reliability, efficiency, and security of deployed models. By the end of this section, readers will have a comprehensive understanding of the strategic and technical aspects involved in deploying generative models, empowering them to navigate the complexities of real-world implementation successfully.

Considerations

When building and deploying generative models, there are several important considerations and best practices to keep in mind.

Compute resources

Generative models can be computationally expensive to train and deploy. It is important to ensure that you have access to sufficient compute resources to support your needs.

For generative models, computational resources are crucial for model training and deployment. The number of computational resources needed will depend on the complexity of the model and the dataset being used.

Training

Generative models can be computationally expensive to train. This is because they often require multiple training runs to converge on a good solution. Additionally, generative models are often trained on large datasets, which can further increase the computational requirements.

To train generative models, researchers typically use cloud computing platforms, such as AWS, GCP, and Microsoft Azure. Cloud computing platforms provide access to a large pool of computing resources that can be scaled up or down as needed.

Additionally, there are several tools and frameworks that can be used to speed up the training of generative models. For example, the TensorFlow library provides a number of distributed training techniques that can be used to train generative models on multiple GPUs or machines.

Deployment

Once a generative model is trained, it needs to be deployed to a production environment so that it can be used to generate outputs. The computational requirements for deployment will depend on the specific platform being used.

For example, deploying a generative model to a web service will require less computational resources than deploying it to a mobile device. Additionally, some generative models can be compressed to reduce their size and computational requirements.

Here are some tips for reducing the computational requirements of generative models:

- **Choose the right architecture**: Some generative model architectures are more computationally efficient than others. For example, **convolutional neural networks (CNNs)** are more computationally efficient than **recurrent neural networks (RNNs)**.

- **Use pre-trained models**: Pre-trained models can be used to initialize generative models, which can reduce the amount of training required.

- **Quantize your model**: Quantizing a model can reduce its size and computational requirements.

- **Deploy your model to a specialized platform**: There are a number of specialized platforms that can be used to deploy generative models, such as Google Cloud TPUs and Amazon **Elastic Compute Cloud (EC2)** F1 instances.

By following these tips, you can reduce the computational requirements of your generative models and make them more deployable.

Here is an example of how to reduce the computational requirements of a generative model:

Let us say that we are training a GAN to generate images of human faces. The GAN architecture consists of a generator and a discriminator. The generator is responsible for generating images, while the discriminator is responsible for distinguishing between real and generated images.

To reduce the computational requirements of the GAN, we can use the following techniques:

- **Choose the right architecture**: We can use a CNN architecture for the generator and the discriminator. CNNs are more computationally efficient than other architectures, such as RNNs.
- **Use pre-trained models**: We can initialize the generator with a pre-trained model, such as a VGG16 model. This will reduce the amount of training required.
- **Quantize the model**: We can quantify the GAN model to reduce its size and computational requirements.
- **Deploy the model to a specialized platform**: We can deploy the GAN model to a specialized platform, such as a Google Cloud TPU or an Amazon EC2 F1 instance.

By using these techniques, we can significantly reduce the computational requirements of the GAN and make it more deployable.

Model size

Generative models can be quite large, especially for complex tasks such as image generation or text generation. This can make it challenging to deploy them to certain platforms. Model size is an important consideration when deploying generative models. Generative models can be quite large, especially for complex tasks such as image generation or text generation. This can make it challenging to deploy them to certain platforms.

There are a number of factors that contribute to the size of a generative model, including:

- **Model architecture**: The architecture of the generative model will have a significant impact on its size. For example, CNNs are typically larger than RNNs.
- **Number of parameters**: The number of parameters in the generative model will also affect its size. Generative models with more parameters will be larger.
- **Dataset size**: The size of the dataset used to train the generative model will also affect its size. Generative models trained on larger datasets will be larger.

The size of a generative model can have a number of implications for deployment:

- **Storage requirements**: Larger generative models require more storage space. This can be a challenge for deploying generative models to mobile devices or embedded systems.
- **Network bandwidth**: They also require more network bandwidth to deploy and use. This can be a challenge for deploying generative models to cloud-based platforms.
- **Compute requirements**: Larger generative models often require more compute resources to run. This can increase the cost of deploying and using generative models.

There are a number of techniques that can be used to reduce the size of generative models, including:

- **Use a smaller model architecture**: There are a number of smaller model architectures that can be used for generative tasks. For example, MobileNets are smaller and more efficient than traditional CNNs.

- **Prune the model**: Model pruning can be used to remove unnecessary parameters from a generative model. This can reduce the size of the model without significantly impacting its performance.

- **Quantize the model**: Quantizing a model can reduce its size by representing the weights and activations of the model with fewer bits.

- **Use a knowledge distillation**: Knowledge distillation can be used to transfer the knowledge of a larger generative model to a smaller generative model. This can be used to create a smaller generative model with comparable performance to the larger model.

By using these techniques, you can reduce the size of your generative model and make it more deployable.

Here is an example of how to reduce the size of a generative model:

Let us say that we have trained a GAN to generate images of human faces. The GAN architecture consists of a generator and a discriminator. The generator is responsible for generating images, while the discriminator is responsible for distinguishing between real and generated images.

To reduce the size of the GAN, we can use the following techniques:

- **Use a smaller model architecture**: We can use a MobileNet architecture for the generator and the discriminator. MobileNets are smaller and more efficient than traditional CNNs.

- **Prune the model**: We can prune the GAN model to remove unnecessary parameters. This can reduce the size of the model without significantly impacting its performance.

- **Quantize the model**: We can quantize the GAN model to reduce its size by representing the weights and activations of the model with fewer bits.

- **Use a knowledge distillation**: We can use knowledge distillation to transfer the knowledge of the original GAN to a smaller GAN. This can be used to create a smaller GAN with comparable performance to the original GAN.

By using these techniques, we can significantly reduce the size of the GAN and make it more deployable.

Model size is an important consideration when deploying generative models. By using the techniques described above, you can reduce the size of your generative model and make it more deployable.

Model latency

Generative models can have high latency, which means that it can take time for them to generate outputs. This is important to consider if your application needs to generate outputs quickly.

There are a number of factors that can contribute to model latency, including:

- **Model architecture**: The architecture of the generative model can also affect its latency. For example, CNNs typically have higher latency than RNNs.
- **Hardware**: The hardware used to deploy the generative model can also affect its latency. For example, generative models deployed on GPUs will typically have lower latency than generative models deployed on CPUs.

There are a number of techniques that can be used to reduce the latency of generative models, including:

- **Using a smaller model architecture**: There are a number of smaller model architectures that can be used for generative tasks. For example, MobileNets are smaller and faster than traditional CNNs.
- **Optimizing the model**: The model can be optimized for latency by using techniques such as quantization and pruning.
- **Deploying the model on specialized hardware**: Generative models can be deployed on specialized hardware, such as GPUs and TPUs, to reduce their latency.
- **Using a model-serving framework**: A model-serving framework can be used to optimize the deployment and execution of generative models.

By using these techniques, you can reduce the latency of your generative model and make it more responsive for users.

Here is an example of how to reduce the latency of a generative model:

Let us say that we have a GAN that generates images of human faces. The GAN architecture consists of a generator and a discriminator. The generator is responsible for generating images, while the discriminator is responsible for distinguishing between real and generated images.

To reduce the latency of the GAN, we can use the following techniques:

- **Using a smaller model architecture**: We can use a MobileNet architecture for the generator and the discriminator as they are smaller and faster than traditional CNNs.

- **Optimizing the model**: We can optimize the GAN model for latency by using techniques such as quantization and pruning.
- **Deploying the model on specialized hardware**: We can deploy the GAN model on a GPU to reduce its latency.
- **Using a model serving framework**: We can use a model serving framework, such as TensorFlow Serving, to optimize the deployment and execution of the GAN.

By using these techniques, we can significantly reduce the latency of the GAN and make it more responsive for users. Model latency is an important consideration when deploying generative models. By using the techniques described above, you can reduce the latency of your generative model and make it more responsive for users.

Model accuracy

Generative models are not perfect. They can sometimes generate outputs that are inaccurate or misleading. It is important to evaluate the accuracy of your model before deploying it to production.

Model accuracy is the measure of how well a generative model can generate outputs that are similar to the real data. It is an important consideration when deploying generative models, especially for applications where the accuracy of the generated outputs is critical.

There are a number of ways to measure the accuracy of a generative model, including:

- **Quantitative metrics**: Quantitative metrics, such as **mean squared error (MSE)** and **peak signal-to-noise ratio (PSNR)**, can be used to measure the accuracy of generated images.
- **Qualitative metrics**: Qualitative metrics, such as human evaluation, can be used to measure the accuracy of generated text or images.

The accuracy of a generative model will depend on a number of factors, including:

- **Model architecture**: The architecture of the generative model will have a significant impact on its accuracy. For example, CNNs are typically more accurate than RNNs for image generation tasks.
- **Dataset size**: The size of the dataset used to train the generative model will also affect its accuracy. Generative models trained on larger datasets will be more accurate.
- **Training time**: The amount of time spent training the generative model will also affect its accuracy. Generative models trained for longer periods of time will be more accurate.

There are a number of techniques that can be used to improve the accuracy of generative models, including:

- **Using a larger dataset**: Training the generative model on a larger dataset will improve its accuracy.
- **Training for longer**: Training the generative model for a longer period of time will improve its accuracy.
- **Using a more complex model architecture**: Using a more complex model architecture, such as a CNN, can improve the accuracy of the generative model.
- **Using regularization techniques**: Regularization techniques, such as dropout and batch normalization, can help to prevent overfitting and improve the accuracy of the generative model.

Here is an example of how to improve the accuracy of a generative model:

Let us say that we are training a GAN to generate images of human faces. The GAN architecture consists of a generator and a discriminator. The generator is responsible for generating images, while the discriminator is responsible for distinguishing between real and generated images.

To improve the accuracy of the GAN, we can use the following techniques:

- **Using a larger dataset**: We can train the GAN on a larger dataset of human face images. This will help the GAN to learn the distribution of human faces more accurately.
- **Training for longer**: We can train the GAN for a longer period of time. This will give the GAN more time to learn the distribution of human faces and generate more accurate images.
- **Using a more complex model architecture**: We can use a more complex model architecture for the generator, such as a CNN. This will help the GAN to generate more realistic images.
- **Using regularization techniques**: We can use regularization techniques, such as dropout and batch normalization, to prevent overfitting and improve the accuracy of the GAN.

By using these techniques, we can significantly improve the accuracy of the GAN and generate more realistic images of human faces.

Model accuracy is an important consideration when deploying generative models. By using the techniques described above, you can improve the accuracy of your generative model and generate outputs that are more similar to the real data.

Model fairness

Generative models can be biased, which can lead to unfair outputs. It is important to test your model for bias and take steps to mitigate it before deploying it to production.

Model fairness is the measure of how impartial and unbiased a generative model is. It is an important consideration when deploying generative models, especially for applications where the fairness of the generated outputs is critical.

There are a number of ways to measure the fairness of a generative model, including:

- **Statistical metrics**: Statistical metrics, such as demographic parity and equalized opportunity, can be used to measure the fairness of generated outputs.
- **Human evaluation**: Human evaluation can be used to measure the fairness of generated outputs, such as text or images.

The fairness of a generative model will depend on a number of factors, including:

- **Dataset**: The dataset used to train the generative model can introduce bias into the model. For example, a dataset of images that is predominantly white and male will likely produce a generative model that generates biased outputs.
- **Model architecture**: The architecture of the generative model can also introduce bias into the model. For example, a generative model that uses a linear architecture may be more likely to generate biased outputs than a generative model that uses a non-linear architecture.
- **Training process**: The training process used to train the generative model can also introduce bias into the model. For example, if the generative model is trained using a loss function that is not fair, then the generative model will likely be biased.

There are a number of techniques that can be used to improve the fairness of generative models, including:

- **Using a debiasing algorithm**: A debiasing algorithm can be used to remove bias from a generative model.
- **Using a fair training process**: The generative model can be trained using a fair training process, such as adversarial training.
- **Using a human-in-the-loop approach**: A human-in-the-loop approach can be used to monitor and correct the outputs of the generative model.

By using these techniques, we can significantly improve the fairness of the GAN and generate outputs that are more impartial and unbiased.

Model fairness is an important consideration when deploying generative models. By using the techniques described above, you can improve the fairness of your generative model and generate outputs that are more impartial and unbiased.

Best practices

Below are some of the best practice considerations regarding the deployment of generative models:

- **Using a cloud platform**: Cloud platforms offer a number of advantages for deploying generative models, such as scalability, elasticity, and pay-as-you-go pricing.

- **Containerizing your model**: Containerizing your model will make it easier to deploy and manage it.

- **Using a model-serving framework**: A model-serving framework will make it easier to deploy and manage your model in production.

- **Monitoring your model**: It is important to monitor your model in production to ensure that it is performing as expected. This includes tracking metrics such as accuracy, latency, and throughput.

- **Updating your model**: It is important to update your model regularly with new data and training to improve its performance.

In addition to the above, here are some other best practices for deploying generative models:

- **Using a sandbox environment**: Before deploying your model to production, it is important to test it in a sandbox environment. This will help you to identify and fix any potential problems.

- **Having a rollback plan**: In case something goes wrong with your deployed model, it is important to have a rollback plan in place. This will allow you to quickly revert to a previous version of your model.

- **Documenting your deployment**: It is important to document your deployment process so that you can easily reproduce it in the future.

- **Monitoring your model for security vulnerabilities**: It is important to monitor your deployed model for security vulnerabilities. This will help you to protect your model from being exploited by attackers.

By following these considerations and best practices, you can deploy your generative models successfully and securely.

When deploying generative models, several crucial considerations and best practices should be taken into account. These encompass factors like ensuring adequate computer resources due to the computational intensity of training and deployment. Handling large model sizes, especially for complex tasks, may pose challenges in deployment. Balancing model latency, accuracy, and fairness is essential, as generative models may exhibit biases. Best practices involve leveraging cloud platforms for scalability, containerizing models for easier deployment, using model-serving frameworks, monitoring performance metrics in production, and regularly updating models to enhance their capabilities and accuracy. These practices collectively contribute to the effective and reliable deployment of generative models.

In the next section, readers can expect a comprehensive exploration of the typical challenges faced when implementing generative models and effective strategies to address them. This section will delve into overcoming hurdles encountered during the development and deployment phases, providing insights and solutions to enhance the implementation process.

Overcoming common challenges in implementation

In the final section of the chapter, we will navigate through the intricate landscape of challenges often encountered when implementing generative models. From issues arising during model development to complexities faced in the deployment phase, this section aims to equip readers with a comprehensive understanding of potential hurdles and, more importantly, effective strategies to surmount them. By the end of this exploration, readers will gain valuable insights into mitigating common challenges, ensuring a more seamless and successful implementation of generative models in diverse applications.

The implementation of generative models can be challenging for a number of reasons. Some of the most common challenges include:

Training data

Generative models require large amounts of training data to learn the distribution of the data and generate realistic outputs. It can be difficult to collect and prepare large datasets, especially for complex tasks such as image generation or text generation. This is because generative models are essentially learning to model the probability distribution of the data. To do this accurately, they need to see a large number of examples of the data. Collecting and preparing large datasets can be a challenge, especially for complex tasks such as image generation or text generation. For example, if you are training a generative model to generate images of human faces, you will need to collect a large dataset of images of human faces. This can be time-consuming and expensive. In addition, the quality of the training data is also important. If the training data is noisy or incomplete, then the generative model will likely learn the noise and incompleteness, and generate noisy and incomplete outputs.

Model architecture

There is no one-size-fits-all model architecture for generative models. The best model architecture will depend on the specific task at hand. It can be challenging to choose the right model architecture and tune its hyperparameters. For example, if you are training a generative model to generate images, then you will need to use a model architecture that is specifically designed for image generation. It can be challenging to choose the right model architecture and tune its hyperparameters. There are a number of different model architectures available, and each architecture has its own strengths and weaknesses. It is important to experiment with different model architectures and hyperparameters to find the best combination for your task.

Training process

The training process for generative models can be complex and time-consuming. It can be difficult to train generative models to converge to a good solution. Generative models are often trained using a technique called gradient descent. Gradient descent is an iterative algorithm that updates the parameters of the model in order to minimize the loss function. The loss function measures how well the model is performing on the training data. For generative models, the loss function is typically a measure of the distance between the distribution of real data and the distribution of generated data. Training a generative model using gradient descent can be challenging. Generative models are often very complex and have a large number of parameters. This can make it difficult for the gradient descent algorithm to converge to a good solution. In addition, generative models can be unstable during training. This means that the gradients can explode, which can cause the model to diverge. There are a number of techniques that can be used to stabilize the training process, such as gradient clipping and regularization.

Model evaluation

It can be difficult to evaluate the performance of generative models. Traditional metrics such as accuracy and precision are not always well-suited for generative models. This is because generative models are not typically trying to classify or predict anything. Instead, they are trying to generate realistic outputs. There are a number of metrics that can be used to evaluate the performance of generative models, such as **Fréchet Inception Distance (FID)** and Inception Score. FID is a metric that measures the distance between the distribution of real data and the distribution of generated data. Inception Score is a metric that measures the diversity and realism of the generated outputs. However, even these metrics are not perfect. FID and Inception Score are both subjective metrics, and they can be influenced by the specific dataset and model architecture used.

Deployment

Once a generative model is trained, it needs to be deployed to a production environment. This can be challenging, especially for large and complex models. Generative models can be very computationally expensive to run, and they can require a lot of memory. It is important to choose a deployment platform that can handle the computational requirements of your generative model. Cloud platforms such as GCP and AWS offer a number of services that can be used to deploy and manage generative models, such as Google TPUs and Amazon EC2 F1 instances. In addition, it is important to consider the scalability of your deployment platform. If you expect your generative model to be used by a large number of users, then you will need to choose a deployment platform that can scale to meet your needs.

Here are some tips for overcoming the common challenges in implementation of generative models:

- **Training data**: If you are unable to collect a large dataset, you can use techniques such as data augmentation to increase the size of your dataset. You can also use pre-trained models to initialize your generative model, which can reduce the amount of training data required.
- **Model architecture**: There are a number of resources available to help you choose the right model architecture for your task. You can also use transfer learning to adapt a pre-trained model to your task.
- **Training process**: There are a number of techniques that can help you train generative models more effectively. For example, you can use batch normalization and dropout to regularize your model and prevent overfitting. You can also use gradient clipping to prevent the gradients from exploding, which can destabilize the training process.
- **Model evaluation**: A number of metrics can be used to evaluate the performance of generative models, such as FID and Inception Score. You can also use human evaluation to assess the quality of the generated outputs.
- **Deployment:** You can use a cloud platform to deploy your generative model. Cloud platforms offer a number of advantages, such as scalability, elasticity, and pay-as-you-go pricing.

By following these tips, you can overcome the common challenges in implementation of generative models and successfully deploy your models to production.

Here is an example of how to overcome one of the common challenges in implementation of generative models:

Challenge: Training a generative model on a limited dataset.

Solution: Use data augmentation to increase the size of the dataset. Data augmentation can be used to create new training data from existing training data by applying transformations such as cropping, flipping, and rotating the images.

For example, if you are training a generative model to generate images of human faces, you can use data augmentation to create new training data from existing training data by cropping the faces to different sizes and flipping them horizontally and vertically. This will increase the size of your dataset and help the generative model to learn the distribution of human faces more accurately.

In this concluding section, we delved into the myriad challenges associated with implementing generative models, spanning from the intricate nuances during model development to the intricate details of deployment. Addressing common issues such as the requirement for large and high-quality training datasets, selecting appropriate model architectures, managing the intricacies of the training process, and grappling with the complexities of model evaluation and deployment, we provided readers with a comprehensive toolkit of strategies to overcome these obstacles effectively. From the importance of data augmentation to the intricacies of model architecture selection, stabilization of the training process, and accurate model evaluation using metrics like FID and Inception Score, each facet was thoroughly explored. Additionally, we emphasized the significance of choosing the right deployment platform, leveraging cloud services like GCP and AWS. Offering practical tips to tackle common challenges, such as training on limited datasets through data augmentation, this section equips readers with valuable insights and practical solutions, ensuring a smoother journey in the implementation of generative models.

Conclusion

In the culminating chapter, readers embarked on a comprehensive journey, starting with a practical guide to developing generative models. This section equipped them with invaluable insights into the complexities of model architecture, training processes, and model evaluation. Transitioning to deployment considerations and best practices, readers gained knowledge on leveraging cloud platforms and employing containerization for effective model deployment. The chapter reached its zenith with an exploration of the common challenges in implementation, offering practical solutions and strategies. From addressing issues related to training data, model architecture, and the training process to navigating the intricacies of model evaluation and deployment, readers were armed with a robust understanding and toolkit for successful implementation of generative models in diverse applications.

With this, we conclude this chapter and book.

Join our book's Discord space

Join the book's Discord Workspace for Latest updates, Offers, Tech happenings around the world, New Release and Sessions with the Authors:

https://discord.bpbonline.com

Index

A

adversarial autoencoders (AAEs) 251
aesthetic revolution, in design 163
   algorithmic design creativity 163
   architectural innovations 163
   product and industrial design 163
   real-world examples 164
   user-centric interfaces 163
AI-generated art
   ethical considerations 137, 138
AI-generated NFT art 160
   artistic collaborations 160
   features 160
   fusion of technology and creativity 160
   impact on art market 161
   tokenized ownership and digital scarcity 161
algorithmic artistry 155
   impact and future trends 157
   real-world examples and case studies 155, 156
algorithmic musical composition 162
   collaborative initiatives 162
   personalized music experiences 162
   real-world examples 162, 163
   unique melodic patterns 162
algorithmic trading strategies
   adaptability to market changes 125
   backtesting and continuous improvement 124
   context and importance 123
   data-driven decision-making 124
   dynamic portfolio optimization 124
   generative AI's role 123
   market sentiment analysis 124

predictive analytics, for market trends 124
real-world impact 123, 124
risk management strategies 124
Amazon 214, 215
Amazon SageMaker 273
　benefits 273, 274
　examples 275
　features 274
　use cases 274, 275
anti-money laundering (AML) 50
application in drug discovery
　example use case 114
　industry adoption 114
　real-world impact 113, 114
architecture and training process 232
　of GANs 232, 233
art and entertainment industry 35, 36
　algorithmic composition 36
　ethical considerations 38
　evolutionary algorithms 36, 37
　generative art 36
　generative art installations 38
　humans and algorithms collaboration 37, 38
　interactive generative art 37
　machine learning and style transfer 37
　procedural generation 37
artificial intelligence (AI) 2
Artificial Intelligence Virtual Artist (AIVA) 36, 167
Autodesk's generative design in architecture 171
　examples and use cases 171
　human-AI collaboration 172
　value 171

autoencoders 87
　implementation framework 90
　key concepts 87-89
autoregressive models 4, 5
　loss function 5
　optimizer 5

B

BatchGAN 250
BERT implementations 95
　future directions and ongoing research 96
　GitHub repository 96
　Hugging Face Transformers library 95
　TensorFlow 2.0 96
bias, in creative AI 177
　addressing 178
　algorithmic bias 177
　consequences 178
　data bias 177
　human bias 177
　real-world examples 177, 178
Bidirectional Encoder Representations from Transformers (BERT) 7, 94
　key concepts 94, 95
BigGAN 248

C

CapsuleGANs 247
challenges and ongoing research, GANs
　computational cost 244, 245
　ethical concerns 246, 247
　mode collapse 242, 243
　training instability 243, 244
conditional GANs (cGANs) 73
Contrastive Language-Image Pretraining (CLIP) 8

convolutional neural networks (CNNs) 6, 96
creative assistance, in content generation 38, 39
  AI-enhanced filmmaking and animation 40, 41
  AI-generated literature and poetry 42
  AI-generated music and composition 39, 40
  automated content generation 43
  chatbots, for customer interaction 44
  content curation and trend analysis 45
  creative chatbots and interactive storytelling 41
  dynamic pricing optimization 45
  email marketing optimization 45
  ethical considerations 42, 43
  interactive and immersive experiences 39
  marketing and content creation 43
  personalized marketing campaigns 44
  predictive analytics, for customer behaviour 44
  sentiment analysis in marketing 45
  social media management 44
  virtual fashion design 41, 42
  visual arts and style transfer 40
  visual content generation 44
creative expression, with generative AI
  aesthetic revolution, in design 163
  algorithmic musical composition 162
  ethical considerations 176
  harmonies, of code and melody 161
  human and AI collaboration 166, 167
  in art, music and design 154

credit scoring and risk assessment
  context and importance 127
  generative AI's role 127
  real-world impact 127-129
customer service chatbots
  context and importance 125
  generative AI's role 125
  real-world impact 125-127
CycleGAN implementations 92
  DeepArt.io 93
  for art style transfer 92
  for object transfiguration 93
  Pix2PixHD 93
  ZooGAN 92
Cycle generative adversarial network (CycleGAN) 8, 63, 91, 250
  key concepts 91, 92
  using 93, 94

D

DALL-E 65, 66
  collaborative approach 66
  continual research contributions 66
  Creative AI 66
  education and outreach 66
  ethical considerations 66
  text-to-image synthesis 66
DeepChem 82, 83
Deep Convolutional GAN (DCGAN) 7, 72
DeepDream 96, 156
  artistic applications 97
  challenges 98
  cultural impact 97
  ethical considerations 98
  origins 96
  working principle 96, 97

DeepDream case study 158
  functioning 158
  impact on artistic community 159
  overview 158
  popularization and accessibility 159
  visual aesthetics and artistic impact 159
deployment considerations 283
  best practices 290, 291
  computational requirements, for generative model 284, 285
  compute resources 283
  model accuracy 288, 289
  model fairness 289, 290
  model latency 287, 288
  model size 285, 286
  training 283, 284
Digital Light Synthesis (DLA) 194
drug discovery platform (DDP) 195
DSGAN 252
DualDGAN 249

E

entertainment case study 140
  AI-enhanced filmmaking and animation 141
  outcomes 141
ethical concerns, in creative AI
  addressing 184
  autonomy 188, 189
  disinformation 185-187
  job displacement 184, 185
  misinformation 185-187
  weaponization 187, 188
ethical considerations, in creative AI 176
  bias 177
  copyright and ownership 178, 179
  ethical concerns 182, 183
  ethical concerns, addressing 184
  privacy concerns 180, 181
  transparency 181, 182
evolutionary trajectory 5-7
explainable AI (XAI) 148

F

Facebook AI 68
  AI research 69
  conditional generative adversarial networks and user interaction 69
  deep generative models 69
  ethical considerations 69
  GANs for style transfer 69
  generative models for video 69
  image synthesis and enhancement 68
  open-source contributions 69
finance and risk management 48, 49
  automated compliance and regulatory reporting 50
  dynamic risk management 50
  insurance underwriting and claims processing 51
  market sentiment analysis 50
  personalized financial advice 49
  portfolio optimization and asset allocation 50
  stress testing and scenario analysis 51
finance case study 139
  fraud detection and prevention, in financial transactions 140
  outcomes 140
Forrester 150, 151
fraud detection and prevention
  context and importance 121
  generative AI's role 122
  real-world impact 122, 123

Fréchet inception distance (FID) 5, 72, 293
future trends and potential disruptions 148

G
GAN deployment 268
  on Google Cloud AI platform 268-270
  on Microsoft Azure 271, 272
GANs examples
  challenges 241
  DeepMind 237, 238
  Google AI 236
  IBM 238, 239
  NVIDIA 236, 237
  ongoing research 241
  PayPal 239, 240
GANs future 247
  network architectures 247, 248
  objective functions 250
  rationale, for new network architectures 248
  rationale, for training algorithms 249
  training algorithms 249
  training algorithms examples 250
GANs, in visual arts 158
  AI-generated NFT art 160
  DeepDream case study 158
  evolution, of style transfer 158
  interactive art installations 159
Gartner 148, 149
GauGAN 248
General Electric (GE) 211
generative adversarial networks (GANs) 2, 61, 63, 64, 259
  application deployment 77-79
  applications 235
  architecture, selecting 72, 73
  data preparation 73, 74
  discriminator network 259
  ethical guidelines 252, 253
  examples 236
  exploring 233
  generator network 259
  model training 75, 76
  NVIDIA 64, 65
  OpenAI 65
  optimization and fine-tuning 76, 77
  problem, defining 71, 72
  real-world examples 234, 235
  success stories 233
  training process 259
  using 71
  working 234
generative AI 1
  anticipated future trajectory 14-16
  applications, in real world 8-12
  autoregressive models 4, 5
  challenges 12-14
  challenges and considerations 60
  defining 2, 3
  evaluation 5
  evolution 2, 3
  future outlook 60
  generative models 3
  in art 154
  in design 154
  in music 154
  key components 3
  mechanisms 5
  significance and impact, on various industries 18
generative AI and business innovation
  existing designs optimization 199, 200

generative AI in product development 193
innovations, in manufacturing and supply chain 207-209
product development and design, enhancing 192, 193
products and services, personalization 200, 201
generative AI in business
  contextual understanding 224, 225
  cross-functional collaboration 221, 222
  data quality and accessibility 222, 223
  ethical considerations 223, 224
  intellectual property management 225, 226
  regulatory compliance 227, 228
  roadmaps, implementing 219-221
  strategies, leveraging 219, 228, 229
  transparency 223, 224
  user feedback integration 226, 227
generative AI in casting mold design
  benefits 210
  future 210
generative AI in demand forecasting and inventory optimization
  benefits 213
  future 214
generative AI in entertainment sector 129
  AI-enhanced filmmaking and animation 135, 136
  AI-generated music and composition 132, 133
  creative chatbots and interactive storytelling 136, 137
  generative art and design 130, 131
  interactive and immersive experiences 131, 132
  visual arts and style transfer 133-135
generative AI in financial sector 120
  algorithmic trading strategies 123
  credit scoring and risk assessment 127
  customer service chatbots 125
  fraud detection and prevention 121
generative AI in healthcare 111
  application in drug discovery 113
  drug discovery and molecular design 113
  medical imaging enhancement 112
  medical text generation 116
  personalized treatment plans 114
  predictive analytics for patient outcomes 117
  synthetic data generation for research 119
generative AI in jet engine production
  benefits 212
  future 212
generative AI in movie and TV show recommendations
  benefits 216
  future 217
generative AI in music recommendations
  benefits 218
  future 218, 219
generative AI in product development
  Eli Lilly and Company 195
  Ford Motor Company 194
  leveraging 193, 194
  Nike 196
  Procter & Gamble (P&G) 197, 198, 199

generative AI in route planning
  benefits 215
  future 215
generative model deployment 260, 261
  AWS Console 264, 265
  AWS SDKs and APIs 265
  examples 261, 262
  GANs networks deployment 262, 263, 264
  SageMaker Studio 264
generative model implementation, challenges
  deployment 293, 294
  model architecture 292, 293
  model evaluation 293
  overcoming 292
  training data 292
  training process 293
generative models
  breakthroughs 7, 8
  generative adversial networks 3, 4
  overview 62, 63
  practical guide, for development 256, 257, 258
  variational autoencoders 4
Generative Pre-trained Transformer (GPT) 4
generative, versus discriminative models
  applications 106
  context in summary 107
  dichotomy, decoding 105, 106
  fundamental differences 105
  trade-offs and synergy 106, 107
  uncertainty handling 106
Google AI Platform (Unified) 275
  examples 278

  features 276, 277
  use cases 277
  value proposition 276
Google Brain 67
  AI ethics and fairness 68
  application in TensorFlow 68
  collaborations 68
  conditional generative adversarial networks 67
  image-to-image translation 67
  interactive generative adversarial networks 67
  progressive generative adversarial networks 67
  publications 68
  style transfer 67
Google's Magenta and music composition 167, 168
  examples and use cases 168
  human-AI collaboration 169
  value 168
Google's Magenta Studio 81, 82

H

healthcare and drug discovery industry
  advancing molecular generation 19, 20
  bias and fairness, addressing 27, 28
  case studies and success stories 24, 25
  enhancing biomedical imaging 20, 21
  ethical considerations and future prospects 26
  global access, to healthcare innovations 32, 33
  informed consent, in personalized medicine 29, 30
  ongoing ethical discourse and governance 33-35

personalized medicine and treatment plans 23, 24
responsible data use and patient privacy 26, 27
targeted drug design and optimization 21-23
transparency, in model decision-making 30-32
healthcare case study 139
  medical imaging enhancement in oncology 139
  outcomes 139
human and AI collaboration, creative AI 166, 167
  Autodesk's generative design in architecture 171
  Magenta and music composition 167, 168
  NVIDIA's DeepArt and DeepDream in visual arts 169
  OpenAI's GPT-3 in creative assistance 172
human resources and recruitment 51
  automated onboarding processes 53
  automated resume screening 52
  candidate matching and recommendations 52
  chatbots, for candidate interaction 53
  diversity and inclusion initiatives 52
  employee retention strategies 53
  performance management enhancements 53, 54
  predictive hiring analytics 52
  skills gap analysis 53
  workforce planning and scalability 54
human resources and recruitment case study 143
  AI-enhanced recruitment in HR 143
  outcomes 144

I

IBM 70
  AI ethics and fairness 71
  creative applications 70
  explainability 70
  GANs for anomaly detection 70
  GANs for data augmentation 70
  generative models in AI research 70
  industry-specific applications 71
  interpretability 70
  quantum machine learning 71
Inception Score (IS) 5
innovations, in manufacturing and supply chain 207-209
  impact 209

J

Jensen-Shannon divergence (JSD) 251
jet engines 211
Joint Photographic Experts Group (JPEG) 89

K

Kullback-Leibler (KL) divergence 80

L

Local Interpretable Model-agnostic Explanations (LIME) 30
long short-term memory networks (LSTMs) 167
loss functions 102
  adversarial loss of generative adversarial networks 102
  balancing act 103
  cycle consistency loss for CycleGAN 103

perceptual loss, for Style Transfer and Image Generation 103
reconstruction loss of variational autoencoders 102

M

Magenta 156
Magenta Studio 162
Magnetic Resonance Imaging (MRI) 112
manufacturing and design case study 141
   generative design, in aerospace engineering 141
   outcomes 142
manufacturing and design industry 46
   additive manufacturing and 3D printing 46
   customization and mass personalization 47
   energy efficiency in manufacturing 47
   generative design, in product development 46
   human-robot collaboration 48
   predictive maintenance and quality control 46
   robotics and automation 47
   simulations, for prototyping and testing 47
   supply chain optimization 47
maximum mean discrepancy (MMD) 251
medical imaging enhancement
   application, in medical imaging 112
   example use case 112
   industry adoption 113
   real-world impact 112
medical text generation 116
   context and challenges 116
   example use case 117

   generative AI's role 116
   industry adoption 117
   real-world impact 116
Microsoft Azure Machine Learning 278
   benefits 281
   examples 280, 281
   features 279
   use cases 280
   value proposition 278
MuseNet 162, 248

N

natural language processing (NLP) 7, 116
Netflix 215, 216
next Rembrandt 155
NVIDIA 64, 65
NVIDIA's DeepArt and DeepDream in visual arts 169
   examples and use cases 170
   human-AI collaboration 170, 171
   value 170

O

objective functions 250
   examples 251
   practical implementation 251, 252
   rationale 251
OpenAI 65
   DALL-E 65, 66
OpenAI's DALL-E 82
OpenAI's GPT-3 in creative assistance 172
   examples and use cases 173
   human-AI collaboration 173-175
   value 173
Open Neural Network Exchange (ONNX) 260

P

personalized treatment plans
  challenges 114
  context 114
  example use case 115
  generative AI's role 115
  industry adoption 115
  real-world impact 115
predictive analytics for patient outcomes
  context and challenges 117
  example use case 118
  generative AI's role 118
  industry adoption 118
  real-world impact 118
products and services personalization 200, 201
  financial services 204-206
  healthcare 206, 207
  media and entertainment 203, 204
  retail 202, 203
ProgressiveGANs 247

R

real-world applications case studies 138
  agriculture 145
  education 146
  energy 146
  entertainment 140
  finance 139
  healthcare 139
  human resources and recruitment 143, 144
  manufacturing and design 141, 142
  retail 147
  robotics and automation 144, 145
  transportation 146
  urban planning and architecture 142, 143
real-world applications, generative API 8
  cross-modal generation in CLIP 12
  data augmentation in machine learning 10
  drug discovery and molecular generation 9
  Image synthesis and Deepfake technology 9
  speech synthesis and voice cloning 11
  style transfer in artistic endeavors 10
  super-resolution imaging 11
  text-to-image synthesis 11
real-world applications, VAEs
  anomaly detection 80
  drug discovery 80
  medical imaging 80
  natural language processing (NLP) 80
real-world examples, aesthetic revolution in design
  AI-driven decision support 164
  AI-Generated art installations 165, 166
  exploration of design options 164
  parametric and performance-driven design 164
  real-world applications 165
recurrent neural networks (RNNs) 6, 162
robotic process automation (RPA) 56
robotics and automation 54
  adaptive and learning robotics 55
  AI-enhanced robotic process automation 56
  automated manufacturing processes 55
  autonomous vehicles and drones 56
  generative design 55

human-robot collaboration 55
intelligent vision systems 56
predictive maintenance for robots 55
warehouse and logistics automation 56, 57
robotics and automation case study 144
  outcomes 145

S

SageMaker Studio 264
Siemens 209, 210
SNGAN 249
Spotify 217
StarGAN 250
StyleGAN 8, 63, 64, 252
StyleGAN2 64
synthetic data generation for research
  context and challenges 119
  example use case 120
  generative AI's role 119
  industry adoption 120
  real-world impact 119

T

TensorFlow Probability (TFP) 85, 86

U

underlying principles 98-100
underlying principles, of generative models 100
  case studies and real-world applications 104, 105
  comparison, with discriminative models 104
  ethical considerations 103
  GANs 101
  generative model evaluation 103
  generative modelling, as mathematical composition 101
  linear algebra 101
  loss functions 102
  mathematical foundations 100
  probability theory 100
  training mechanisms 102
  transfer learning, in generative models 104
  variational autoencoders 101
urban planning and architecture 57
  community-driven design through AI feedback 59
  crisis and disaster response planning 58
  environmental sustainability 58
  generative design 57
  heritage preservation and adaptive reuse 59
  mixed-use development planning 58
  public space design and accessibility 59
  smart infrastructure planning 57
  traffic flow optimization 58
urban planning and architecture case study 142
  outcomes 143
  urban planning, with generative AI 142

V

VAE deployment 265, 266
  example script 266, 267
  on AWS SageMaker via console 267
  on Google Cloud AI platform 270, 271
  on Microsoft Azure 272, 273
VAEs implementations
  DeepChem 82, 83
  Google's Magenta Studio 81, 82

implementation framework 86, 87
OpenAI's DALL-E 82
PyTorch's variational autoencoders
 implementation 83-85
TensorFlow Probability (TFP) 85, 86
variational autoencoders
 (VAEs) 2, 4, 61, 79, 259, 260
  advancements 81
  architecture 79
  challenges 81
  image generation example 80
  implementations 81
  real-world applications 80
  training process 80
virtual and augmented reality
 (VR/AR) applications 131
virtual reality (VR) 39

W

Walmart 212, 213
Wasserstein GAN (WGAN) 72
WGAN-D 252
WGAN-GP 249

Z

ZooGAN 92

Printed by Amazon Italia Logistica S.r.l.
Torrazza Piemonte (TO), Italy